D1453188

APACHE MEDICINE-MEN

JOHN G. BOURKE

DOVER PUBLICATIONS, INC.
NEW YORK

Published in Canada by General Publishing Company, Ltd., 30 Lesmill Road, Don Mills, Toronto, Ontario.

Published in the United Kingdom by Constable and Company, Ltd., 3 The Lanchesters, 162–164 Fulham Palace Road, London W6 9ER.

Bibliographical Note

This Dover edition, first published in 1993, is an unabridged republication of an Accompanying Paper, "The Medicine-Men of the Apache" (original pages 443–603), in the *Ninth Annual Report of the Bureau of Ethnology to the Secretary of the Smithsonian Institution, 1887–'88*, as originally published by the United States Government Printing Office, Washington, D.C., in 1892.

Library of Congress Cataloging-in-Publication Data

Bourke, John Gregory, 1846–1896.
   [Medicine-men of the Apache]
   Apache medicine-men / John G. Bourke
      p.   cm.
   Originally published: The medicine-men of the Apache. Washington, D.C. : U.S.G.P.O., 1892.
   Includes bibliographical references and index.
   ISBN 0-486-27842-5 (pbk. : alk. paper)
   1. Apache Indians—Medicine. 2. Shamans—New Mexico. 3. Apache Indians—Rites and ceremonies. 4. Apache Indians—Religion and mythology. I. Title.
E99.A6B8 1993
615.8′82′09789—dc20   93-36083
                                                 CIP

Manufactured in the United States of America
Dover Publications, Inc., 31 East 2nd Street, Mineola, N.Y. 11501

CONTENTS.

Page.

CHAPTER I. The medicine-men, their modes of treating disease, their superstitions, paraphernalia, etc 1

Medicine-women 18
Remedies and modes of treatment 21
Hair and wigs 24
Mudheads 25
Scalp shirts... 26
The rhombus, or bull roarer.. 26
The cross... 29
Necklaces of human fingers... 30
Necklaces of human teeth... 37
The scratch stick 40
The drinking reed 43

CHAPTER II. Hoddentin, the pollen of the tule, the sacrificial powder of the Apache; with remarks upon sacred powders and offerings in general 49

The "kunque" of the Zuñi and others.. 57
Use of the pollen by the Israelites and Egyptians 67
Hoddentin a prehistoric food.. 68
Hoddentin the yiauhtli of the Aztecs 71
"Bledos" of ancient writers—its meaning 72
Tzoalli 73
General use of the powder among Indians 78
Analogues of hoddentin 80
The down of birds in ceremonial observances 83
Hair powder.. 85
Dust from churches—its use.. 87
Clay-eating.. 87
Prehistoric foods used in covenants... 90
Sacred breads and cakes 91
Unleavened bread 93
The hot cross buns of Good Friday 94
Galena 98

CHAPTER III. The izze-kloth or medicine cord of the Apache................... 100

Analogues to be found among the Aztecs, Peruvians, and others.......... 108
The magic wind-knotted cords of the Lapps and others 110
Rosaries and other mnemonic cords... 111
The sacred cords of the Parsis and Brahmans 113
Use of cords and knots and girdles in parturition.......................... 120
"Medidas," "measuring cords," "wresting threads," etc.................... 122
Unclassified superstitions upon this subject................................. 125
The medicine hat 130

iii

CONTENTS.

Page.

CHAPTER III—Continued.
The spirit or ghost dance headdress 135
Amulets and talismans 137
The "tzi-daltai" 137
Chalchihuitl 138
Phylacteries 141
Bibliography 146
Index 154

ILLUSTRATIONS.

			Facing Page
PLATE	I.	Scalp shirt of Little Big Man	26
	II.	Necklace of human fingers	30
	III.	Apache medicine hat used in ghost or spirit dance	136
	IV.	Apache medicine shirt	138
	V.	Apache medicine shirt	139
	VI.	Apache medicine shirt	142

			Page
FIG.	1.	Medicine arrow used by Apache and Pueblo women	18
	2.	Rhombus of the Apache	27
	3.	Rhombus of the Apache	28
	4.	The scratch stick and drinking reed	44
	5.	Bag containing hoddentin	50
	6.	Nan-ta-do-tash's medicine hat	53
	7.	Single-strand medicine cord (Zuñi)	100
	8.	Four-strand medicine cord (Apache)	101
	9.	Three-strand medicine cord (Apache)	102
	10.	Two-strand medicine cord	103
	11.	Four-strand medicine cord (Apache)	104
	12.	Apache war bonnet	131
	13.	Ghost dance headdress	132
	14.	Apache kan or gods. (Drawn by Apache)	136
	15.	Tzi-daltai amulets (Apache)	137
	16.	Tzi-daltai amulet (Apache)	138
	17.	Tzi-daltai amulet (Apache)	139
	18.	Tzi-daltai amulet (Apache)	139
	19.	Phylacteries	142
	20.	Apache medicine sash	143

LETTER OF TRANSMITTAL.

WASHINGTON, D. C., *February 27, 1891.*

SIR: Herewith I have the honor to submit a paper upon the paraphernalia of the medicine-men of the Apache and other tribes.

Analogues have been pointed out, wherever possible, especially in the case of the hoddentin and the izze-kloth, which have never to my knowledge previously received treatment.

Accompanying the paper is a bibliography of the principal works cited.

I have the honor to be, very respectfully, your obedient servant,

JOHN G. BOURKE,
Captain, Third Cavalry, U. S. Army.

Hon. J. W. POWELL,
Director Bureau of Ethnology.

CHAPTER I.

THE MEDICINE-MEN, THEIR MODES OF TREATING DISEASE, THEIR SUPERSTITIONS, PARAPHERNALIA, ETC.

The Caucasian population of the United States has been in intimate contact with the aborigines for a period of not less than two hundred and fifty years. In certain sections, as in Florida and New Mexico, this contact has been for a still greater period; but claiming no earlier date than the settlement of New England, it will be seen that the white race has been slow to learn or the red man has been skillful in withholding knowledge which, if imparted, would have lessened friction and done much to preserve and assimilate a race that, in spite of some serious defects of character, will for all time to come be looked upon as "the noble savage."

Recent deplorable occurrences in the country of the Dakotas have emphasized our ignorance and made clear to the minds of all thinking people that, notwithstanding the acceptance by the native tribes of many of the improvements in living introduced by civilization, the savage has remained a savage, and is still under the control of an influence antagonistic to the rapid absorption of new ideas and the adoption of new customs.

This influence is the "medicine-man."

Who, and what are the medicine-men (or medicine-women), of the American Indians? What powers do they possess in time of peace or war? How is this power obtained, how renewed, how exercised? What is the character of the remedies employed? Are they pharmaceutical, as we employ the term, or are they the superstitious efforts of empirics and charlatans, seeking to deceive and to misguide by pretended consultations with spiritual powers and by reliance upon mysterious and occult influences?

Such a discussion will be attempted in this paper, which will be restricted to a description of the personality of the medicine-men, the regalia worn, and the powers possessed and claimed. To go farther,

1

and enter into a treatment of the religious ideas, the superstitions, omens, and prayers of these spiritual leaders, would be to open a road without end.

As the subject of the paraphernalia of the medicine-men has never, to my knowledge, been comprehensively treated by any writer, I venture to submit what I have learned during the twenty-two years of my acquaintance with our savage tribes, and the studies and conclusions to which my observations have led. While treating in the main of the medicine-men of the Apache, I do not intend to omit any point of importance noted among other tribes or peoples.

First, in regard to the organization of the medicine-men of the Apache, it should be premised that most of my observations were made while the tribe was still actively engaged in hostilities with the whites, and they cannot be regarded as, and are not claimed to be, conclusive upon all points. The Apache are not so surely divided into medicine lodges or secret societies as is the case with the Ojibwa, as shown by Dr. W. J. Hoffman; the Siouan tribes, as related by Mr. J. Owen Dorsey; the Zuñi, according to Mr. F. H. Cushing; the Tusayan, as shown by myself, and other tribes described by other authorities.

The Navajo, who are the full brothers of the Apache, seem to have well defined divisions among their medicine-men, as demonstrated by Dr. Washington Matthews, U. S. Army; and I myself have seen great medicine lodges, which must have contained at least a dozen Apache medicine-men, engaged in some of their incantations. I have also been taken to several of the sacred caves, in which solemn religious dances and other ceremonies were conducted under the same superintendence, but never have I witnessed among the Apache any rite of religious significance in which more than four or five, or at the most six, of the medicine-men took part.

The difficulty of making an accurate determination was increased by the nomadic character of the Apache, who would always prefer to live in small villages containing only a few brush shelters, and not needing the care of more than one or two of their "doctors." These people show an unusual secretiveness and taciturnity in all that relates to their inner selves, and, living as they do in a region filled with caves and secluded nooks, on cliffs, and in deep canyons, have not been compelled to celebrate their sacred offices in "estufas," or "plazas," open to the inspection of the profane, as has been the case with so many of the Pueblo tribes.

Diligent and persistent inquiry of medicine-men whose confidence I had succeeded in gaining, convinced me that any young man can become a "doctor." ("diyi" in the Apache language, which is translated "sabio" by the Mexican captives). It is necessary to convince his friends that he "has the gift," as one of my informants expressed it; that is, he must show that he is a dreamer of dreams, given to long fasts and vigils, able to interpret omens in a satisfactory manner, and do other things of that general nature to demonstrate the possession of

an intense spirituality. Then he will begin to withdraw, at least tem-
porarily, from the society of his fellows and devote himself to long ab-
sences, especially by night, in the "high places" which were inter-
dicted to the Israelites. Such sacred fanes, perched in dangerous and
hidden retreats, can be, or until lately could be, found in many parts
in our remote western territory. In my own experiences I have found
them not only in the country of the Apache, but two-thirds of the way
up the vertical face of the dizzy precipice of Tâaiyalana, close to Zuñi,
where there is a shrine much resorted to by the young men who seek to
divine the result of a contemplated enterprise by shooting arrows into
a long cleft in the smooth surface of the sandstone; I have seen them
in the Wolf Mountains, Montana; in the Big Horn range, Wyoming; on
the lofty sides of Cloud Peak, and elsewhere. Maj. W. S. Stanton,
Corps of Engineers, U. S. Army, ascended the Cloud Peak twice, and,
reaching the summit on the second attempt, he found that beyond the
position first attained and seeming then to be the limit of possible ascent,
some wandering Indian had climbed and made his "medicine."

While it is regarded as a surer mode of learning how to be a medicine-
man to seek the tuition of some one who has already gained power and
influence as such, and pay him liberally in presents of all kinds for a
course of instruction lasting a year or longer, I could learn of nothing
to prohibit a man from assuming the rôle of a prophet or healer of the
sick, if so disposed, beyond the dread of punishment for failure to cure
or alleviate sickness or infirmity. Neither is there such a thing as
settled dogma among these medicine-men. Each follows the dictates
of his own inclinations, consulting such spirits and powers as are
most amenable to his supplications and charms; but no two seem
to rely upon identically the same influences. Even in the spirit dance,
which is possibly the most solemn function in which the Apache medicine-men can engage, the head-dresses and kilts adhered closely enough
to the one pattern, but the symbolism employed by each medicine-man
was entirely different from that adopted by his neighbors.

Schultze, Perrin du Lac, Adair, and others allude to "houses of mercy,"
the "right of asylum" in certain lodges and buildings, or even whole
villages, to which if the pursued of the tribe or even an enemy could
obtain admission his life was secure. Frank Gruard and others who
have lived for years among the Sioux, the Cheyenne, and other tribes
of the plains have assured me that the same right of asylum obtains
among them for the fugitive who takes shelter in the medicine lodge or
the council lodge, and almost parallel notions prevail among the
Apache. I have heard that the first American who came into one of
their villages, tired and hungry, was not molested in the slightest degree.

It is stated by Kelly[1] that all warriors who go through the sun dance
of the Sioux rank thereafter as medicine-men. This statement seems

---

[1] Narrative of Captivity, Cincinnati, 1871. p. 141.

to me to be overdrawn. Nothing of the kind was learned by me at the sun dance of the Sioux which I noted in 1881, and in any event the remark would scarcely apply to the medicine-men of the Apache, who have nothing clearly identifiable with the sun dance, and who do not cut, gash, or in any manner mutilate themselves, as did the principal participants in the sun dance, or as was done in still earlier ages by the galli (the priests of Cybele) or the priests of Mexico.

Herodotus tells us that the priests of Egypt, or rather the doctors, who were at one time identified with them, were separated into classes; some cured the eyes, some the ears, others the head or the belly. Such a differentiation is to be observed among the Apache, Mohave, and other tribes; there are some doctors who enjoy great fame as the bringers of rain, some who claim special power over snakes, and some who profess to consult the spirits only, and do not treat the sick except when no other practitioner may be available. Among the Mohave, the relatives of a dead man will consult one of these spirit-doctors and get him to interview the ghosts who respond to his call and learn from them whether the patient died from ignorance or neglect on the part of the doctor who had charge of the case. If the spirits assert that he did, then the culprit doctor must either flee for his life or throw the onus of the crime upon some witch. This differentiation is not carried so far that a medicine-man, no matter what his class, would decline a large fee.

The right of sanctuary was conceded to all criminals who sought shelter in the vanquech or temple of Chinigchinich.[1]

The castration of the galli, or priests of Cybele, is described by Dupuis.[2]

Diego Duran asserts that the Mexican priests "se endian por medio los miembros viriles y se hacian mil cosas para volverse impotentes por no ofender á sus Dioses."[3]

The hierophants at Athens drank of the hemlock to render themselves impotent, that when they came to the pontificate they might cease to be men.[4]

One class of the Peruvian priests, the Huachus, made auguries from grains of corn or the excrement of animals.[5]

Balboa tells us[5] that the Peruvian priesthood was divided into classes, each with its appropriate functions—the Guacos made the idols for the temples, or rather, they made the idols speak; the others were necromancers and spoke only with the dead; the Huecheoc divined by means of tobacco and coco; the Caviocac became drunk before they attempted to divine, and after them came the Rumatinguis and the Huachus already mentioned.

[1] Padre Boscana, Chinigchinich, in Robinson's California, p. 261.
[2] Origine de tous les Cultes, vol. 2, pt. 2, pp. 87. 88.
[3] Diego Duran, vol. 3, pp. 237, 238.
[4] Higgins, Anacalypsis, lib. 2, p. 77.
[5] Balboa, Hist. du Pérou, in Ternaux-Compans, Voy., vol. 15.

The Oregon tribes have spirit doctors and medicine doctors.[1]

The Chinese historians relate that the shamans of the Huns possessed the power "to bring down snow, hail, rain, and wind."[2]

In all nations in the infancy of growth, social or mental, the power to coax from reluctant clouds the fructifying rain has been regarded with highest approval and will always be found confided to the most important hierophants or devolving upon some of the most prominent deities; almighty Jove was a deified rain-maker or cloud-compeller. Rain-makers flourished in Europe down to the time of Charlemagne, who prohibited these "tempestiarii" from plying their trade.

One of the first requests made of Vaca and his comrades by the people living in fixed habitations near the Rio Grande was "to tell the sky to rain," and also to pray for it.[3]

The prophet Samuel has been alluded to as a rain-maker.[4]

There does not seem to have been any inheritance of priestly functions among the Apache or any setting apart of a particular clan or family for the priestly duties.

Francis Parkman is quoted as describing a certain family among the Miami who were reserved for the sacred ritualistic cannibalism perpetrated by that tribe upon captives taken in war. Such families devoted more or less completely to sacred uses are to be noted among the Hebrews (in the line of Levi) and others; but they do not occur in the tribes of the Southwest.

One of the ceremonies connected with the initiation, as with every exercise of spiritual functions by the medicine-man, is the "ta-a-chi," or sweat-bath, in which, if he be physically able, the patient must participate.

The Apache do not, to my knowledge, indulge in any poisonous intoxicants during their medicine ceremonies; but in this they differ to a perceptible degree from other tribes of America. The "black drink" of the Creeks and the "wisoccan" of the Virginians may be cited as cases in point; and the Walapai of Arizona, the near neighbors of the Apache, make use of the juice, or a decoction of the leaves, roots, and flowers of the *Datura stramonium* to induce frenzy and exhilaration. The laurel grows wild on all the mountain tops of Sonora and Arizona, and the Apache credit it with the power of setting men crazy, but they deny that they have ever made use of it in their medicine or religion. Picart[5] speaks of the drink (wisoccan) which took away the brains of the young men undergoing initiation as medicine-men among the tribes of Virginia, but he does not say what this "wisoccan" was.

In Guiana,[6] the candidate for the office of medicine-man must, among

---

[1] Ross, Fur Hunters, quoted by Spencer, Desc. Soc.

[2] Max Müller, Science of Religion, p. 88.

[3] Davis, Spanish Conq. of N. M., p. 98.

[4] I Samuel, XII, 17, 18.

[5] Cérémonies et Coutumes, vol. 6, p. 75.

[6] Everard im Thurn, Indians of Guiana, London, 1883, p. 334.

other ordeals, "drink fearfully large drafts of tobacco juice, mixed with water." The medicine-men of Guiana are called peaiman.

I have never seen tobacco juice drank by medicine-men or others, but I remember seeing Shunca-Luta (Sorrel Horse) a medicine-man of the Dakota, chewing and swallowing a piece of tobacco and then going into what seemed to be a trance, all the while emitting deep grunts or groans. When he revived he insisted that those sounds had been made by a spirit which he kept down in his stomach. He also pretended to extract the quid of tobacco from underneath his ribs, and was full of petty tricks of legerdemain and other means of mystifying women and children.

All medicine-men claim the power of swallowing spear heads or arrows and fire, and there are at times many really wonderful things done by them which have the effect of strengthening their hold upon the people.

The medicine-men of the Ojibwa thrust arrows and similar instruments down their throats. They also allow themselves to be shot at with marked bullets.[1]

While I was among the Tusayan, in 1881, I learned of a young boy, quite a child, who was looked up to by the other Indians, and on special occasions made his appearance decked out in much native finery of beads and gewgaws, but the exact nature of his duties and supposed responsibilities could not be ascertained.

Diego Duran[2] thought that the priesthood among the Mexicans was to a great extent hereditary, much like the right of primogeniture among the people of Spain. Speaking of the five assistants who held down the human victim at the moment of sacrifice, he says:

Los nombres de los cinco eran Chachalmeca, que en nuestra Lengua quiere tanto decir como Levita ó ministro de cosa divina ó sagrada. Era esta dignidad entre ellos muy suprema y en mucha tenida, la cual se heredaba de hijos á padres como cosa de mayorazgo, sucediendo los hijos á los Padres en aquella sangrienta Dignidad endemoniada y cruel.

Concerning the medicine-men of Peru, Dorman[3] says:

The priestly office among the Peruvians appears to have been hereditary; some attained it by election; a man struck by lightning was considered as chosen by heaven; also those who became suddenly insane. Mr. Southey says that among the Moxos of Brazil, who worshiped the tiger, a man who was rescued from but marked by the claws of the animal, was set apart for the priesthood, and none other.

I shall have occasion to introduce a medicine-woman of the Apache, Tze-go-juni, or "Pretty-mouth," whose claims to preeminence among her people would seem to have had no better foundation than her escape from lightning stroke and from the bites of a mountain lion, which had seized her during the night and had not killed her.

I remember the case of an old Navajo medicine-man who was killed

---

[1] Tanner's Narrative, p. 390.

[2] Diego Duran, lib. 3, cap. 3, p. 201.

[3] Dorman, Primitive Superstitions, p. 384.

by lightning. The whole tribe participated in the singing, drumming, and dancing incident to so important an event, but no white men were allowed to be present. My information was derived from the dead man's young nephew, while I was among that tribe.

Among the Arawak of South America there are hereditary conjurers who profess to find out the enemy who by the agency of an evil spirit has killed the deceased.[1]

Picart says of the medicine-men of the tribes along Rio de la Plata: " Pour être Prêtre ou Médecin parmi eux, il faut avoir jeûné longtems & souvent. Il faut avoir combatu plusieurs fois contre les bêtes Sauvages, principalement contre les Tigres, & tout au moins en avoir été mordu ou égratigné. Après cela on peut obtenir l'Ordre, de Prêtrise; car le Tigre est chez eux un animal presque divin."[2]

The medicine-men of the Apache are not confined to one gens or clan, as among the Shawnee and Cherokee, according to Brinton,[3] neither do they believe, as the Cherokee do, according to the same authority, that the seventh son is a natural-born prophet with the gift of healing by touch, but upon this latter point I must be discreet, as I have never known an Apache seventh son.

The Cherokee still preserve the custom of consecrating a family of their tribe to the priesthood, as the family of Levi was consecrated among the Jews.[4]

The neophytes of the isthmus of Darien were boys from ten to twelve years " selected for the natural inclination or the peculiar aptitude and intelligence which they displayed for the service."[5]

Peter Martyr says of the Chiribchis of South America: " Out of the multitude of children they chuse some of 10 or 12 yeeres old, whom they know by conjecture to be naturally inclined to that service."[6]

The peculiarity of the Moxos was that they thought none designated for the office of medicine-man but such as had escaped from the claws of the South American tiger which, indeed, it is said they worshiped as a god.[7]

Contrary to what Spencer says, the chiefs of the tribes of the Southwest, at least, are not ipso facto medicine-men; but among the Tonto Apache the brother of the head chief, Cha-ut-lip-un, was the great medicine-man, and generally the medicine-men are related closely to the prominent chiefs, which would seem to imply either a formal deputation of priestly functions from the chiefs to relatives, or what may be practically the same thing, the exercise of family influence to bring about a recognition of the necromantic powers of some aspirant; but among

[1] Spencer, Desc. Sociology.
[2] Picart, Cérémonies et Coutumes Religieuses, Amsterdam, 1735, vol. 6, p. 122.
[3] Myths of the New World, p. 281.
[4] Domenech, Deserts, vol. 2, p. 392.
[5] Bancroft, Nat. Races, vol, 1, p. 777.
[6] Hakluyt, Voyages, vol. 5, p. 462.
[7] Brinton, Myths of the New World, p. 281.

the Apache there is no priest caste; the same man may be priest, warrior, etc.[1]

"The juice of the Datura seed is employed by the Portuguese women of Goa: they mix it, says Linschott, in the liquor drank by their husbands, who fall, for twenty-four hours at least, into a stupor accompanied by continued laughing; but so deep is the sleep that nothing passing before them affects them; and when they recover their senses, they have no recollection of what has taken place."[2]

"The Darien Indians used the seeds of the *Datura sanguinea* to bring on in children prophetic delirium, in which they revealed hidden treasure. In Peru the priests who talked with the "huaca" or fetishes used to throw themselves into an ecstatic condition by a narcotic drink called "tonca," made from the same plant."[3]

The medicine-men of the Walapai, according to Charlie Spencer, who married one of their women and lived among them for years, were in the habit of casting bullets in molds which contained a small piece of paper. They would allow these bullets to be fired at them, and of course the missile would split in two parts and do no injury. Again, they would roll a ball of sinew and attach one end to a small twig, which was inserted between the teeth. They would then swallow the ball of sinew, excepting the end thus attached to the teeth, and after the heat and moisture of the stomach had softened and expanded the sinew they would begin to draw it out yard after yard, saying to the frightened squaws that they had no need of intestines and were going to pull them all out. Others among the Apache have claimed the power to shoot off guns without touching the triggers or going near the weapons; to be able to kill or otherwise harm their enemies at a distance of 100 miles. In nearly every boast made there is some sort of a saving clause, to the effect that no witchcraft must be made or the spell will not work, no women should be near in a delicate state from any cause, etc.

Mickey Free has assured me that he has seen an Apache medicine-man light a pipe without doing anything but hold his hands up toward the sun. This story is credible enough if we could aver that the medicine-man was supplied, as I suspect he was, with a burning glass.

That the medicine-man has the faculty of transforming himself into a coyote and other animals at pleasure and then resuming the human form is as implicitly believed in by the American Indians as it was by our own forefathers in Europe. This former prevalence of lycanthropy all over Europe can be indicated in no more forcible manner than by stating that until the reign of Louis XIV, in France, the fact of being a were-wolf was a crime upon which one could be arraigned before a court; but with the discontinuance of the crime the were-wolves them-

[1] Spencer, Ecclesiastical Institutions, cap. v.
[2] Salverte, Philosophy of Magic, vol. 2, pp. 6–7.
[3] Tylor, Primitive Culture, London, 1871, vol. 2, p. 377.

selves seem to have retired from business.[1] In Abyssinia, at the present day, blacksmiths are considered to be were-wolves, according to Winstanley. The Apache look upon blacksmiths as being allied to the spirits and call them "pesh-chidin"—the witch, spirit, or ghost, of the iron. The priestly powers conceded to the blacksmith of Gretna Green need no allusion here.

According to Sir Walter Scott,[2] trials for lycanthropy were abolished in France by an edict of Louis XIV.

Parkman[3] describes, from the Relations of Pére Le Jeune, how the Algonkin medicine-man announced that he was going to kill a rival medicine-man who lived at Gaspé, 100 leagues distant.

The Abipones of Paraguay, according to Father Dobrizhoffer, "credit their medicine-men with power to inflict disease and death, to cure all disorders, to make known distant and future events; to cause rain, hail, and tempest; to call up the shades of the dead and consult them concerning hidden matters; to put on the form of a tiger; to handle every kind of serpent without danger, etc.; which powers they imagine are not obtained by art, but imparted to certain persons by their grandfather, the devil."

The medicine-men of Honduras claimed the power of turning themselves into lions and tigers and of wandering in the mountains.[4]

"Grandes Hechiceros i Bruxos, porque se hacian Perros, Puercos i Ximios."[5]

Gomara also calls attention to the fact that the medicine-men, "hechiceros" and "brujos," as he calls them, of the Nicaraguans, possessed the power of lycanthropy; "segun ellos mismos decian, se hacen perros, puercos y gimias."[6]

Great as are the powers claimed by the medicine-men, it is admitted that baleful influences may be at work to counteract and nullify them. As has already been shown, among these are the efforts of witches, the presence of women who are sometimes supposed to be so "antimedicinal," if such a term may be applied, that the mere stepping over a warrior's gun will destroy its value.

There may be other medicine-men at work with countercharms, and there may be certain neglects on the part of the person applying for aid which will invalidate all that the medicine-man can do for him. For example, while the "hoop-me-koff" was raging among the Mohave the fathers of families afflicted with it were forbidden to touch coffee or salt, and were directed to bathe themselves in the current of the Colorado. But the whooping cough ran its course in spite of all that the medicine-

---

[1] "St. Patrick, we are told, floated to Ireland on an altar stone. Among other wonderful things, he converted a marauder into a wolf and lighted a fire with icicles."—James A. Froude, Reminiscences of the High Church Revival. (Letter V.)

[2] Demonology and Witchcraft, p. 184.

[3] Jesuits in North America, pp. 34, 35.

[4] Herrera, dec. 4, lib. 8, cap. 5. 159.

[5] Ibid., dec. 3, lib. 4, p. 121.

[6] Hist. de las Indias, p. 283.

men could do to check its progress. When the Walapai were about to engage in a great hunt continence was enjoined upon the warriors for a certain period.

Besides all these accidental impairments of the vigor of the medicine-men, there seems to be a gradual decadence of their abilities which can be rejuvenated only by rubbing the back against a sacred stone projecting from the ground in the country of the Walapai, not many miles from the present town of Kingman, on the Atlantic and Pacific Railroad. Another stone of the same kind was formerly used for the same purpose by the medicine-men of the pueblos of Laguna and Acoma, as I have been informed by them. I am unable to state whether or not such recuperative properties were ever ascribed to the medicine stone at the Sioux agency near Standing Rock, S. Dak., or to the great stone around which the medicine-men of Tusayan marched in solemn procession in their snake dance, but I can say that in the face of the latter, each time that I saw it (at different dates between 1874 and 1881), there was a niche which was filled with votive offerings.

Regnard, a traveler in Lapland, makes the statement that when the shamans of that country began to lose their teeth they retired from practice. There is nothing of this kind to be noted among the Apache or other tribes of North America with which I am in any degree familiar. On the contrary, some of the most influential of those whom I have known have been old and decrepit men, with thin, gray hair and teeth gone or loose in their heads. In a description given by Corbusier of a great "medicine" ceremony of the Apache-Yuma at Camp Verde, it is stated that the principal officer was a "toothless, gray-haired man."[1]

Among many savage or barbarous peoples of the world albinos have been reserved for the priestly office. There are many well marked examples of albinism among the Pueblos of New Mexico and Arizona, especially among the Zuñi and Tusayan; but in no case did I learn that the individuals thus distinguished were accredited with power not ascribable to them under ordinary circumstances. Among the Cheyenne I saw one family, all of whose members had the crown lock white. They were not medicine-men, neither were any of the members of the single albino family among the Navajo in 1881.

It is a well known fact that among the Romans epilepsy was looked upon as a disease sent direct from the gods, and that it was designated the "sacred disease"—morbus sacer. Mahomet is believed to have been an epileptic. The nations of the East regard epileptics and the insane as inspired from on high.

Our native tribes do not exactly believe that the mildly insane are gifted with medical or spiritual powers; but they regard them with a feeling of superstitious awe, akin to reverence. I have personally known several cases of this kind, though not within late years, and am not able to say whether or not the education of the younger generation

---

[1] American Antiquarian, November, 1886, p. 334.

in our schools has as yet exercised an influence in eradicating this sentiment.

Strange to say, I was unable to find any observance of lucky or unlucky days among the Apache. The Romans in the period of their greatest enlightenment had their days, both "fasti" and "nefasti." Neither was I able to determine the selection of auspicious days for marriage; indeed, it was stated that the medicine-men had nothing to do with marriage. Among the Zapotecs the wedding day was fixed by the priests.[1] In this the Apache again stands above the Roman who would not marry in the month dedicated to the goddess Maia (May), because human sacrifice used to be offered in that month. This superstition survived in Europe until a comparatively recent period. According to Picart the Hebrew rabbis designated the days upon which weddings should take place.

Herbert Spencer[2] says that the medicine-men of the Arawaks claimed the "jus primæ noctis." There is no such privilege claimed or conceded among the North American tribes, to my knowledge, and the Arawaks would seem to be alone among the natives of the whole continent in this respect.

In the town of Cumaná, in Amaracapanna, apparently close to Carthagena, in the present republic of Colombia, South America, the medicine-men, according to Girolamo Benzoni, exercised the "jus primæ noctis."[3]

To recover stolen or lost property, especially ponies, is one of the principal tasks imposed upon the medicine-men. They rely greatly upon the aid of pieces of crystal in effecting this   I made a friend of an Apache medicine-man by presenting him with a large crystal of denticulated spar, much larger than the one of whose mystical properties he had just been boasting to me. I can not say how this property of the crystal is manifested. Na-a-cha, the medicine-man alluded to, could give no explanation, except that by looking into it he could see everything he wanted to see.

The name of an American Indian is a sacred thing, not to be divulged by the owner himself without due consideration. One may ask a warrior of any tribe to give his name and the question will be met with either a point-blank refusal or the more diplomatic evasion that he can not understand what is wanted of him. The moment a friend approaches, the warrior first interrogated will whisper what is wanted, and the friend can tell the name, receiving a reciprocation of the courtesy from the other. The giving of names to children is a solemn matter, and one in which the medicine-men should always be consulted. Among the Plains tribes the children were formerly named at the moment of piercing their ears, which should occur at the first sun dance after their birth, or rather as near their first year as possible.

---

[1] Dorman, Primitive Superstitions, p. 380, quoting Herrera, dec. 3, p. 262.

[2] Descriptive Sociology.

[3] Admiral Smyth's translation in Hakluyt Society, London, 1857, vol. 21, p. 9.

The wailing of the children at the sun dance as their ears were slit will always be to me a most distressing memory.

The warriors of the Plains tribes used to assume agnomens or battle names, and I have known some of them who had enjoyed as many as four or five; but the Apache name once conferred seems to remain through life, except in the case of the medicine-men, who, I have always suspected, change their names upon assuming their profession, much as a professor of learning in China is said to do.

The names of mothers-in-law are never mentioned and it would be highly improper to ask for them by name; neither are the names of the dead, at least not for a long period of time. But it often happens that the child will bear the name of its grandfather or some other relative who was a distinguished warrior.

All charms, idols, talismans, medicine hats, and other sacred regalia should be made, or at least blessed, by the medicine-men. They assume charge of all ceremonial feasts and dances—such as the nubile dance, which occurs when any maiden attains marriageable age, and war dances preceding battle. Nearly all preparations for the warpath are under their control, and when on the trail of the enemy their power is almost supreme. Not a night passes but that the medicine-men get into the "ta-a-chi," or sweat bath, if such a thing be possible, and there remain for some minutes, singing and making "medicine" for the good of the party. After dark they sit around the fire and sing and talk with the spirits and predict the results of the campaign. I have alluded quite fully to these points in a previous work.

When a man is taken sick the medicine-men are in the zenith of their glory. One or two will assume charge of the case, and the clansmen and friends of the patient are called upon to supply the fire and help out in the chorus. On such occasions the Apache use no music except a drum or a rawhide. The drum is nearly always improvised from an iron camp kettle, partially filled with water and covered with a piece of cloth, well soaped and drawn as tight as possible. The drumstick does not terminate in a ball, as with us, but is curved into a circle, and the stroke is not perpendicular to the surface, but is often given from one side to the other. The American Indian's theory of disease is the theory of the Chaldean, the Assyrian, the Hebrew, the Greek, the Roman—all bodily disorders and ailments are attributed to the maleficence of spirits who must be expelled or placated. Where there is only one person sick, the exercises consist of singing and drumming exclusively, but dancing is added in all cases when an epidemic is raging in the tribe. The medicine-men lead off in the singing, to which the assistants reply with a refrain which at times has appeared to me to be antiphonal. Then the chorus is swelled by the voices of the women and larger children and rises and falls with monotonous cadence. Prayers are recited, several of which have been repeated to me and transcribed; but very frequently the words are ejaculatory and confined to such expressions as "ugashe" (go away), and again there is to be noted the same mumbling of incoherent phrases which has been the stock in trade of medicine-men in all ages and places. This use of gibberish was admitted by the medicine-men, who claimed that the words employed and known only to themselves (each individual seemed to have his own vocabulary) were mysteriously effective in dispelling sickness of any kind. Gibberish was believed to be more potent in magic than was language which the practitioner or his dupes could comprehend. In Saxon Leechdoms, compiled by Cockayne, will be seen a text of gibberish to be recited by those wishing to stanch the flow of blood. (See p. 14.)

In the following citations it will be observed that Adair and Catlin were grievously in error in their respective statements. Adair denies that Indians on the warpath or elsewhere depend upon their "augurs" for instruction and guidance.[1] Gomara is authority for the statement that the natives of Hispaniola never made war without consulting their medicine-men—"no sin respuesta de los ídolos ó sin la de los sacerdotes, que adevinan."[2]

The medicine-men of Chicora (our present South Carolina) sprinkled the warriors with the juice of a certain herb as they were about to engage in battle.[3]

In Chicora "Mascaban los Sacerdotes una Ierva, i con el çumo de ella rociaban los Soldados, quando querian dàr batalla, que era bendecirlos."[4]

"Among the Abipones [of Paraguay] the medicine-man teaches them the place, time, and manner proper for attacking wild beasts or the enemy."[5]

"The North American Indians are nowhere idolaters."[6]

Idols were always carried to war by the natives of Hispaniola: "Atanse á la frente ídolos chiquitos cuando quieren pelear."[7]

"Among the primitive Germans * * * the maintenance of discipline in the field as in the council was left in great measure to the priests; they took the auguries and gave the signal for onset."[8]

"In New Caledonia * * * the priests go to battle, but sit in the distance, *fasting* and praying for victory."[9]

Our hunting songs and war songs may be a survival of the incantations of Celtic or Teutonic medicine-men.

The adoption or retention of obsolete phraseology as a hieratic language which has been noted among many nations of the highest comparative development is a manifestation of the same mental process.

[1] American Indians, p. 26.

[2] Gomara, Hist. de las Indias, p. 173.

[3] "Estos mascan cierta yerba, y con el zumo rocian las soldados estando para dar batalla." Gomara, ibid., p. 179.

[4] Herrera, dec. 2, lib. 10, p. 260.

[5] Father Dobrizhoffer, quoted by Spencer, Eccles. Institutions, cap. 10, sec. 630.

[6] Catlin, N. A. Indians, London, 1845, vol. 2, p. 232.

[7] Gomara, op. cit., p. 173.

[8] Spencer, Eccles. Institutions, cap. 10, pp. 780, 781, quoting Stubb's Constitutional History of England.

[9] Ibid., sec. 630, p. 781, quoting Turner (Geo.), Nineteen Years in Polynesia.

Gibberish was so invariable an accompaniment of the sacred antics of the medicine-men of Mexico that Fray Diego Duran warns his readers that if they see any Indian dancing and singing, "ó diciendo algunas palabras que no son inteligibles, pues es de saber que aquellos representaban Dioses."[1]

Henry Youle Hind says:

The Dakotahs have a common and a sacred language. The conjurer, the war prophet, and the dreamer employ a language in which words are borrowed from other Indian tongues and dialects; they make much use of descriptive expressions, and use words apart from the ordinary signification. The Ojibways abbreviate their sentences and employ many elliptical forms of expression, so much so that half-breeds, quite familiar with the colloquial language, fail to comprehend a medicine-man when in the full flow of excited oratory.[2]

"Blood may be stanched by the words sicyeuma, cucuma, ucuma, cuma, uma, ma, a."[3] There are numbers of these gibberish formulæ given, but one is sufficient.

"The third part of the magic[4] of the Chaldeans belonged entirely to that description of charlatanism which consists in the use of gestures, postures, and mysterious speeches, as byplay, and which formed an accompaniment to the proceedings of the thaumaturgist well calculated to mislead."[5]

Sahagun[6] calls attention to the fact that the Aztec hymns were in language known only to the initiated.

It must be conceded that the monotonous intonation of the medicine-men is not without good results, especially in such ailments as can be benefited by the sleep which such singing induces. On the same principle that petulant babies are lulled to slumber by the crooning of their nurses, the sick will frequently be composed to a sound and beneficial slumber, from which they awake refreshed and ameliorated. I can

---

[1] Vol. 3, p. 176.

" In every part of the globe fragments of primitive languages are preserved in religious rites." Humboldt, Researches, London, 1814, vol. 1, p. 97.

" Et même Jean P c, Prince de la Mirande, escrit que les mots barbares & non entendus ont plus de puissance en la Magie que ceux qui sont entendus." Picart, vol. 10, p. 45.

The medicine-men of Cumana (now the United States of Colombia, South America) cured their patients "con palabras muy revesadas y que aun el mismo médico no las entiende." Gomara, Hist. de las Indias, p. 208.

The Tlascaltecs had "oradores" who employed gibberish—"hablaban Gerigonça." Herrera, dec. 2, lib. 6, p. 163.

In Peru, if the fields were afflicted with drought, the priests, among other things, "chantaient un cantique dont le sens était inconnu du vulgaire." Balboa, Hist. du Pérou, p. 128, in Ternaux-Compans, vol. 15.

[2] Assiniboine and Saskatchewan Exped., London, 1860, vol. 2, p. 155.

[3] Cockayne, Leechdoms, vol. 1, p. xxx.

[4] "The belief in the magic power of sacred words, whether religious formulas or the name of gods, was also acknowledged [i. e. in Egypt] and was the source of a frightful amount of superstition. . . . The superstitious repetition of names (many of which perhaps never had any meaning at all) is particularly conspicuous in numerous documents much more recent than the Book of the Dead."—Hibbert, Lectures, 1879, pp. 192, 193.

[5] Salverte, Philosophy of Magic, vol. 1, p. 134.

[6] Kingsborough, lib. 2, vol. 7, p. 102.

recall, among many other cases, those of Chaundezi ("Long Ear," or "Mule") and Chemihuevi-Sal, both chiefs of the Apache, who recovered under the treatment of their own medicine-men after our surgeons had abandoned the case. This recovery could be attributed only to the sedative effects of the chanting.

Music of a gentle, monotonous kind has been prescribed in the medical treatment of Romans, Greeks, and even of comparatively modern Europeans. John Mason Goode, in his translation of Lucretius' De Natura Rerum, mentions among others Galen, Theophrastus, and Aulus Gellius. An anonymous writer in the Press of Philadelphia, Pa., under date of December 23, 1888, takes the ground that its use should be resumed.

The noise made by medicine-men around the couch of the sick is no better, no worse, than the clangor of bells in Europe. Bells, we are told, were rung on every possible occasion. Brand is full of quaint information on this head. According to him they were rung in Spain when women were in labor,[1] at weddings,[2] to dispel thunder, drive away bad spirits, and frustrate the deviltry of witches;[3] throughout Europe on the arrival of emperors, kings, the higher nobility, bishops, etc.,[4] to ease pain of the dead,[5] were solemnly baptized, receiving names,[6] and became the objects of superstition, various powers being ascribed to them.[7]

Adair, who was gifted with an excellent imagination, alludes to the possession of an "ark" by the medicine-men of the Creeks and other tribes of the Mississippi country, among whom he lived for so many years as a trader. The Apache have no such things; but I did see a sacred bundle or package, which I was allowed to feel, but not to open, and which I learned contained some of the lightning-riven twigs upon which they place such dependence. This was carried by a young medicine-man, scarcely out of his teens, during Gen. Crook's expedition into the Sierra Madre, Mexico, in 1883, in pursuit of the hostile Chiricahua Apache. Maj. Frank North also told me that the Pawnee had a sacred package which contained, among other objects of veneration, the skin of an albino buffalo calf.

There are allusions by several authorities to the necessity of confession by the patient before the efforts of the medicine-men can prove efficacious.[8]

---

[1] Popular Antiquities, vol. 2, p. 70.

[2] Ibid., p. 160.

[3] Ibid., p. 217.

[4] Ibid., p. 218.

[5] Ibid., p. 219.

[6] Ibid., pp. 214, 215.

[7] Ibid., p. 216.

[8] "When the Carriers are severely sick, they often think that they shall not recover, unless they divulge to a priest or magician, every crime which they may have committed, which has hitherto been kept secret."—[Harmon's Journal, p. 300. The Carriers or Ta-kully are Tinneh.

This confession, granting that it really existed, could well be compared to the warpath secret, which imposed upon all the warriors engaged the duty of making a clean breast of all delinquencies and secured them immunity from punishment for the same, even if they had been offenses against some of the other warriors present.

The Sioux and others had a custom of "striking the post" in their dances, especially the sun dance, and there was then an obligation upon the striker to tell the truth. I was told that the medicine-men were wont to strike with a club the stalagmites in the sacred caves of the Apache, but what else they did I was not able to ascertain.

Under the title of "hoddentin" will be found the statement made by one of the Apache as to the means employed to secure the presence of a medicine-man at the bedside of the sick. I give it for what it is worth, merely stating that Kohl, in his Kitchi-Gami, if I remember correctly, refers to something of the same kind where the medicine-man is represented as being obliged to respond to every summons made unless he can catch the messenger within a given distance and kick him.

There is very little discrepancy of statement as to what would happen to a medicine-man in case of failure to cure; but many conflicting stories have been in circulation as to the number of patients he would be allowed to kill before incurring risk of punishment. My own conclusions are that there is no truth whatever in the numbers alleged, either three or seven, but that a medicine-man would be in danger, under certain circumstances, if he let only one patient die on his hands. These circumstances would be the verdict of the spirit doctors that he was culpably negligent or ignorant. He could evade death at the hands of the patient's kinsfolk only by flight or by demonstrating that a witch had been at the bottom of the mischief.[1]

Medicine-men, called "wizards" by Falkner, sometimes were killed by the Patagonians, when unsuccessful in their treatment, and were also obliged to wear women's clothing. They were selected in youth for supposed qualifications, especially if epileptic.[2]

In Hispaniola we are told that when a man died his friends resorted to necromancy to learn whether he had died through the neglect of the attending medicine-man to observe the prescribed fasts. If they found the medicine-man guilty, they killed him and broke all his bones. In spite of this the medicine-man often returned to life and had to be killed again, and mutilated by castration and otherwise.[3]

Herrera repeats the story about a patient who died and whose relatives felt dissatisfied with the medicine-man:

Para saber si la muerte fue por su cúlpa, tomaban el çumo de cierta Ierva, i cortaban las vñas del muerto, i los cabellos de encima de la frente, i los hacian polvos,

---

[1] For identical notions among the Arawaks of Guiana, Tupis of Brazil, Creeks, Patagonians, Kaffirs, Chiquitos, and others, see the works of Schoolcraft, Herbert Spencer, Schultze, and others.

[2] Extract from the Jesuit Falkner's account of Patagonia, in Voyages of the *Adventure* and *Beagle*, London, 1839, vol. 2, p. 163.

[3] "Nul de ces médecins ne peut mourir si'ls ne lui enlevent les testicules." Brasseur de Bourbourg, Trans. of Fra Roman Pane, Des Antiquités des Indiens, Paris, 1864, p. 451.

i mezclados con el çumo, se lo daban à beber al muerto por la boca, i las narices, i luego le preguntaban muchas veces, si el Medico guardò dieta, hasta que hablando el demonio, respondia tan claro, como si fuera vivo, i decia, que el Medico no hiço dieta, i luego le bolvian à la sepultura.

Then the relatives attacked the medicine-man: "I le daban tantos palos, que le quebraban los braços, i las piernas, i à otros sacaban los ojos, i los cortaban sus miembros genitales."[1]

Alexander the Great expressed his sorrow at the death of his friend Hephæstion by crucifying the poor physicians who had attended the deceased.[2]

The medicine-men of the Natchez were put to death when they failed to cure.[3]

The Apache attach as much importance to the necessity of "laying the manes" of their dead as the Romans did. They have not localized the site of the future world as the Mohave have, but believe that the dead remain for a few days or nights in the neighborhood of the place where they departed from this life, and that they try to communicate with their living friends through the voice of the owl. If a relative hears this sound by night, or, as often happens, he imagines that he has seen the ghost itself, he hurries to the nearest medicine-man, relates his story, and carries out to the smallest detail the prescription of feast, singing, dancing, and other means of keeping the spirit in good humor on the journey which it will now undertake to the "house of spirits," the "chidin-bi-kungua." Nearly all medicine-men claim the power of going there at will, and not a few who are not medicine-men claim the same faculty.

The medicine-men of the Apache are paid by each patient or by his friends at the time they are consulted. There is no such thing as a maintenance fund, no system of tithes, nor any other burden for their support, although I can recall having seen while among the Zuñi one of the medicine-men who was making cane holders for the tobacco to be smoked at a coming festival, and whose fields were attended and his herds guarded by the other members of the tribe.

Among the Eskimo "the priest receives fees beforehand."[4]

"Tous ces sorciers ne réfusaient leurs secours à personne, pourvu qu'on les payait."[5]

"Among other customs was that of those who came to be cured, giving their bow and arrows, shoes, and beads to the Indians who accompanied Vaca and his companions."[6] (But we must remember that Vaca and his comrades traveled across the continent as medicine-men.)

"Las sementeras que hacen los Assenais son tambien de comunidad

[1] Hist. Gen., dec. 1, lib. 3, p. 69.
[2] Madden, Shrines and Sepulchres, vol. 1, p. 14.
[3] Gayarre, Louisiana; its Colonial History, p. 355.
[4] Spencer, Desc. Sociology.
[5] Balboa, Hist. du Pérou, Ternaux-Compans, vol. 15.
[6] Davis. Conq. of New Mexico, p. 86.

y comienzan la primera en la casa de su Chemisi que es su sacerdote principal y el que cuida de la Casa del Fuego." [1]   The Asinai extended as far east as the present city of Natchitoches (Nacogdoches).

Spencer quotes Bernan and Hilhouse to the effect that the poor among the Arawaks of South America (Guiana) have no names because they can not pay the medicine-men. [2]

As a general rule, the medicine-men do not attend to their own families, neither do they assist in cases of childbirth unless specially needed.   To both these rules there are exceptions innumerable.   While I was at San Carlos Agency, Surgeon Davis was sent for to help in a case of uterine inertia, and I myself have been asked in the pueblo of Nambé, New Mexico, to give advice in a case of puerperal fever.

The medicine-men are accused of administering poisons to their enemies.   Among the Navajo I was told that they would put finely pounded glass in food.

<h3 style="text-align:center">MEDICINE-WOMEN.</h3>

There are medicine-women as well as medicine-men among the Apache, with two of whom I was personally acquainted.   One named "Captain Jack" was well advanced in years and physically quite feeble, but bright in intellect and said to be well versed in the lore of

her people.   She was fond of instructing her grandchildren, whom she supported, in the prayers and invocations to the gods worshiped by her fathers, and I have several times listened carefully and unobserved to these recitations and determined that the prayers were the same as those which had already been given to myself as those of the tribe.   The other was named Tze-go-juni, a Chiricahua, and a woman with a most romantic history.   She had passed five years in captivity among the Mexicans in Sonora and had learned to speak Spanish with facility.   A mountain lion had severely mangled her in the shoulder and knee, and once she had been struck by lightning; so that whether by reason of superior attainments or by an appeal to the superstitious reverence of her comrades, she wielded considerable influence.   These medicine-women devote their attention principally to obstetrics, and have

Fig. 1.—Medicine arrow used by Apache and Pueblo women.

many peculiar stories to relate concerning pre-natal influences and matters of that sort.   Tze-go-juni wore at her neck the stone amulet, shaped like a spear, which is figured in the illustrations of this paper.   The material was the silex from the top of a mountain, taken from a ledge at the foot of a tree which had been struck by lightning. The fact that siliceous rock will emit sparks when struck by another hard body appeals to the reasoning powers of the savage as a proof that the fire must have been originally deposited therein by the bolt of light-

---

[1] Cronica Serafica y Apostolica, Espinosa, Mexico, 1746, p. 421.
[2] Desc. Sociology.

ning. A tiny piece of this arrow or lance was broken off and ground into the finest powder, and then administered in water to women during time of gestation. I have found the same kind of arrows in use among the women of Laguna and other pueblos. This matter will receive more extended treatment in my coming monograph on "Stone Worship."

Mendieta is authority for the statement that the Mexicans had both medicine-men and medicine-women. The former attended to the sick men and the latter to the sick women. "Á las mujeres siempre las curaban otras mujeres, y á los hombres otros hombres."[1] Some of the medicine-women seem to have made an illicit use of the knowledge they had acquired, in which case both the medicine-woman and the woman concerned were put to death. "La mujer preñada que tomaba con que abortar y echar la criatura, ella y la física que le habia dado con que la lanzase, ambas morian."[2]

Gomara asserts that they were to be found among the Indians of Chicora (South Carolina).[3] He calls them "viejas" (old women). "Los Medicos eran Mugeres viejas, i no havia otras."[4] In Nicaragua, "Las Viejas curaban los Enfermos."[5]

There were medicine-women in Goazacoalco: "Tienen Medicos para curar las enfermedades, i los mas eran Mugeres, grandes Herbolarias, que hacian todas las curas con Iervas."[6]

Bernal Diaz, in 1568, speaks of having, on a certain occasion, at the summit of a high mountain, found "an Indian woman, very fat, and having with her a dog of that species, which they breed in order to eat, and which do not bark. This Indian was a witch; she was in the act of sacrificing the dog, which is a signal of hostility."[7]

"The office of medicine-man though generally usurped by males does not appertain to them exclusively, and at the time of our visit the one most extensively known was a black (or meztizo) woman, who had acquired the most unbounded influence by shrewdness, joined to a hideous personal appearance, and a certain mystery with which she was invested."[8] Creeks have medicine-women as well as medicine-men. The Eskimo have medicine-men and medicine-women.[9] The medicine-men and women of the Dakota "can cause ghosts to appear on occasion."[10]

Speaking of the Chippewa, Spencer says: "Women may practice soothsaying, but the higher religious functions are performed only by men."[11]

---

[1] Mendieta, Hist. Eclesiástica Indiana, p. 136.

[2] Ibid., p. 136.

[3] Hist. de las Indias, p. 179.

[4] Herrera, dec. 2, lib. 10, p. 260.

[5] Ibid., dec. 3, lib. 4, p. 121.

[6] Ibid., dec. 4, lib. 9, cap. 7, p. 188.

[7] Keating's translation, p. 352, quoted by Samuel Farmar Jarvis, Religion of the Indian Tribes, in Coll. New York Historical Soc., vol. 3, 1819, p. 262.

[8] Smith, Araucanians, pp. 238, 239.

[9] Richardson, Arctic Searching Expedition, vol. 1, p. 366.

[10] Schultze, Fetichism, New York, 1885, p. 49.

[11] Spencer, Desc. Sociology.

The medicine-men of the Apacne do not assume to live upon food different from that used by the laity. There are such things as sacred feasts among the tribes of North America—as, for example, the feast of stewed puppy at the sun dance of the Sioux—but in these all people share.

In the mortuary ceremonies of the medicine-men there is a difference of degree, but not of kind. The Mohave, however, believe that the medicine-men go to a heaven of their own. They also believe vaguely in four different lives after this one.

Cabeza de Vaca says that the Floridians buried their ordinary dead, but burned their medicine-men, whose incinerated bones they preserved and drank in water.[1] "After they [the medicine-men and women of the Dakota] have four times run their career in human shape they are annihilated."[2] Schultze says that the medicine-men of the Sioux and the medicine-women also, after death "may be transformed into wild beasts."[2]

Surgeon Smart shows that among other offices entrusted to the medicine-men of the Apache was the reception of distinguished strangers.[3] Long asserts that the medicine-men of the Otoe, Omaha, and others along the Missouri pretended to be able to converse with the fetus in utero and predict the sex.[4] Nothing of that kind has ever come under my notice. Adair says that the medicine-men of the Cherokee would not allow snakes to be killed.[5] The Apache will not let snakes be killed within the limits of the camp by one of their own people, but they will not only allow a stranger to kill them, but request him to do so. They made this request of me on three occasions.

Several of the most influential medicine-men whom I have known were blind, among others old Na-ta-do-tash, whose medicine hat figures in these pages. Whether this blindness was the result of old age or due to the frenzy of dancing until exhausted in all seasons I am unable to conjecture. Schultze says of the shamans of Siberia: "This artificial frenzy has such a serious effect upon the body, and more particularly the eyes, that many of the shamans become blind; a circumstance which enhances the esteem in which they are held."[6] Some of the medicine-men of Peru went blind from overexertion in their dances, although Gomara assigns as a reason that it was from fear of the demon with whom they talked. "Y aun algunos se quiebran los ojos para semejante hablar [i. e., talk with the devil]; y creo que lo hacian de miedo, porque todos ellos se atapan los ojos cuando hablan con el."[7]

Dunbar tells us that the medicine-men of the Pawnee swallowed arrows and knives, and had also the trick of apparently killing a man

---

[1] Ternaux-Compans, vol. 7, p. 110.

[2] Schultze, Fetichism, New York, 1885, p. 49.

[3] Smithsonian Report for 1867.

[4] Long's Expedition, Philadelphia, 1823, p. 238.

[5] Hist. of the American Indians, p. 238.

[6] Schultze, Fetichism, New York, 1885, p. 52.

[7] Hist. de las Indias, p. 232.

and bringing him back to life. The same power was claimed by the medicine-men of the Zuñi, and the story told me by old Pedro Pino of the young men whom they used to kill and restore to life, will be found in "The Snake Dance of the Moquis."

REMEDIES AND MODES OF TREATMENT.

The materia medica of the Apache is at best limited and comprehends scarcely anything more than roots, leaves, and other vegetable matter. In gathering these remedies they resort to no superstitious ceremonies that I have been able to detect, although I have not often seen them collecting. They prefer incantation to pharmacy at all times, although the squaws of the Walapai living near old Camp Beale Springs in 1873, were extremely fond of castor oil, for which they would beg each day.

The main reliance for nearly all disorders is the sweat bath, which is generally conducive of sound repose. All Indians know the benefit to be derived from relieving an overloaded stomach, and resort to the titillation of the fauces with a feather to induce nausea. I have seen the Zuñi take great drafts of lukewarm water and then practice the above as a remedy in dyspepsia.

When a pain has become localized and deep seated, the medicine-men resort to suction of the part affected, and raise blisters in that way. I was once asked by the Walapai chief, Sequanya, to look at his back and sides. He was covered with cicatrices due to such treatment, the medicine-men thinking thus to alleviate the progressive paralysis from which he had been long a sufferer, and from which he shortly afterwards died. After a long march, I have seen Indians of different bands expose the small of the back uncovered to the fierce heat of a pile of embers to produce a rubefacient effect and stimulate what is known as a weak back. They drink freely of hot teas or infusions of herbs and grasses for the cure of chills. They are all dextrous in the manufacture of splints out of willow twigs, and seem to meet with much success in their treatment of gunshot wounds, which they do not dress as often as white practitioners, alleging that the latter, by so frequently removing the bandages, unduly irritate the wounds. I have known them to apply moxa, and I remember to have seen two deep scars upon the left hand of the great Apache chief Cochise, due to this cause.

It should not be forgotten that the world owes a large debt to the medicine-men of America, who first discovered the virtues of coca, sarsaparilla, jalap, cinchona, and guiacum. They understand the administration of enemata, and have an apparatus made of the paunch of a sheep and the hollow leg bone.

Scarification is quite common, and is used for a singular purpose. The Apache scouts when tired were in the habit of sitting down and lashing their legs with bunches of nettles until the blood flowed. This, according to their belief, relieved the exhaustion.

The medicine-men of the Floridians, according to Vaca, sucked and blew on the patient, and put hot stones on his abdomen to take away pain; they also scarified, and they seemed to have used moxas. "Ils cautérisent aussi avec le feu." [1]

The medicine-men of Hispaniola cured by suction, and when they had extracted a stone or other alleged cause of sickness it was preserved as a sacred relic, especially by the women, who looked upon it as of great aid in parturition. [2] Venegas speaks of a tube called the "chacuaco," formed out of a very hard black stone, used by the medicine-men of California in sucking such parts of the patient's body as were grievously afflicted with pains. In these tubes they sometimes placed lighted tobacco and blew down upon the part affected after the manner of a moxa, I suppose. [3]

The men of Panuco were so addicted to drunkenness that we are told: "Lorsqu'ils sont fatigués de boire leur vin par la bouche, ils se couchent, élèvent les jambes en l'air, et s'en font introduire dans le fondement au moyen d'unè canule, tant que le corps peut en contenir." [4] The administration of wine in this manner may have been as a medicine, and the Aztecs of Panuco may have known that nutriment could be assimilated in this way. It shows at least that the Aztecs were acquainted with enemata.

"Quando la enfermedad les parecia que tenia necesidad de evacuacion, usaban del aiuda ò clister [clyster], con cocimientos de Iervas, i polvos, en Agua, i tomandola en la boca, con vn cañuto de hueso de pierna de Garça, la hechaban, i obraba copiosamente: i en esto pudo esta Gente ser industriada de la Cigueña, que con su largo pico se cura, como escriven los Naturales." [5] Smith says that the medicine-men of the Araucanians "are well acquainted with the proper use of emetics, cathartics, and sudorifics. For the purpose of injection they make use of a bladder, as is still commonly practiced among the Chilenos." [6] Oviedo says of the medicine-men: "Conoçian muchas hiervas de que usaban y eran apropiadas á diversas enfermedades." [7] One of the most curious remedies presented in Bancroft's first volume is the use of a poultice of mashed poison-ivy leaves as a remedy for ringworm by the Indians of Lower California.

The Indians of Topia (in the Sierra Madre, near Sinaloa), were in the habit of scarifying their tired legs and aching temples. [8] The Arawaks, of Guiana, also scarified, according to Spencer. [9] The inhabitants of

---

[1] Ternaux-Compans, vol. 7, pp. 114, 115.
[2] Notes from Gomara, Hist. de las Indias, pp. 172–173.
[3] History of California, vol. 1, p. 97.
[4] Ternaux-Compans, vol. 10, p. 85.
[5] Herrera, dec. 4, lib. 9, cap. 8, p. 188.
[6] Smith, Araucanians, p. 234.
[7] Bancroft, Native Races, vol. 1, p. 779.
[8] Alegre, Historia de la Compañia de Jesus en Nueva-España, vol. 1, p. 401.
[9] Desc. Sociology.

Kamchatka use enemata much in the same way as the Navajo and Apache do.[1] They also use moxa made of a fungus.[2]

It has never been my good fortune to notice an example of trephining among our savage tribes, although I have seen a good many wounded, some of them in the head. Trephining has been practiced by the aborigines of America, and the whole subject as noted among the primitive peoples of all parts of the globe has been treated in a monograph by Dr. Robert Fletcher, U. S. Army.[3]

Dr. Fordyce Grinnell, who was for some years attached to the Wichita Agency as resident physician, has published the results of his observations in a monograph, entitled "The healing art as practiced by the Indians of the Plains," in which he says: "Wet cupping is resorted to quite frequently. The surface is scarified by a sharp stone or knife, and a buffalo horn is used as the cupping glass. Cauterizing with red-hot irons is not infrequently employed." A cautery of "burning pith" was used by the Araucanians.[4]

"It may be safely affirmed that a majority of the nation [Choctaw] prefer to receive the attentions of a white physician when one can be obtained. * * * When the doctor is called to his patient he commences operations by excluding all white men and all who disbelieve in the efficacy of his incantations."[5] "The [Apache] scouts seem to prefer their own medicine-men when seriously ill, and believe the weird singing and praying around the couch is more effective than the medicine dealt out by our camp 'sawbones.'"[6] The promptness with which the American Indian recovers from severe wounds has been commented upon by many authorities. From my personal observation I could, were it necessary, adduce many examples. The natives of Australia seem to be endowed with the same recuperative powers.[7]

After all other means have failed the medicine-men of the Southwest devote themselves to making altars in the sand and clay near the couch of the dying, because, as Antonio Besias explained, this act was all the same as extreme unction. They portray the figures of various animals, and then take a pinch of the dust or ashes from each one and rub upon the person of the sick man as well as upon themselves. Similar altars or tracings were made by the medicine-men of Guatemala when they were casting the horoscope of a child and seeking to determine what was to be its medicine in life. This matter of sand altars has been fully treated by Matthews in the report of the Bureau of Ethnology for 1883–'84, and there are several representations to be found in my Snake Dance of the Moquis. "Writing on sand" is a mode of divination among the

---

[1] Kraskenninikoff, History of Kamtchatka and the Kurilski Islands, Grieve's translation, p. 219.

[2] Ibid., p. 220.

[3] Contributions to North American Ethnology, vol. 5.

[4] Smith, Araucanians, p. 233.

[5] Dr. Edwin G. Meek, Toner Collection, Library of Congress.

[6] Lieut. Pettit in Jour. U. S. Mil. Serv. Instit., 1886, pp. 336–337

[7] Smyth, Aborigines of Victoria, vol. 1, p. 155.

Chinese.[1]   Padre Boscana represents the "puplem" or medicine-men
of the Indians of California as making or sketching "a most uncouth
and ridiculous figure of an animal on the ground," and presumably of
sands, clays, and other such materials.[2]

HAIR AND WIGS.

The medicine-men of the Apache were, at least while young, extremely
careful of their hair, and I have often seen those who were very properly proud of their long and glossy chevelure.   Particularly do I recall
to mind the "doctor" at San Carlos in 1885, who would never allow
his flowing black tresses to be touched.   But they do not roach their
hair, as I have seen the Pawnee do; they do not add false hair to their
own, as I have seen among the Crow of Montana and the Mohave of the
Rio Colorado; they do not apply plasters of mud as do their neighbors
the Yuma, Cocopa, Mohave and Pima, and in such a manner as to
convince spectators that the intent was ceremonial; and they do not
use wigs in their dances.   Wigs made of black wool may still be found
occasionally among the Pueblos, but the Apache do not use them, and
there is no reference to such a thing in their myths.

It is to be understood that these paragraphs are not treating upon
the superstitions concerning the human hair, as such, but simply of the
employment of wigs, which would seem in former days among some of
the tribes of the Southwest to have been made of human hair presented by patients who had recovered from sickness or by mourners
whose relatives had died.[3]   Wigs with masks attached were worn by
the Costa Ricans, according to Gabb.[4]

Some of the Apache-Yuma men wear long rolls of matted hair behind,
which are the thickness of a finger, and two feet or more in length, and
composed of old hair mixed with that growing on the head, or are in the
form of a wig, made of hair that has been cut off when mourning the
dead, to be worn on occasions of ceremony.[5]

Observations of the same kind have been made by Speke upon the
customs of the people of Africa in his Nile,[6] concerning the Kidi people
at the head of the Nile; by Cook, in Hawkesworth's Voyages,[7] speaking
of Tahiti, and by Barcia,[8] speaking of Greenland.   Sir Samuel Baker
describes the peculiar wigs worn by the tribes on Lake Albert Nyanza,

---

[1] Dennys, Folk Lore of China, p. 57.

[2] "Chinigchinich" in Robinson's California, pp. 271, 272.

[3] The reader interested in this matter may find something bearing upon it in Diego Duran, lib. 1, cap.
36, p. 387; Torquemada, Mon. Indiana, lib. 9, cap. 3; Venegas, History of California, vol. 1, p. 105;
Gomara, Conq. de Mexico, p. 443; Herrera, dec. 4, lib. 8, p. 158; Maximilian of Wied, p. 431, and others;
The "pelucas" mentioned of the Orinoco tribes by Padre Gumilla would seem to be nothing more than
feather head-dresses; p. 66.

[4] Tribes and Languages of Costa Rica, Proc. Am. Philos. Soc., Philadelphia, 1875, p. 503.

[5] Corbusier, in American Antiquarian, Sept., 1886, p. 279.

[6] Source of the Nile, p. 567.

[7] Vol. 2, p. 193.

[8] Ensayo Cronologico, p. 139.

formed of the owner's hair and contributions from all sources plastered with clay into a stiff mass.[1]

Melchior Diaz reported that the people of Cibola "élèvent dans leurs maisons des animaux velus, grands comme des chiens d'Espagne. Ils les tondent, ils en font des perruques de couleurs." This report was sent by the Viceroy Mendoza to the Emperor Charles V. Exactly what these domesticated animals were, it would be hard to say; they may possibly have been Rocky Mountain sheep,[2] though Mr. Cushing, who has studied the question somewhat extensively, is of the opinion that they may have been a variety of the llama.

The Assinaboine used to wear false hair, and also had the custom of dividing their hair into "joints" of an inch or more, marked by a sort of paste of red earth and glue;[3] The Mandan did the same.[4] In this they both resemble the Mohave of the Rio Colorado. "The Algonquins believed also in a malignant Manitou. * * * She wore a robe made of the hair of her victims, for she was the cause of death."[5]

The Apache, until within the last twenty years, plucked out the eyelashes and often the eyebrows, but only a few of them still persist in the practice. Kane says that the Winnebagoes "have the custom of pulling out their eyebrows."[6] Herrera says that among the signs by which the Tlascaltecs recognized their gods when they saw them in visions, were "vianle sin cejas, i sin pestañas."[7]

MUDHEADS.

Reference has been made to a ceremonial plastering of mud upon the heads of Indians. When General Crook was returning from his expedition into the Sierra Madre, Mexico, in 1883, in which expedition a few of the enemy had been killed, the scouts upon reaching the San Bernardino River made a free use of the sweat bath, with much singing and other formulas, the whole being part of the lustration which all warriors must undergo as soon as possible after being engaged in battle. The Apache proper did not apply mud to their heads, but the Apache-Yuma did.

Capt. Grossman, U. S. Army,[8] says of the Pima method of purification after killing an Apache, that the isolation of the warrior lasts for sixteen days, during which period no one speaks to him, not even the old woman who brings him his food. The first day he touches neither food nor drink, and he eats sparingly for the whole time, touch-

---

[1] For the Shamans of Kodiak, see Lisiansky, Voyage, London, 1814, p. 208; for the Mexicans, Padre José Acosta, Paris, 1600, cap. 26, p. 256; Society Islands, Malte-Brun, Univ. Geography, vol. 3, lib. 58, p. 634, Boston, 1825. Sir Samuel Baker, The Albert 'Nyanza, vol. 1, p. 211.

[2] Ternaux-Compans, vol. 9, p. 294.

[3] Catlin, North American Indians, London, 1845, vol. 1, p. 55.

[4] Ibid., p. 95.

[5] Parkman, Jesuits in North America, p. lxxxiv.

[6] Wanderings of an Artist in North America, p. 40.

[7] Dec. 2, lib. 6, p. 161.

[8] Smithsonian Report for 1871.

ing neither meat nor salt; he bathes frequently in the Gila River and nearly the whole time keeps his head covered with a plaster of mud and mesquite.

"The boyes [of the Massagueyes] of seven or eight yeeres weare clay fastned on the hayre of the head, and still renewed with new clay, weighing sometimes five or six pounds. Nor may they be free hereof till in warre or lawfull fight hee hath killed a man." [1]

According to Padre Geronimo Boscana, the traditions of the Indians of California show that they "fed upon a kind of clay." [2] But this clay was often plastered upon their heads "as a kind of ornament." These were the Indians of San Juan Capistrano, who strongly resembled the Mohave. After all, the "mudheads" of the Mohave are no worse than those people in India who still bedaub their heads with "the holy mud of the Ganges." Up to this time the mud has been the "blue mud" of the Colorado and other rivers, but when we find Herbert Spencer mentioning that the heads of the Comanche are "besmeared with a dull red clay" we may suspect that we have stumbled upon an analogue of the custom of the Aztec priests, who bedaubed their heads with the coagulating lifeblood of their human victims. We know that there has been such a substitution practiced among the Indians of the Pueblo of Jemez, who apply red ocher to the mouth of the stone mountain lion, in whose honor human blood was once freely shed. The practice of so many of the Plains tribes of painting the median line of the head with vermilion seems to be traceable back to a similar custom.

SCALP SHIRTS.

The shirt depicted on Pl. I, made of buckskin and trimmed with human scalps, would seem to belong to the same category with the mantles made of votive hair, mentioned as being in use among the California tribe a little more than a century ago. It was presented to me by Little Big Man, who led me to believe that it had once belonged to the great chief of the Sioux, Crazy Horse, or had at least been worn by him. Of its symbolism I am unable to find the explanation. The colors yellow and blue would seem to represent the earth and water or sky, the feathers attached would refer to the birds, and the round circle on the breast is undoubtedly the sun. There is a cocoon affixed to one shoulder, the significance of which I do not know.

THE RHOMBUS, OR BULL ROARER.

The rhombus was first seen by me at the snake dance of the Tusayan, in the village of Walpi, Ariz., in the month of August, 1881. Previous to that date I had heard of it vaguely, but had never been able to see it in actual use. The medicine-men twirled it rapidly, and with a uniform motion, about the head and from front to rear, and succeeded

---

[1] Purchas, lib. 9, cap. 12, sec. 4, p. 1555, edition of 1622.
[2] Chinigchinich, p. 253.

SCALP SHIRT OF "LITTLE BIG MAN" (SIOUX).

in faithfully imitating the sound of a gust of rain-laden wind. As explained to me by one of the medicine-men, by making this sound they compelled the wind and rain to come to the aid of the crops. At a later date I found it in use among the Apache, and for the same purpose. The season near the San Carlos Agency during the year 1884 had been unusually dry, and the crops were parched. The medicine-men arranged a procession, two of the features of which were the rhombus and a long handled cross, upon which various figures were depicted. Of the latter, I will speak at another time.

Again, while examining certain ruins in the Verde Valley, in central Arizona, I found that the "Cliff Dwellers," as it has become customary to call the prehistoric inhabitants, had employed the same weapon of persuasion in their intercourse with their gods. I found the rhombus also among the Rio Grande Pueblo tribes and the Zuñi. Dr. Washington Matthews has described it as existing among the Navajo and Maj. J. W. Powell has observed it in use among the Utes of Nevada and Utah. As will be shown, its use in all parts of the world seems to have been as general as that of any sacred implement known to primitive man, not even excepting the sacred cords or rosaries discussed in this paper. Three forms of the rhombus have come under my own observation, each and all apparently connected in symbolism with the lightning. The first terminates in a triangular point, and the general shape is either that of a long, narrow, parallelogram, capped with an equilateral triangle, or else the whole figure is that

FIG. 2.—Rhombus of the Apache.

of a slender isosceles triangle. Where the former shape was used, as at the Tusayan snake dance, the tracing of a snake or lightning in blue or yellow followed down the length of the rhombus and terminated in the small triangle, which did duty as the snake's head. The second pattern was found by Dr. Matthews among the Navajo, and by myself in the old cliff dwellings. The one which I found was somewhat decayed, and the extremity of the triangle was broken off. There was no vestige of painting left. The second form was serrated on both edges to simulate the form of the snake or lightning. The third form, in use among the Apache, is an oblong of 7 or 8 inches in length, one and a quarter inches in width by a quarter in thickness. One extremity, that through which the cord passes, is rounded to rudely represent a human head, and the whole bears a close resemblance to the drawings of schoolboys which are intended for the human figure. The Apache explained that the lines on the front side of the rhombus were the entrails and those on the rear side the hair of their wind god. The hair is of several colors, and represents the lightning. I did not ascertain positively that such

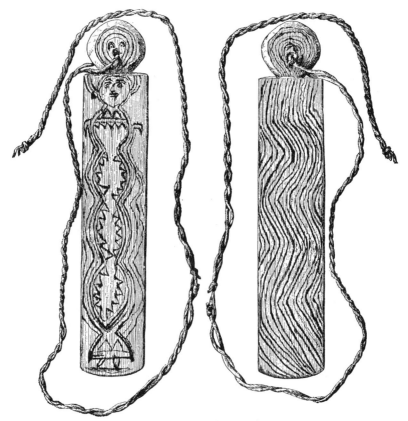

Fig. 3.—Rhombus of the Apache.

was the case, but was led to believe that the rhombus of the Apache was made by the medicine-men from wood, generally pine or fir, which had been struck by lightning on the mountain tops. Such wood is held in the highest estimation among them, and is used for the manufacture of amulets of especial efficacy. The Apache name for the rhombus is tzi-ditindi, the "sounding wood." The identification of the rhombus or "bull roarer" of the ancient Greeks with that used by the Tusayan in their snake dance was first made by E. B. Tylor in the Saturday Review in a criticism upon "The Snake Dance of the Moquis of Arizona."

The Kaffirs have the rhombus among their playthings:

The nodiwu is a piece of wood about 6 or 8 inches long, and an inch and a half or 2 inches wide, and an eighth or a quarter of an inch thick in the middle. Towards the edges it is beveled off, so that the surface is convex, or consists of two inclined planes. At one end it has a thong attached to it by which it is whirled rapidly round. * * * There is a kind of superstition connected with the nodiwu, that playing with it invites a gale of wind. Men will, on this account, often prevent boys from using it when they desire calm weather for any purpose. This superstition is identical with that which prevents many sailors from whistling at sea.[1]

Of the Peruvians we are informed that " their belief was that there was a man in the sky with a sling and a stick, and that in his power were the rain, the hail, the thunder, and all else that appertains to the regions of the air, where clouds are formed."[2]

The sacred twirler of the snake dance is found in Greece, America, Africa and New Zealand. It survives as a toy in England and the United States.[3] The same peculiar instrument has been noticed in the religious ceremonials of the Australians, especially in the initiatory rites of the " bora." It is called the " tirricoty."[4] The twirling of the tzi-ditindi in medicine or prayer corresponds to the revolution of the prayer wheel of the Lamas.

THE CROSS.

The sign of the cross appears in many places in Apache symbolism. The general subject of the connection of the cross with the religion of the aborigines of the American continent has been so fully traversed by previous authors that I do not care to add much more to the subject beyond saying that my own observation has assured me that it is related to the cardinal points and the four winds, and is painted by warriors upon their moccasins upon going into a strange district in the hope of keeping them from getting on a wrong trail.

In October, 1884, I saw a procession of Apache men and women, led by the medicine-men bearing two crosses, made as follows: The vertical arm was 4 feet 10 inches long, and the transverse between 10 and 12 inches, and each was made of slats about 1½ inches wide, which looked as if they had been long in use. They were decorated with blue polka dots upon the unpainted surface. A blue snake meandered down the longer arm. There was a circle of small willow twigs at top; next below that, a small zinc-cased mirror, a bell, and eagle feathers. Nosey, the Apache whom I induced to bring it to me after the ceremony, said that they carried it in honor of Guzanutli to induce her to send rain, at that time much needed for their crops. It is quite likely that this particular case represents a composite idea; that the original beliefs of the

---

[1] Theal, Kaffir Folk-lore, pp. 209–210.

[2] Clements R. Markham, Note on Garcilasso de la Vega, in Hakluyt Soc., vol. 41, p. 183, quoting Acosta, lib. 5, cap. 4.

[3] Andrew Lang, Custom and Myth, New York, 1885, chapter entitled " The bull roarer," pp. 29–44.

[4] John Fraser, The Aborigines of Australia; their Ethnic Position and Relations, pp. 161–162.

Apache have been modified to some extent by the crude ideas of the Mexican captives among them, who still remember much that was taught them in the churches of the hamlets in northern Mexico, from which they were kidnapped years ago; but, on the other hand, it is to be remembered that the cross has always formed a part of the Apache symbolism; that the snake does not belong to the Christian faith, and that it has never been allowed to appear upon the cross since the time of the Gnostics in the second and third centuries. Therefore, we must regard that as a Pagan symbol, and so must we regard the circle of willow twigs, which is exactly the same as the circle we have seen attached to the sacred cords for the cure of headache.[1]

The cross was found in full vogue as a religious emblem among the aborigines all over America. Father Le Clercq[2] speaks of its very general employment by the Gaspesians: " Ils ont parmi eux, tout infideles qu'ils soient, la Croix en singuliere veneration, qu'ils la portent figurée sur leurs habits & sur leur chair; qu'ils la tiennent à la main dans tous leurs voïages, soit par mer, soit par terre; & qu'enfin ils la posent au dehors & au dedans de leurs Cabannes, comme la marque d'honneur qui les distingue des autres Nations du Canada." He narrates[3] that the Gaspé tradition or myth was, that the whole tribe being ravaged by a plague, the medicine-men had recourse to the Sun, who ordered them to make use of the cross in every extremity.

Herrera relates that the followers of Hernandez de Cordoba found at Cape Catoche "unos Adoratorios . . . i Cruces pintadas que les causò gran admiracion."[4] He also says that Juan de Grijalva on the island of Cozumel found a number of oratories and temples, but one in particular was made in the form of a square tower, with four openings. Inside this tower was a cross made of lime, which the natives reverenced as the god of the rain; "una Cruz de Cal, de tres varas en alto à la qual tenian por el Dios de la lluvia."[5]

NECKLACES OF HUMAN FINGERS.

The necklace of human fingers, an illustration of which accompanies this text (Pl. II), belonged to the foremost of the medicine-men of a brave tribe—the Cheyenne of Montana and Wyoming. They were the backbone of the hostility to the whites, and during the long and arduous campaign conducted against them by the late Maj. Gen. George Crook, which terminated so successfully in the surrender of 4,500 of the allied Sioux and Cheyenne, at Red Cloud and Spotted Tail agencies, in the early spring of 1877, it was a noted fact that wherever a band of the

---

[1] " When the rain-maker of the Lenni Lennape would exert his power, he retired to some secluded spot and drew upon the earth the figure of a cross (its arms toward the cardinal points?), placed upon it a piece of tobacco, a gourd, a bit of some red stuff, and commenced to cry aloud to the spirits of the rains."—Brinton, Myths of the New World, New York, 1868, p. 96 (after Loskiel).

[2] Père Chrestien Le Clercq, Gaspesie, Paris, 1691, p. 170.

[3] Ibid., cap. x, pp. 172–199.

[4] Dec. 2, lib. 2, p. 48.

[5] Ibid., p. 59.

Plate II

NECKLACE OF HUMAN FINGERS.

Cheyenne was to be found there the fighting was most desperate. It is a matter now well established that the Cheyenne are an offshoot of the Algonquian family, speaking a dialect closely resembling that of the Cree, of British America.

It may interest some readers to listen to a few words descriptive of the manner in which such a ghastly relic of savagery came into my possession. On the morning of the 25th of November, 1876, the cavalry and Indian scouts (Sioux, Shoshoni, Arapaho, Pawnee, and a few of the Cheyenne themselves), of Gen. Crook's command, under the leadership of the late Brig. Gen. Ranald S. Mackenzie, then colonel of the Fourth Cavalry, surprised and destroyed the main village of the Cheyenne, on the headwaters of the Powder River, in the Big Horn Mountains, Wyoming. The onslaught was irresistible, the destruction complete, and the discomfited savages were forced to flee from their beds, half naked and with nothing save their arms and ammunition. More than half of the great herd of ponies belonging to the savages were killed, captured, or so badly wounded as to be of no use to the owners. The cold became so intense that on the night after the fight eleven papooses froze to death in their mothers' arms, and the succeeding night, three others. This blow, the most grievous ever inflicted upon the plains tribes, resulted in the surrender, first of the Cheyenne, and later on of the principal chief of the Sioux, the renowned Crazy Horse; after which the Sioux troubles were minimized into the hunt for scattered bands. Undoubtedly, among the bitterest losses of valuable property suffered by the Cheyenne on this occasion were the two necklaces of human fingers which came into my possession, together with the small buckskin bag filled with the right hands of papooses belonging to the tribe of their deadly enemies, the Shoshoni. These were found in the village by one of our scouts—Baptiste Pourrier, who, with Mr. Frank Gruard, was holding an important and responsible position in connection with the care of the great body of Indian scouts already spoken of. From these two gentlemen I afterwards obtained all the information that is here to be found regarding the Cheyenne necklace.

The second necklace, consisting of four fingers, was buried, as Gen. Crook did not wish to have kept more than one specimen, and that only for scientific purposes. Accordingly, the necklace here depicted was sent first to the U. S. Military Academy at West Point, New York, and later to the National Museum in Washington, where it was believed it could better fulfill its mission of educating students in a knowledge of the manners and customs of our aborigines.

The buckskin bag, with the papooses' hands, was claimed by the Shoshoni scouts, who danced and wailed all night, and then burned the fearful evidence of the loss sustained by their people.

The necklace is made of a round collar of buckskin, incrusted with the small blue and white beads purchased from the traders, these being arranged in alternate spaces of an inch or more in length. There are also attached numbers of the perforated wampum shell beads of native manufacture. Pendant from this collar are five medicine arrows, the exact nature of which, it was, of course, impossible to determine from the owner himself. Both Frank and Baptiste agreed that an arrow might become " medicine " either from having been shot into the person of the owner himself or into the body of an enemy, or even from having been picked up under peculiar circumstances. The owner, High Wolf or Tall Wolf, admitted as much after he had surrendered at the Red Cloud Agency and had made every effort to obtain the return of his medicine, which was this necklace.

The four medicine bags to be seen in the picture are worthy of attention. They were carefully examined under a powerful glass by Dr. H. C. Yarrow, U. S. Army, in the city of Washington, and pronounced to be human scrota. The first of these contained a vegetable powder, somewhat decomposed, having a resemblance to hoddentin; the second was filled with killikinnick; the third with small garnet-colored seeds like the chia in use among the Apache, and the fourth with a yellow, clayey-white vegetable matter not identified. The fifth, also, remained unidentified.

Besides the above, there are artificial teeth, resembling those of the fossil animals abundant in the Bad Lands of South Dakota, but cut out of soft stone.

The fingers—eight altogether—are the left-hand middle fingers of Indians of hostile tribes, killed by High Wolf. I obtained the list and could insert it here were it worth while to do so. The fingers have not been left in the natural state, but have been subjected to very careful and elaborate antiseptic treatment in order thoroughly to desiccate them. They were split longitudinally on the inner side and after the bone had been extracted the surface of the skin, both inside and out, received a treatment with a wash or paint of ocherous earth, the same as is used for the face. I was told that the bones were not replaced but that sticks were inserted to maintain the fingers in proper shape.

Of the reason for making use of such a trophy or relic, there is not much to be said; even the savages know little and say less. From the best information that I have been able to gather, it would seem to be based partly upon a vainglorious desire to display the proofs of personal prowess, and partly upon the vague and ill defined, but deeply rooted, belief in the talismanic or " medicinal" potency possessed by all parts of the human body, especially after death. It was such a belief which impelled the Mandan, Aztecs, and others of the American tribes to preserve the skulls of their dead as well as (among the Aztecs) those of the victims sacrificed in honor of their gods. As has been shown in another place, the Zuñi and others take care to offer food at stated periods to the scalps of their enemies.

The use of necklaces of human fingers or of human teeth is to be found in many parts of the world, and besides the fingers themselves, we find the whole arm, or in other cases only the nails. The Cheyenne did not always restrict themselves to fingers; they generally made use of the whole hand, or the arm of the slaughtered enemy. In a colored picture drawn and painted by one of themselves I have a representation of a scalp dance, in which the squaws may be seen dressed in their best, carrying the arms of enemies elevated on high poles and lances. There is no doubt in my mind that this custom of the Cheyenne of cutting off the arm or hand gave rise to their name in the sign language of the "Slashers," or "Wrist Cutters," much as the corresponding tribal peculiarity of the Dakota occasioned their name of the "Coupe Gorge" or "Throat Cutters."

The necklace of human fingers is found among other tribes. A necklace of four human fingers was seen by the members of the Lewis and Clarke expedition among the Shoshoni at the headwaters of the Columbia, in the early years of the present century. Early in the spring of 1858 Henry Youle Hind refers to the allies of the Ojibwa on Red River as having "two fingers severed from the hands of the unfortunate Sioux."[1] In Eastman's "Legends of the Sioux," we read of "Harpsthinah, one of the Sioux women, who wore as long as she could endure it, a necklace made of the hands and feet of Chippewah children."[2] We read that in New Zealand, "Several rows of human teeth, drawn on a thread, hung on their breasts."[3] Capt. Cook speaks of seeing fifteen human jaw bones attached to a semicircular board at the end of a long house on the island of Tahiti. "They appeared to be fresh, and there was not one of them that wanted a single tooth;"[4] and also, "the model of a canoe, about three feet long, to which were tied eight human jaw bones; we had already learnt that these were trophies of war."[5] Capt. Byron, R. N., saw in the Society Islands, in 1765, a chief who "had a string of human teeth about his waist, which was probably a trophy of his military prowess."[6]

"The wild Andamanese, who live only on the fruits of their forests and on fish, so far revere their progenitors that they adorn their women and children with necklaces and such like, formed out of the finger and toe-nails of their ancestors."[7]

Bancroft says[8] that the Californians did not generally scalp, but they did cut off and keep the arms and legs of a slain enemy or, rather, the hands and feet and head. They also had the habit of plucking out and preserving the eyes.

Kohl assures us that he has been informed that the Ojibwa will frequently cut fingers, arms, and limbs from their enemies and preserve

---

[1] Assinniboine and Saskatchewan Expedition, vol. 2, p. 123.
[2] New York, 1849, pp. x, xxix, 47.
[3] Forster, Voyage Round the World, vol. 1. pp. 219, 519.
[4] Hawkesworth. op. cit., vol. 2, p. 161.
[5] Ibid., p. 257.
[6] Ibid., vol. 1, p. 113.
[7] Forlong, Rivers of Life, vol. 1, pp. 541, 542.
[8] Nat. Races, vol. 1, p. 380.

these ghastly relics for use in their dances. Sometimes the warriors will become so excited that they will break off and swallow a finger.[1]

Tanner says of the Ojibwa: "Sometimes they use sacks of human skin to contain their medicines, and they fancy that something is thus added to their efficacy."[2]

Of the savages of Virginia we read: "Mais d'autres portent pour plus glorieuse parure une main seiche de quelqu'un de leurs ennemis."[3]

Of the Algonkin we read: "Il y en a qui ont une partie du bras et la main de quelque Hiroquois qu' ils ont tué; cela est si bien vuidée que les ongles restent toutes entieres."[4]

The Mohawk "place their foe against a tree or stake and first tear all the nails from his fingers and run them on a string, which they wear the same as we do gold chains. It is considered to the honor of any chief who has vanquished or overcome his enemies if he bite off or cut off some of their members, as whole fingers."[5]

The Cenis (Asinai) of Texas, were seen by La Salle's expedition in 1687–1690, torturing a captive squaw. "They then tore out her hair, and cut off her fingers."[6]

In volume 2 of Kingsborough's Mexican Antiquities, in the plates of the Vatican manuscript, is to be seen a representation of an Aztec priest or other dignitary holding out in his hands two human arms. In plate 76 of the same is a priest offering up a human sacrifice, the virile member of the victim cut off.

Teoyamaqui, the wife of Huitzlipochtli, the Aztec god of war, was depicted with a necklace of human hands.[7] Squier also says that Darga or Kali, the Hindu goddess, who corresponds very closely to her, was represented with "a necklace of skulls" and "a girdle of dissevered human hands."

The Hindu goddess Kali was decorated with a necklace of human skulls.[8] In the Propaganda collection, given in Kingsborough,[9] are to be seen human arms and legs.

"On the death of any of the great officers of state, the finger bones and hair are also preserved; or if they have died shaven, as sometimes occurs, a bit of their mbŭgŭ dress will be preserved in place of the hair."[10] "Their families guard their tombs."[11]

The principal war fetiches of Uganda "consist of dead lizards, bits,

---

[1] Kohl, Kitchi-gami, pp, 345, 346.

[2] Tanner's Narrative, p. 372.

[3] John de Laet, lib. 3, cap. 18, p. 90, quoting Capt. John Smith.

[4] Le Jeune in Jesuit Relations, 1633, vol.1, Quebec, 1858.

[5] Third Voyage of David Peter De Vries to New Amsterdam, in Trans. N. Y. Hist. Soc., vol. 3, p. 91.

[6] Charlevoix, New France, New York, 1866, vol. 4, p. 105.

[7] Squier, Serpent Symbol, p. 197.

[8] Coleman, Mythology of the Hindus, London, 1832, p. 63.

[9] Vol. 3.

[10] Speke, Source of the Nile. London, 1863, p. 500.

[11] Ibid.

of wood, hide, nails of dead people, claws of animals, and beaks of birds." Stanley saw them displayed before King Mtesa.[1]

"Some of the women in Gippsland wear round the neck human hands, which, Mr. Hull says, were beautifully prepared. He moreover informs me that they sometimes wear the parts of which the 'Lingam' and 'Priapus' were the emblems."[2] "The Gippsland people keep the relics of the departed. They will cut off the hands to keep as a remembrance, and these they will attach to the string that is tied round the neck."[3]

Smyth also relates that the women of some of the Australian tribes preserve "the hands of some defunct member of the tribe—that of some friend of the woman's, or perhaps one belonging to a former husband. This she keeps as the only remembrance of one she once loved; and, though years may have passed, even now, when she has nothing else to do, she will sit and moan over this relic of humanity. Sometimes a mother will carry about with her the remains of a beloved child, whose death she mourns."[4] The Australians also use the skulls of their "nearest and dearest relatives" for drinking vessels; thus, a daughter would use her mother's skull, etc.[5]

"One of the most extraordinary of their laws is that a widow, for every husband she marries after the first, is obliged to cut off a joint of a finger, which she presents to her husband on the wedding day, beginning at one of the little fingers."[6]

In the Army and Navy Journal, New York, June 23, 1888, is mentioned a battle between the Crow of Montana and the Piegan, in which the former obtained some of the hands and feet of dead warriors of the first-named tribe and used them in their dances.

Catlin shows that the young Sioux warriors, after going through the ordeal of the sun dance, placed the little finger of the left hand on the skull of a sacred buffalo and had it chopped off.[7]

"The sacrifices [of American Indians] at the fasts at puberty sometimes consist of finger joints."[8]

In Dodge's Wild Indians is represented (Pl. VI, 13) a Cheyenne necklace of the bones of the first joint of the human fingers, stripped of skin and flesh. I have never seen or heard of anything of the kind, although I have served with the Cheyenne a great deal and have spoken about their customs. My necklace is of human fingers mummified, not of bones.

Fanny Kelly says of a Sioux chief: "He showed me a puzzle or game he had made from the finger bones of some of the victims that

[1] Stanley, Through the Dark Continent, vol. 1, p. 327.
[2] Miles, Demigods and Dæmonia, in Jour. Ethnol. Soc., London, vol. 3, p. 28, 1854.
[3] Smyth, Aborigines of Victoria, vol. 1, p. 30.
[4] Ibid., p. 131.
[5] Ibid., p. 348.
[6] Peter Kolben, speaking of the Hottentots, in Knox, vol. 2, p. 394.
[7] O-kee-pa, pp. 28–29.
[8] Frazer, Totemism, Edinburgh, 1887, pp. 54, 55; after Maximilian.

had fallen beneath his own tomahawk. The bones had been freed from the flesh by boiling, and, being placed upon a string, were used for playing some kind of Indian game."[1]

Strabo recounts in his third book that the Lusitanians sacrificed prisoners and cut off their right hands to consecrate them to their gods.

Dulaure says that the Germans attached the heads and the right hands of their human victims to sacred trees.[2]

Adoni-bezek cut off the thumbs and great toes of seventy kings of Syria.[3]

The necklace of human fingers is not a particle more horrible than the ornaments of human bones to be seen in the cemetery of the Capuchins in Rome at the present day. I have personally known of two or three cases where American Indians cut their enemies limb from limb. The idea upon which the practice is based seems to be the analogue of the old English custom of sentencing a criminal to be "hanged, drawn, and quartered."

Brand gives a detailed description of the "hand of glory," the possession of which was believed by the peasantry of Great Britain and France to enable a man to enter a house invisible to the occupants. It was made of the hand of an executed (hanged) murderer, carefully desiccated and prepared with a great amount of superstitious mummery. With this holding a candle of "the fat of a hanged man" burglars felt perfectly secure while engaged in their predatory work.[4] The belief was that a candle placed in a dead man's hand will not be seen by any but those by whom it is used. Such a candle introduced into a house kept those who were asleep from awakening.

The superstition in regard to the "hand of glory" was widely diffused throughout France, Germany, Spain, and Great Britain. As late as the year 1831 it was used by Irish burglars in the county Meath.

Dr. Frank Baker delivered before the Anthropological Society of Washington, D. C., a lecture upon these superstitions as related to the "hand of glory," to which the student is respectfully referred.[5]

An Aztec warrior always tried to procure the middle finger of the left hand of a woman who had died in childbirth. This he fastened to his shield as a talisman.[6] The great weapon of the Aztec witches was the left arm of a woman who had died in her first childbirth.[7] Pliny mentions "still-born infants cut up limb by limb for the most abominable practices, not only by widwives, but by harlots even as well!"[8]

---

[1] Kelly, Narrative of Captivity, Cincinnati, 1871, p. 143.

[2] Différens Cultes, vol. 1, p. 57.

[3] Judges, I, 7.

[4] Brand, Pop. Ant., London, 1882, vol. 3, p. 278.

[5] American Anthropologist, Washington, D. C., January, 1888.

[6] Kingsborough, vol. 8, p, 70. The Aztec believed that the woman who died in childbirth was equal to the warrior who died in battle and she went to the same heaven. The middle finger of the left hand is the finger used in the necklace of human fingers.

[7] Sahagun, in Kingsborough, vol. 7, p. 147.

[8] Pliny, Nat. Hist., lib. 28, cap. 20. Holland's translation

The opinions entertained in Pliny's time descended to that of the Reformation—

> Finger of birth-strangled babe,
> Ditch-deliver'd by a drab.[1]

"Scrofula, imposthumes of the parotid glands, and throat diseases, they say, may be cured by the contact of the hand of a person who has been carried off by an early death;" but, he goes on to say, any dead hand will do, "provided it is of the same sex as the patient and that the part affected is touched with the back of the left hand."[2] A footnote adds that this superstition still prevails in England in regard to the hand of a man who has been hanged.

The use of dead men's toes, fingers, spinal vertebræ, etc., in magical ceremonies, especially the fabrication of magical lamps and candles, is referred to by Frommann.[3]

Grimm is authority for the statement that in both France and Germany the belief was prevalent that the fingers of an unborn babe were "available for magic."[4]

In England witches were believed to "open graves for the purpose of taking out the joints of the fingers and toes of dead bodies . . . in order to prepare a powder for their magical purposes."[5]

Saint Athanase dit même, que ces parties du corps humain [i.e., hands, feet, toes, fingers, etc.] étoient adorées comme des dieux particuliers."[6]

According to the sacred lore of the Brahmans "the Tîrtha sacred to the Gods lies at the root of the little finger, that sacred to the Rishis in the middle of the fingers, that sacred to Men at the tips of the fingers, that sacred to Agni (fire) in the middle of the hand."[7]

In the Island of Ceylon "debauchees and desperate people often play away the ends of their fingers."[8]

Hone shows that "every joint of each finger was appropriated to some saint."[9]

NECKLACES OF HUMAN TEETH.

A number of examples are to be found of the employment of necklaces of human teeth. In my own experience I have never come across any specimens, and my belief is that among the Indians south of the Isthmus such things are to be found almost exclusively. I have found no reference to such ornamentation or "medicine" among the tribes of North America, but there are many to show the very general dissemination of the custom in Africa and in the islands of the South Sea. Gomara says that the Indians of Santa Marta wore at their necks, like

---

[1] Shakespeare, Macbeth, act 4, scene 1.
[2] Pliny, Nat. Hist., lib. 28, cap. 11.
[3] Tractatus de Fascinatione, Nuremberg, 1675, p. 681.
[4] Teutonic Mythology, vol. 3, p. 1073.
[5] Brand, Pop. Ant., vol. 3, p. 10.
[6] Montfaucon, l'Antiquité expliquée, vol. 2, liv. 4, cap. 6, p. 249.
[7] Vâsishtha, cap. 3, pars. 64–68, p. 25 (Sacred Books of the East, Oxford, 1882, Max Müller's edition).
[8] Travels of Two Mohammedans through India and China, in Pinkerton's Voyages, vol. 7, p. 218.
[9] Every-Day Book, vol. 2, col. 95.

dentists, the teeth of the enemies they had killed in battle.[1] Many of the Carib, we are told by a Spanish writer, ostentatiously wear necklaces made of strings of the teeth of the enemies whom they have slain.[2] Padre Fray Alonzo Fernandez says of the Carib: "Traen los dientes con los cabellos de los que mataron por collares, como hazian antiguamente los Scitas."[3] The people of New Granada "traen al cuello dientes de los que matavan."[4] Picart says that the natives of New Granada and Cumana "portent au col les dents des ennemis qu'ils ont massacrez."[5] The Spaniards found in the temple of the Itzaes, on the island of Peten, an idol made of "yesso," which is plaster, and in the head, which was shaped like the sun, were imbedded the teeth of the Castilians whom they had captured and killed.[6]

"They strung together the teeth of such of their enemies as they had slain in battle and wore them on their legs and arms as trophies of successful cruelty."[7]

Stanley says, referring to the natives of the Lower Congo country: "Their necklaces consisted of human, gorilla, and crocodile teeth, in such quantity, in many cases, that little or nothing could be seen of the neck."[8]

"The necklaces of human teeth which they [Urangi and Rubunga, of the Lower Congo] wore."[9] Again, "human teeth were popular ornaments for the neck."[10] When a king dies they [the Wahŭma, of the head of the Nile] cut out his lower jaw and preserve it covered with beads.[11]

Schweinfurth[12] speaks of having seen piles of "lower jawbones from which the teeth had been extracted to serve as ornaments for the neck" by the Monbuttoo of Africa. "A slaughtered foe was devoured from actual bloodthirstiness and hatred by the Niam-Niams of Central Africa. . . . They make no secret of their savage craving, but ostentatiously string the teeth of their victims round their necks, adorning the stakes erected beside their dwellings for the habitation of the trophies with the skulls of the men they have devoured. Human fat is universally sold."[13]

---

[1] "Traen los dientes al cuello (como sacamuelas) por bravosidad."—Gomara, Historia de las Indias, p. 201.

[2] "Los Caberres y muchos Caribes, usan por gala muchas sartas de dientes y muelas de gente para dar á entender que son muy valientes por los despojos que allí ostentan ser de sus enemigos que mataron."—Gumilla, Orinoco, Madrid, 1741, p. 65.

[3] Padre Fray Alonzo Fernandez, Historia Eclesiastica, Toledo, 1611, p. 17.

[4] Ibid., p. 161.

[5] Cérémonies et Coûtumes, Amsterdam, 1735, vol. 6, p. 114.

[6] "Formada la cara como de Sol, con rayos de Nacar al rededor, y perfilada de lo mismo; y en la boca embutidos los dientes, que quitaron à los Españoles, que avian muerto."—Villaguitierre, Hist. de la Conquista de la Provincia de el Itza, Madrid, 1701, p. 500. (Itza seems to have been the country of the Lacandones.)

[7] Edwards, speaking of the Carib, quoted by Spencer, Desc. Sociology. The same custom is ascribed to the Tupinambi of Brazil. Ibid, quoting from Southey.

[8] Through the Dark Continent, vol. 2, p. 286.

[9] Ibid, p. 288.

[10] Ibid., p. 290.

[11] Speke, Source of the Nile, London, 1863, p. 500.

[12] Heart of Africa, vol 2, p. 54.

[13] Ibid., vol. 1, p. 285.

The four front teeth were extracted by the men and women of the Latooka and other tribes of the White Nile, but no explanation is given of the custom.[1]

In Dahomey, strings of human teeth are worn.[2]

Freycinet saw in Timor, Straits of Malacca, "a score of human jaw-bones, which we wished to purchase; but all our offers were met by the word 'pamali,' meaning sacred."[3]

In one of the "morais" or temples entered by Kotzebue in 1818, on the Sandwich Islands, there were two great and ugly idols, one representing a man, the other a woman. "The priests made me notice that both statues, which had their mouths wide open, were furnished with a row of human teeth."[4]

The Sandwich Islanders kept the jaw bones of their enemies as trophies.[5] King Tamaahmaah had a "spitbox which was set round with human teeth, and had belonged to several of his predecessors."[6]

Among some of the Australian tribes the women wear about their necks the teeth which have been knocked out of the mouths of the boys at a certain age.[7] This custom of the Australians does not obtain among the North American tribes, by whom the teeth, as they fall out, are carefully hidden or buried under some tree or rock. At least, I have been so informed by several persons, among others by Chato, one of the principal men of the Chiricahua Apache.

Molina speaks of the customs of the Araucanians, who, after torturing their captives to death, made war flutes out of their bones and used the skulls for drinking vessels.[8] The Abipones of Paraguay make the bones of their enemies into musical instruments.[9]

The preceding practice is strictly in line with the "medicinal" and "magical" values attached in Europe to human teeth, human skin, etc. The curious reader may find much on this subject in the works of Frommann, Beckherius, Etmuller, Samuel Augustus Flemming, and others of the seventeenth century, where it will be shown that the ideas of the people of Europe of that period were only in name superior to those of the savages of America, the islands of the South Seas, and of Central Africa. In my work upon "The Scatalogic Rites of all Nations" I have treated this matter more in extenso, but what is here adduced will be sufficient for the present article.

The skin of Ziska, the Bohemian reformer, was made into a "medicine drum" by his followers.

[1] Sir Samuel Baker, The Albert N'yanza, Philadelphia, 1869, p. 154 et seq.

[2] Burton, Mission to Gelele, vol. 1, p. 135 et seq.

[3] Voyage Round the World, London, 1823, pp. 209, 210.

[4] Kotzebue, Voyage, London, 1821, vol. 2, p. 202. See also Villaguitierre, cited above.

[5] Capt. Cook's First Voyage, in Pinkerton's Voyages, London, 1812, vol. 11, pp. 513, 515.

[6] Campbell, Voyage Round the World, N. Y., 1819, p. 153.

[7] Frazer, Totemism, Edinburgh, 1887, p. 28.

[8] Historia de Chile, Madrid, 1795, vol. 2, p. 80.

[9] Spencer, Desc. Sociology.

THE SCRATCH STICK.

When Gen. Crook's expedition against the Chiricahua Apache reached the heart of the Sierra Madre, Mexico, in 1883, it was my good fortune to find on the ground in Geronimo's rancheria two insignificant looking articles of personal equipment, to which I learned the Apache attached the greatest importance. One of these was a very small piece of hard wood, cedar, or pine, about two and a half to three inches long and half a finger in thickness, and the other a small section of the cane indigenous to the Southwest and of about the same dimensions. The first was the scratch stick and the second the drinking reed.

The rule enjoined among the Apache is that for the first four times one of their young men goes out on the warpath he must refrain from scratching his head with his fingers or letting water touch his lips. How to keep this vow and at the same time avoid unnecessary personal discomfort and suffering is the story told by these petty fragments from the Apache's ritual. He does not scratch his head with his fingers; he makes use of this scratch stick. He will not let water touch his lips, but sucks it into his throat through this tiny tube. A long leather cord attached both stick and reed to the warrior's belt and to each other. This was all the information I was able to obtain of a definite character. Whether these things had to be prepared by the medicine-men or by the young warrior himself; with what ceremonial, if any, they had to be manufactured, and under what circumstances of time and place, I was unable to ascertain to my own satisfaction, and therefore will not extend my remarks or burden the student's patience with incoherent statements from sources not absolutely reliable. That the use of the scratch stick and the drinking reed was once very general in America and elsewhere, and that it was not altogether dissociated from ritualistic or ceremonial ideas, may be gathered from the citations appended.

In her chapter entitled "Preparatory ceremony of the young warrior" Mrs. Emerson says: "He does not touch his ears or head with his hand," explaining in a foot note, "the head was sometimes made a sacrificial offering to the sun."[1] Tanner relates that the young Ojibwa warrior for the "three first times" that he accompanies a war party "must never scratch his head or any other part of his body with his fingers, but if he is compelled to scratch he must use a small stick."[2] Kohl states that the Ojibwa, while on the warpath, "will never sit down in the shade of a tree or scratch their heads; at least, not with their fingers. The warriors, however, are permitted to scratch themselves with a piece of wood or a comb."[3] Mackenzie states regarding the Indians whom he met on the Columbia, in 52° 38′, N. lat., "instead of a

---

[1] Indian Myths, Boston, 1884, p. 256.
[2] Tanner's Narrative, p. 122.
[3] Kitchi-gami, p. 344.

comb they [the men] have a small stick hanging by a string from one of the locks [of hair], which they employ to alleviate any itching or irritation in the head."[1]

The Tlinkit of British North America use these scratchers made of basalt or other stone.

"The pipe-stem carrier (i. e., the carrier of the sacred or 'medicine' pipe) of the Crees, of British North America, dares not scratch his own head, without compromising his own dignity, without the intervention of a stick, which he always carries for that purpose."[2]

Bancroft[3] quotes Walker as saying that " a Pima never touches his skin with his nails, but always with a small stick for that purpose, which he renews every fourth day and wears in his hair."

As part of the ceremony of "initiating youth into manhood" among the Creeks, the young neophyte "during the twelve moons · · · is also forbidden to pick his ears or scratch his head with his fingers, but must use a small splinter to perform these operations."[4]   The Apache-Yuma men carry in their hair "a slender stick or bone about 8 inches long, which serves them as a comb."[5]

The idea that these scratch sticks replace combs is an erroneous one; Indians make combs in a peculiar way of separate pieces of wood, and they are also very fond of brushing their long locks with the coarse brushes, which they make of sacaton or other grass.

"One other regulation, mentioned by Schomburgk, is certainly quaint; the interesting father may not scratch himself with his finger nails, but may use for this purpose a splinter, especially provided, from the midrib of a cokerite palm."[6]

When a Greenlander is about to enter into conversation with the spirits "no one must stir, not so much as to scratch his head."[7]

In the New Hebrides most of the natives "wear a thin stick or reed, about 9 inches long, in their hair, with which they occasionally disturb the vermin that abound in their heads."[8]

Alarcon, describing the tribes met on the Rio Colorado, in 1541, says: "They weare certaine pieces of Deeres bones fastened to their armes, wherewith they strike off the sweate."[9]

In German folk-lore there are many references to the practice in which the giants indulged frequently in scratching themselves, sometimes as a signal to each other. Just what significance to attach to these stories I can not presume to say, as Grimm merely relates the fact without comment.[10]

[1] Voyages, p. 323.

[2] Kane, Wanderings of an Artist in North America, p. 399.

[3] Native Races, vol. 1, p. 553.

[4] Hawkins, quoted by Gatschet, Migration Legend of the Creeks, Philadelphia, 1884, vol. 1, p. 185.

[5] Corbusier, in American Antiquarian, September, 1886, p. 279.

[6] Everard F. im Thurn, Indians of Guiana, p. 218.

[7] Crantz, History of Greenland, London, 1767, vol. 1, pp. 210–211.

[8] Forster, Voyage Round the World, vol. 2, pp. 275, 288.

[9] Hakluyt, Voyages, vol. 3, p. 508.

[10] Grimm, Teutonic Mythology, vol. 2, p. 544.

Of the Abyssinians, Bruce says: "Their hair is short and curled like that of a negro's in the west part of Africa, but this is done by art not by nature, each man having a wooden stick with which he lays hold of the lock and twists it round like a screw till it curls in the form he desires."[1] In a foot note, he adds: "I apprehend this is the same instrument used by the ancients, and censured by the prophets, which in our translation is rendered crisping-pins."

Possibly the constant use of the scratch stick in countries without wood suggested that it should be carried in the hair, and hence it would originate the fashion of wearing the hair crimped round it, and after a while it would itself be used as a crimping-pin.

Thus far, the suggestion of a religious or ceremonial idea attaching to the custom of scratching has not been apparent, unless we bear in mind that the warrior setting out on the warpath never neglects to surround himself with all the safeguards which the most potent incantations and "medicine" of every kind can supply. But Herbert Spencer tells us in two places that the Creeks attach the idea of a ceremonial observance to the custom. He says that "the warriors have a ceremony of scratching each other as a sign of friendship;"[2] and again, "scratching is practiced among young warriors as a ceremony or token of friendship. When they have exchanged promises of inviolable attachment, they proceed to scratch each other before they part."[3]

Dr. J. Hampden Porter remarks that this ceremonial scratching may be a "survival" of the blood covenant, and that in earlier times the young warriors, instead of merely scratching each other's arms, may have cut the flesh and exchanged the blood. The idea seems to be a very sensible one.

Father Alegre describes a ceremonial scratching which may have been superseded by the scratch stick, to which the medicine-men of certain tribes subjected the young men before they set out on the warpath. Among the Pima and Opata the medicine-men drew from their quivers the claws of eagles, and with these gashed the young man along the arms from the shoulders to the wrists.[4]

This last paragraph suggests so strongly certain of the practices at the sun dance of the tribes farther to the north that it may be well to compare it with the other allusions in this paper to that dance.

It will be noticed that the use of the scratch-stick, at least among the tribes of America, seems to be confined to the male sex; but the information is supplied by Mr. Henshaw, of the Bureau of Ethnology, that the Indians of Santa Barbara, Cal., made their maidens at the

---

[1] Travels to discover the source of the Nile in the years 1768, etc., Dublin, 1791, vol. 3, p. 410.
[2] Desc. Sociology.
[3] Ibid., quoting Schoolcraft.
[4] "Saca de su carcax algunos pies y uñas de águila secos y endurecidos, con los cuales, comienza á sajarle desde los hombros hasta las muñecas."—Historia de la Compañia de Jesus en Nueva España, Mexico,1842, vol. 2, pp. 218, 219.

time of attaining womanhood wear pendant from the neck a scratcher of abalone shell, which they had to use for an indefinite period when the scalp became irritable.

Prof. Otis T. Mason, of the National Museum, informs me that there is a superstition in Virginia to the effect that a young woman enciente for the first time must, under no circumstances, scratch her head with her fingers, at least while uncovered; she must either put on gloves or use a small stick.

The Parsi have a festival at which they serve a peculiar cake or bread called "draona," which is marked by scratches from the finger nails of the woman who has baked it.[1]

No stress has been laid upon the appearance in all parts of the world of "back scratchers" or "scratch my backs," made of ivory, bone, or wood, and which were used for toilet purposes to remove irritation from between the shoulder blades or along the spine where the hand itself could not reach. They are to the present day in use among the Chinese and Japanese, were once to be found among the Romans and other nations of Europe, and instances of their occasional employment until a very recent date might be supplied.

THE DRINKING REED.

Exactly what origin to ascribe to the drinking reed is now an impossibility, neither is it probable that the explanations which the medicine-men might choose to make would have the slightest value in dispelling the gloom which surrounds the subject. That the earliest conditions of the Apache tribe found them without many of the comforts which have for generations been necessaries, and obliged to resort to all sorts of expedients in cooking, carrying, or serving their food is the most plausible presumption, but it is submitted merely as a presumption and in no sense as a fact. It can readily be shown that in a not very remote past the Apache and other tribes were compelled to use bladders and reeds for carrying water, or for conveying water, broth, and other liquid food to the lips. The conservative nature of man in all that involves his religion would supply whatever might be needed to make the use of such reeds obligatory in ceremonial observances wherein there might be the slightest suggestion of religious impulse. We can readily imagine that among a people not well provided with forks and spoons, which are known to have been of a much later introduction than knives, there would be a very decided danger of burning the lips with broth, or of taking into the mouth much earthy and vegetable matter or ice from springs and streams at which men or women might wish to drink, so the use of the drinking reed would obviate no small amount of danger and discomfort.

---

[1] Shâyast lâ-shâyast, cap. 3, par. 32, p. 284 (Max Müller edition, Oxford, 1880). When the "drôn" has been marked with three rows of finger-nail scratches it is called a "frasast."

Water was carried in reeds by the Dyaks of Borneo, according to Bock.[1] The manner in which the natives of the New Hebrides and other islands of the South Pacific Ocean carry water in bamboo joints recalls the Zuñi method of preserving the sacred water of the ocean in hollow reeds.[2]

Fig. 4.—The scratch stick and drinking reed.

Mr. F. H. Cushing shows that "so far as language indicates the character of the earliest water vessels which to any extent met the requirements of the Zuñi ancestry, they were tubes of wood or sections of canes."[3] Long after these reeds had disappeared from common use, the priests still persisted in their use for carrying the water for the sacred ceremonies. The mother of the king of Uganda gave to Speke "a beautifully-worked pombé sucking-pipe."[4] For ordinary purposes these people have "drinking gourds." In Ujiji, Cameron saw an old chief sucking pombé, the native beer, through a reed;[5] and, later on in his narrative, we learn that the reed is generally used for the purposes of drinking. "The Malabars reckoned it insolent to touch the vessel with their lips when drinking."[6] They made use of vessels with a spout, which were no more and no less than the small hollow-handled soup ladles of the Zuñi and Tusayan, through which they sipped their hot broth.

In an ancient grave excavated not far from Salem, Massachusetts, in 1873, were found five skeletons, one of which was supposed to be that of the chief Nanephasemet, who was killed in 1605 or 1606. He was the king of Namkeak. On the breast of this skeleton were discovered "several small copper tubes . . . from 4 to 8 inches in length, and from one-eighth to one-fourth of an inch in diameter, made of copper rolled up, with the edges lapped."[7]

Alarcon relates that the tribes seen on the Rio Colorado by him in 1541, wore on one arm "certain small pipes of cane." But the object or purpose of wearing these is not indicated.[8]

The natives of the Friendly Islands carried in their ears little cylinders of reed, although we learn that these were "filled with a red solid

[1] Head-Hunters of Borneo, London, 1881, p. 139.

[2] See, for the New Hebrides, Forster, Voyage Round the World, vol. 2, p. 255.

[3] Report of the Bureau of Ethnology, 1882–'83, p. 482.

[4] Speke, Source of the Nile, London, 1863, pp. 306, 310.

[5] Cameron, Across Africa, London, 1877, vol. 1, p. 276.

[6] De Gama's Discovery of the East Indies, in Knox, Voyages, London, 1767, vol, 2, p. 324.

[7] Andrew K. Ober, in the Salem Gazette, Salem, Mass.

[8] Hakluyt, Voyages, vol. 3, p. 508; also, Ternaux-Compans, Voy., vol. 9, pp. 307, 308.

substance."[1] Among the Narrinyeri of Australia, when young men are to be initiated into the rank of warriors, during the ceremonies "they are allowed to drink water, but only by sucking it up through a reed."[2] Admiral von Wrangel says of the Tchuktchi of Siberia: "They suck their broth through a small tube of reindeer bone," which " each individual carries about with him."[3] Padre Sahagun says that the human victim whom the Aztecs offered up in sacrifice was not allowed to touch water with his lips, but had to suck it through a reed."[4]

"The Mexicans had a forty-days' fast in memory of one of their sacred persons who was tempted *forty* days on a mountain. He drinks through a reed. He is called the Morning Star."[5] The Mexicans, according to Fray Diego Duran, placed before the statues of their dead bowls of "vino," with "rosas," tobacco (this seems to be the proper translation of the word "humazos," smokes), and a reed called the "drinker of the sun," through which the spirit could imbibe.[6]

" The suction pipes of steatite," mentioned by Schoolcraft, as found in the mounds, may have been the equivalents of our drinking reeds, and made of steatite to be the more readily preserved in the ritual of which they formed part.

Copper cylinders $1\frac{1}{4}$ inches long and $\frac{2}{3}$ of an inch in diameter were found in the mounds of the Mississippi Valley by Squier and Davis. The conjecture that they had been used "for ornaments" does not seem warranted.[7]

We should not forget that there was a semideification of the reed itself by the Aztec in their assignment of it to a place in their calendar under the name of "acatl."[8]

Mrs. Ellen Russell Emerson speaks of the custom the warriors of the northern tribes had which suggests that she had heard of the drinking reed without exactly understanding what it meant. She says that warriors carry bowls of birch bark "from one side of which the warrior drinks in going to battle—from the other, on his return. These bowls are not carried home, but left on the prairie, or suspended from trees within a day's journey of his village."[9]

Among the Brahmans practices based upon somewhat similar ideas are to be found: every morning, upon rising, "ils prennent trois fois de l'eau dans la main, & en jettent trois fois dans leur bouche, évitant d'y toucher avec la main."[10]

---

[1] Forster, Voyage Round the World, vol. 1, p. 435.

[2] Smyth, Aborigines of Victoria, vol. 1. p. 66.

[3] English edition, New York, 1842, p. 271.

[4] Kingsborough, vol. 6, p. 100.

[5] Godfrey Higgins, Anacalypsis, vol. 2, book 1, cap. 4, sec. 9, p. 31.

[6] Y ponía delante un canuto grande y queso [grueso?] para con que bebiese: este canuto llamaban "bebedero del Sol."—Diego Duran, vol. 1, cap. 38, p. 386.

[7] Smithsonian Contributions, vol. 1, p. 151.

[8] The reed, which is the proper meaning of the word "acatl," is the hieroglyphic of the element water. Veytia, quoted by Thomas, in 3rd Ann. Rep., Bu. Eth.. 1881–1882, p. 42 et seq.

[9] Indian Myths, Boston, 1884, p. 260.

[10] Picart, Cérémonies et Coûtumes Réligieuses de tous les Peuples du Monde. Amsterdam, 1735, vol. 6, part 2, p. 103

The fundamental reason upon which the use of the drinking reed is based is that the warrior or devotee shall not let water touch his lips. It is strange to find among the regulations with regard to taking water by the warrior caste: "He shall not sip water while walking, standing, lying down, or bending forward."[1]

The Dharma-sûtra, traditionally connected with the Rishi-Vasishtha, of the Seventh Mandala of the Rig-Veda, is a relic of a Vedic school of the highest antiquity. Its seat was in the present northwestern provinces of India, and, like the Dharmasâstra of Gautama, it is the sole surviving record from this source.[2]

There was another service performed by reeds or tubes in the domestic economy of nations around the north pole. As the Apache are derived from an Arctic ancestry it does not seem amiss to allude to it. Lord Lonsdale, in describing the capture of a whale which he witnessed, says that the Eskimo women "first of all gathered up the harpoons and then pulled out all the spears. As each spear was withdrawn a blow-pipe was pushed into the wound and the men blew into it, after which the opening was tied up. When every wound had been treated in this manner the whale resembled a great windbag and floated high in the water."

In the National Museum at Washington, D. C., there are many pipes made of the bones of birds, which were used by the Inuit as drinking tubes when water had to be taken into the mouth from holes cut in the ice. These drinking tubes seem to be directly related to our subject, although they may also have been used as Lonsdale describes the pipes for blowing the dead whale full of air. Another point to be mentioned is that the eagle pipe kept in the mouth of the young warrior undergoing the torture of the sun dance among the Sioux and other tribes on the plains is apparently connected with the "bebedero del Sol" of the peoples to the south.[3]

The use of this drinking reed, shown to have been once so intimately associated with human sacrifice, may have disappeared upon the introduction of labrets, which seem, in certain cases at least, to be associated with the memory of enemies killed in battle, which would be only another form of human sacrifice. This suggestion is advanced with some misgivings, and only as a hypothesis to assist in determining for what purpose labrets and drinking tubes have been employed. The Apache have discontinued the use of the labret, which still is to be found among their congeners along the Lower Yukon, but not among those living along the lower river.[4] According to Dall the custom was probably adopted from the Inuit; he also shows that whenever labrets are worn in a tribe they are worn by both sexes, and that the women assume them at the first appearance of the catamenia.

---

[1] Vâsishtha, cap. 3, pars. 26–30, pp. 20–21. Sacred Books of the East, Oxford, 1882, vol. 14; edition of Max Müller.

[2] Ibid.

[3] Diego Duran, loc. cit.

[4] See Dall, Masks and Labrets, p. 151.

"This is to be noted, that how many men these Savages [Brazilians] doe kill, so many holes they will have in their visage, beginning first in their nether lippe, then in their cheekes, thirdly, in both their eye-browes, and lastly in their eares."[1]

Cabeza de Vaca speaks of the Indians near Malhado Island, "They likewise have the nether lippe bored, and within the same they carrie a piece of thin Cane about halfe a finger thicke."[2] Herrera relates very nearly the same of the men of "Florida": "Traìan una tetilla oradada, metido por el agujero un pedaço de Caña, i el labio baxero tambien agujereado, con otra caña en èl."[3] But Herrera probably obtained his data from the narrative of Vaca.

In looking into this matter of labrets as connected or suspected as being in some way connected with the drinking reed, we should not expect to find the labret adhering very closely to the primitive form, because the labret, coming to be regarded more and more as an ornament, would allow greater and greater play to the fancy of the wearer or manufacturer, much the same as the crosses now worn by ladies, purely as matter of decoration, have become so thoroughly examples of dexterity in filagree work as to have lost the original form and significance as a declaration of faith. But it is a subject of surprise to find that the earlier writers persistently allude to the labrets in the lips of the Mexican deities, which probably were most tenacious of primitive forms, as being shaped like little reeds—"cañutillos."

Herrera says of Tescatlipoca: "Que era el Dios de la Penitencia, i de los Jubileos . . . Tenia Çarcillo de Oro, i Plata en el labio baxo, con un cañutillo cristalino, de un geme de largo."[4] The high priest, he says, was called topilçin, and in sacrificing human victims he wore "debaxo del labio, junto al medio de la barba, una pieça como cañutillo, de una piedra açul."[5]

Father Acosta also speaks of the tube (canon) of crystal worn by Tezcatlipoca in the lower lip: "En la leure d'embas un petit canon de crystal, de la longueur d'un xeme ou demy pied."[6]

Speaking of Quetzalcoatl Clavigero says: "From the under lip hung a crystal tube."[7] From Diego Duran's account of this "bezote" or labret it must have been hollow, as he says it contained a feather: "En el labio bajo tenia un bezote de un veril cristalino y en el estaba metida una pluma verde y otras veces azul."[8]

In the Popul Vuh is to be found a myth which gives an account of the origin of labrets. It relates that two night watchers over the flowers

---

[1] Peter Carder, an Englishman captive among the Brazilians, 1578–1586, in Purchas, vol. 4, lib. 6, cap. 5, p. 1189.

[2] Purchas, vol. 4, lib. 8, cap. 1, sec. 2, p. 1508.

[3] Dec. 4, lib. 4, p. 69.

[4] Dec. 3, lib. 2, p. 67.

[5] Ibid., p. 70.

[6] Histoire Naturelle des Indes, Paris, 1600, lib. 5, cap, 9, p. 224.

[7] History of Mexico, Philadelphia, 1817, vol. 2, p. 6.

[8] Duran, op. cit., vol. 3, cap. 4, p. 211.

in the garden of Xibalba had in some manner proved derelict in duty, and had their lips split as a punishment.[1]

In Paraguay a tribe called the Chiriguanes, "se percent la levre inférieure & ils y attachent un petit Cilindre d'étain ou d'argent, ou de Resine transparente. Ce prétendu ornement s'appelle *Tembeta*."[2]

---

[1] Brasseur de Bourbourg's translation, cap. 12, p. 175.

[2] Picart, Cérémonies et Coûtumes Réligieuses de tous les Peuples du Monde, Amsterdam, 1743, vol. 8, p. 287.

CHAPTER II.

HODDENTIN, THE POLLEN OF THE TULE, THE SACRIFICIAL
POWDER OF THE APACHE; WITH REMARKS UPON SACRED
POWDERS AND BREAD OFFERINGS IN GENERAL.

"Trifles not infrequently lead to important results. In every walk of
science a trifle disregarded by incurious thousands has repaid the
inquisitiveness of a single observer with unhoped-for knowledge."[1]

The taciturnity of the Apache in regard to all that concerns their
religious ideas is a very marked feature of their character; probably no
tribe with which our people have come in contact has succeeded more
thoroughly in preserving from profane inquiry a complete knowledge
of matters relating to their beliefs and ceremonials. How much of this
ignorance is to be attributed to interpreters upon whom reliance has
necessarily been placed, and how much to the indisposition of the
Apache to reveal anything concerning himself, it would be fruitless to
inquire, but, in my own experience, when I first went among them in
New Mexico and Arizona twenty-three years ago, I was foolish enough
to depend greatly upon the Mexican captives who had lived among
the Apache since boyhood, and who might be supposed to know exactly
what explanation to give of every ceremony in which the Apache might
engage. Nearly every one of these captives, or escaped captives, had
married among the Apache, and had raised families of half-breed
children, and several of them had become more Apache than the Apache
themselves. Yet I was time and again assured by several of these interpreters that the Apache had no religion, and even after I had made
some progress in my investigations, at every turn I was met by the
most contradictory statements, due to the interpreter's desire to inject
his own views and not to give a frank exposition of those submitted by
the Apache. Thus, an Apache god would be transmuted into either a
"santo" or a "diablo," according to the personal bias of the Mexican
who happened to be assisting me. "Assanutlije" assumed the disguise
of "Maria Santissima," while ceremonies especially sacred and beneficent in the eyes of the savages were stigmatized as "brujeria" and
"hechiceria" (witchcraft) in open defiance of the fact that the Apache
have as much horror and dread of witches as the more enlightened of
their brethren who in past ages suffered from their machinations in

---

[1] Deane, Serpent Worship, London, 1833, p. 410.

Europe and America. The interpreters had no intention to deceive; they were simply unable to disengage themselves from their own prejudices and their own ignorance; they could not, and they would not,

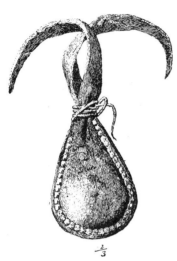

FIG. 5.—Bag containing hoddentin.

credit the existence of any such thing as religion, save and excepting that taught them at their mothers' knees in the petty hamlets of Sonora and of which they still preserved hazy and distorted recollections. One of the first things to be noticed among the Apache, in this connection, was the very general appearance of little bags of buckskin, sometimes ornamented, sometimes plain, which were ordinarily attached to the belts of the warriors, and of which they seemed to be especially careful.[1]

What follows in this chapter was not learned in an hour or a day, but after a long course of examination and a comparison of statements extracted from different authorities.

The bags spoken of revealed when opened a quantity of yellow colored flour or powder, resembling cornmeal, to which the Apache gave the name of " hoddentin," or " hadntin," the meaning of which word is " the powder or pollen of the tule," a variety of the cat-tail rush, growing in all the little ponds and cienegas of the Southwest.

I made it the touchstone of friendship that every scout or other Apache who wished for a favor at my hands should relate something concerning his religious belief. I did not care much what topic he selected; it might be myths, clan laws, war customs, medicine—anything he pleased, but it had to be something and it had to be accurate. Hoddentin having first attracted my attention, I very naturally made many of my first inquiries about it, and, while neglecting no opportunity for independent observation, drew about me the most responsible men and women, heard what each had to say, carefully compared and contrasted it with the statements of the others, and now give the result.

I noticed that in the dances for the benefit of the sick the medicine-men in the intervals between chants applied this yellow powder to the forehead of the patient, then in form of a cross upon his breast, then in a circle around his couch, then upon the heads of the chanters and of sympathizing friends, and lastly upon their own heads and into their own mouths. There is a considerable difference in method, as medicine-men allow themselves great latitude, or a large " personal equa-

---

[1] The medicine sack or bag of the Apache, containing their "hoddentin," closely resembles the "bullæ" of the Romans—in which "On y mettait des préservatifs contre les maléfices." Musée de Naples, London, 1836, p. 4. Copy shown me by Mr. Spofford, of the Library of Congress.

tion," in all their dealings with the supernatural. No Apache would, if it could be avoided, go on the warpath without a bag of this precious powder somewhere upon his person, generally, as I have said, attached to his ammunition belt. Whenever one was wounded, hurt, or taken sick while on a scout, the medicine-man of the party would walk in front of the horse or mule ridden by the patient and scatter at intervals little pinches of hoddentin, that his path might be made easier. As was said to me: " When we Apache go on the warpath, hunt, or plant, we always throw a pinch of hoddentin to the sun, saying ' with the favor of the sun, or permission of the sun, I am going out to fight, hunt, or plant,' as the case may be, ' and I want the sun to help me.'"

I have noticed that the Apache, when worn out with marching, put a pinch of hoddentin on their tongues as a restorative.

"Hoddentin is eaten by sick people as a remedy."[1]

" Before starting out on the warpath, they take a pinch of hoddentin, throw it to the sun, and also put a pinch on their tongues and one on the crown of the head. . . . When they return, they hold a dance, and on the morning of that day throw pinches of hoddentin to the rising sun, and then to the east, south, west, and north, to the four winds."[2]

I am unable to assert that hoddentin is used in any way at the birth of a child; but I know that as late as 1886 there was not a babe upon the San Carlos reservation, no matter how tender its age, that did not have a small bag of hoddentin attached to its neck or dangling from its cradle. Neither can I assert anything about its use at time of marriage, because, among the Apache, marriage is by purchase, and attended with little, if any, ceremony. But when an Apache girl attains the age of puberty, among other ceremonies performed upon her, they throw hoddentin to the sun and strew it about her and drop on her head flour of the piñon, which flour is called by the Chiricahua Apache " nostchi," and by the Sierra Blanca Apache " opé."[3]

" Upon attaining the age of puberty, girls fast one whole day, pray, and throw hoddentin to the sun."[4] When an Apache dies, if a medicine-man be near, hoddentin is sprinkled upon the corpse. The Apache buried in the clefts of rocks, but the Apache-Mohave cremated. " Before lighting the fire the medicine-men of the Apache-Mohave put hoddentin on the dead person's breast in the form of a cross, on the forehead, shoulders, and scattered a little about."[5]

The very first thing an Apache does in the morning is to blow a little pinch of hoddentin to the dawn. The Apache worship both dawn and darkness, as well as the sun, moon, and several of the planets.

---

[1] Information of Tze-go-juni.
[2] Information of Concepcion.
[3] See notes, a few pages farther on, from Kohl; also those from Godfrey Higgins. The word "opé" suggests the name the Tusayan have for themselves, Opi, or Opika, " bread people."
[4] Information of Tze-go-juni.
[5] Information of Mike Burns.

" When the sun rises we cast a pinch of hoddentin toward him, and
we do the same thing to the moon, but not to the stars, saying 'Gun-
ju-le, chigo-na-ay, si-chi-zi, gun-ju-le, inzayu, ijanale,' meaning 'Be good,
O Sun, be good.' 'Dawn, long time let me live'; or, 'Don't let me die
for a long time,' and at night, 'Gun-ju-le, chil-jilt, si-chi-zi, gun-ju-le,
inzayu, ijanale,' meaning 'Be good, O Night; Twilight, be good; do not
let me die." "In going on a hunt an Apache throws hoddentin and
says 'Gun-ju-le, chigo-na-ay, cha-ut-si, ping, kladitza,' meaning 'Be
good, O Sun, make me succeed deer to kill.'"[1]

The name of the full moon in the Apache language is "klego-na-ay,"
but the crescent moon is called "tzontzose" and hoddentin is always
offered to it.[2]

" Hoddentin is thrown to the sun, moon (at times), the morning star,
and occasionally to the wagon."[3] "The Apache offer much hoddentin
to 'Na-u-kuzze,' the Great Bear."[4] "Our custom is to throw a very
small pinch of hoddentin at dawn to the rising sun."[5] "The women of
the Chiricahua throw no hoddentin to the moon, but pray to it, saying:
" Gun-ju-le, klego-na-ay," (be good, O Moon).[6]

When the Apache plant corn the medicine-men bury eagle-plume
sticks in the fields, scatter hoddentin, and sing. When the corn is
partially grown they scatter pinches of hoddentin over it.[7]

The "eagle-plume sticks" mentioned in the preceding paragraph suggests the "ke-thawn" mentioned by Matthews in "The Mountain
Chant."[8]

" When a person is very sick the Apache make a great fire, place the
patient near it, and dance in a circle around him and the fire, at the
same time singing and sprinkling him with hoddentin in the form of a
cross on head, breast, arms, and legs."[9]

In November, 1885, while at the San Carlos agency, I had an interview with Nantadotash, an old blind medicine-man of the Akañe or
Willow gens, who had with him a very valuable medicine-hat which he
refused to sell, and only with great reluctance permitted me to touch.
Taking advantage of his infirmity, I soon had a picture drawn in my
notebook, and the text added giving the symbolism of all the ornamentation attached. Upon discovering this, the old man became much
excited, and insisted upon putting a pinch of hoddentin upon the drawing, and then recited a prayer, which I afterwards succeeded in getting
verbatim. After the prayer was finished, the old man arose and
marked with hoddentin the breast of his wife, of Moses, of Antonio,

[1] Information of Mickey Free.
[2] Information of Alchise, Mike, and others.
[3] Information of Francesca and other captive Chiricahua squaws.
[4] Information of Moses Henderson.
[5] Information of Chato.
[6] Information of Tze-go-juni.
[7] Information of Moses Henderson and other Apache at San Carlos.
[8] Bureau of Ethnology, Report for 1883-'84.
[9] Information of Francesca and others.

of other Apache present, and then of myself, putting a large pinch over my heart and upon each shoulder, and then placed the rest upon his own tongue. He explained that I had taken the "life" out of his medicine hat, and, notwithstanding the powers of his medicine, returned in less than a month with a demand for $30 as damages. His hat never was the same after I drew it. My suggestion that the application of a little soap might wash away the clots of grease, soot, and earth adhering to the hat, and restore its pristine efficacy were received with the scorn due to the sneers of the scoffer.

"In time of much lightning, the Apache throw hoddentin and say: 'Gun-ju-le, ittindi,' be good, Lightning."[1]

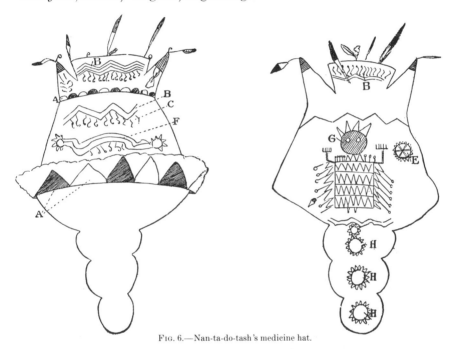

Fig. 6.—Nan-ta-do-tash's medicine hat.

Tzit-jizinde, "the Man who likes Everybody," who said he belonged to the Inoschujochin—Manzanita or Bearberry clan—showed me how to pray with hoddentin in time of lightning or storm or danger of any kind. Taking a small pinch in his fingers, he held it out at arm's length, standing up, and repeated his prayer, and then blew his breath hard. I was once with a party of Apache while a comet was visible. I called their attention to it, but they did not seem to care. On the other hand, Antonio told me that the "biggest dance" the Apache ever had was during the time that "the stars all fell out of the sky" (1833).

"The only act of a religious character which I observed . . . was shortly after crossing the river they [i. e., the American officers] were

---

met by a small party of the Indians, one of whom chalked a cross on the breast of each, with a yellow earth, which he carried in a satchel at his belt. Previous to doing so he muttered some words very solemnly with his hands uplifted and eyes thrown upwards. Again, on arriving at the camp of the people, the chief and others in greeting them took a similar vow, touching thereafter the yellow chalked cross. Sonora may have furnished them with some of their notions of a Deity."[1]

"The yellow earth," seen by Dr. Smart was, undoubtedly, hoddentin, carried in a medicine bag at the belt of a medicine-man. Some years ago I went out with Al. Seiber and a small party of Apache to examine three of their "sacred caves" in the Sierra Pinal and Sierra Ancha. No better opportunity could have been presented for noting what they did. The very last thing at night they intoned a "medicine" song, and at early dawn they were up to throw a pinch of hoddentin to the east.

Moses and John, two of the Apache mentioned above, requested permission to go off in the mountains after deer and bear, supposed to be plentiful in the higher altitudes. Before leaving camp, Moses blew a pinch of hoddentin toward the sun, repeating his prayer for success, and ending it with a sharp, snappy "ek," as if to call attention. In one of the sacred caves visited on this trip, the Apache medicine-men assembled for the purpose of holding their snake dance. This I have never seen among the Apache, but that they celebrate it and that it is fully the equal of the repulsive rite which I have witnessed and noted among the Tusayan[2] I am fully assured. I may make reference to some of its features in the chapter upon animal worship and ophic rites.

From a multiplicity of statements, the following are taken: Concepcion had seen the snake dance over on the Carrizo, near Camp Apache; the medicine-men threw hoddentin upon the snakes. He said: "After getting through with the snake, the medicine-man suffered it to glide off, covered with the hoddentin, thrown by admiring devotees."

Mike Burns had no remembrance of seeing hoddentin thrown to the sun. He had seen it thrown to the snake, "in a kind of worship."

Nott and Antonio stated that "when they find that a snake has wriggled across the trail, especially the trail to be followed by a war party, they throw hoddentin upon the trail." Nott took a pinch of hoddentin, showed how to throw it upon the snake, and repeated the prayer, which I recorded.

Corbusier instances a remedy in use among the Tonto Apache. This consisted in applying a rattlesnake to the head or other part suffering from pain. He continues : "After a time the medicine-man rested the snake on the ground again, and, still retaining his hold of it with his right hand, put a pinch of yellow pollen into its mouth with his left, and rubbed some along its belly."[3]

[1] Smart, in Smithsonian Report for 1867, p. 419.

[2] Snake Dance of Moquis of Arizona, New York, 1884.

[3] In the third volume of Kingsborough, on plate 17 (Aztec picture belonging to M. Pejernavy, Pesth, Hungary), an Aztec, probably a priest, is shown offering food to a snake, which eats it out of his hand.

He then held his hand out to a man, who took a pinch of the powder and rubbed it on the crown of a boy's head. Yellow pollen treated in this manner is a common remedy for headache, and may frequently be seen on the crowns of the heads of men and boys."[1]

Hoddentin is used in the same manner as a remedy for headache among the San Carlos Apache, but the medicine-men apply a snake to the person of a patient only when their "diagnosis" has satisfied them that he has been guilty of some unkindness to a snake, such as stepping upon it, in which case they pretend that they can cure the man by applying to the part affected the portion of the reptile's body upon which he trampled.

The Apache state that when their medicine-men go out to catch snakes for their snake dance, they recite a prayer and lay their left hand, in which is some hoddentin, at the opening of the snake's den, through which the reptile must crawl, and, after a short time the snake will come out and allow himself to be handled.

Hoddentin is also offered to other animals, especially the bear, of which the Apache, like their congeners the Navajo, stand in great awe and reverence. When a bear is killed, the dance which is held becomes frenzied; the skin is donned by all the men, and much hoddentin is thrown, if it can be obtained. One of these dances which I saw in the Sierra Madre, Mexico, in 1883, lasted all night, without a moment's cessation in the singing and prancing of the participants.

A great deal of hoddentin is offered to the "ka-chu" (great or jack rabbit).[2]

The Apache medicine-man, Nakay-do-klunni, called by the whites "Bobbydoklinny," exercised great influence over his people at Camp Apache, in 1881. He boasted of his power to raise the dead, and predicted that the whites should soon be driven from the land. He also drilled the savages in a peculiar dance, the like of which had never been seen among them. The participants, men and women, arranged themselves in files, facing a common center, like the spokes of a wheel, and while thus dancing hoddentin was thrown upon them in profusion. This prophet or "doctor" was killed in the engagement in the Cibicu canyon, August 30, 1881.

In a description of the "altars" made by the medicine-men of the Apache-Yuma at or near Camp Verde, Arizona, it is shown that this sacred powder is freely used. Figures were drawn upon the ground to represent the deities of the tribe, and the medicine-men dropped on all, except three of them, a pinch of yellow powder (hoddentin) which was taken from a small buckskin bag. This powder was put upon the head, chest, or other part of the body of the patient.

Surgeon Corbusier, U. S. Army,[3] says that the ceremony just described was " a most sacred one and entered into for the purpose of averting the

[1] Corbusier, in American Antiquarian, November, 1886, pp. 336-37.
[2] Information of Moses Henderson.
[3] American Antiquarian, Sept. and Nov., 1886.

diseases with which the Apache at Camp Verde had been afflicted the summer previous."

I am not sure that the Apache-Yuma have not borrowed the use of hoddentin from the Apache. My reason for expressing this opinion is that I have never seen an Apache without a little bag of hoddentin when it was possible for him to get it, whereas I have never seen an Apache-Yuma with it except when he was about to start out on the warpath. The "altars" referred to by Corbusier are made also by the Apache, Navajo, Zuñi, and Tusayan. Those of the Apache, as might be inferred from their nomadic state, were the crudest; those of the Navajo, Zuñi, and Tusayan display a wonderful degree of artistic excellence. The altars of the Navajo have been described and illustrated by Dr. Washington Matthews,[1] and those of the Tusayan by myself.[2]

Moses Henderson, wishing me to have a profitable interview with his father, who was a great snake doctor among the Apache, told me that when he brought him to see me I should draw two lines across each other on his right foot, and at their junction place a bead of the chalchihuitl, the cross to be drawn with hoddentin. The old man would then tell me all he knew.

The Apache, I learned, at times offer hoddentin to fire, an example of pyrodulia for which I had been on the lookout, knowing that the Navajo have fire dances, the Zuñi the Feast of the Little God of Fire, and the Apache themselves are not ignorant of the fire dance.

Hoddentin seems to be used to strengthen all solemn compacts and to bind faith. I had great trouble with a very bright medicine-man named Na-a-cha, who obstinately refused to let me look at the contents of a phylactery which he constantly wore until I let him know that I, too, was a medicine-man of eminence. The room in which we had our conversation was the quarters of the post surgeon, at that time absent on scout. The chimney piece was loaded with bottles containing all kinds of drugs and medicines. I remarked carelessly to Na-a-cha that if he doubted my powers I would gladly burn a hole through his tongue with a drop of fluid from the vial marked "Acid, nitric," but he concluded that my word was sufficient, and after the door was locked to secure us from intrusion he consented to let me open and examine the phylactery and make a sketch of its contents. To guard against all possible trouble, he put a pinch of hoddentin on each of my shoulders, on the crown of my head, and on my chest and back. The same performance was gone through with in his own case. He explained that hoddentin was good for men to eat, that it was good medicine for the bear, and that the bear liked to eat it. I thought that herein might be one clew to the reason why the Apache used it as a medicine. The bear loves the tule swamp, from which, in days primeval, he sallied out to attack the squaws and children gathering the tule powder or tule bulb. Poorly

---

[1] Ann. Rep. Bu. Eth., 1883–'84.
[2] Snake Dance of the Moquis.

armed, as they then were, the Apache must have had great trouble in resisting him; hence they hope to appease him by offering a sacrifice acceptable to his palate. If acceptable to the chief animal god, as the bear seems to have been, as he certainly was the most dangerous, then it would have been also acceptable to the minor deities like the puma, snake, eagle, etc., and, by an easy transition, to the sun, moon, and other celestial powers. This opinion did not last long, as will be shown. From its constant association with all sacrifices and all acts of worship, hoddentin would naturally become itself sanctified and an object of worship, just as rattles, drums, standards, holy grails, etc., in different parts of the world have become fetichistic. I was not in the least surprised when I heard Moses Henderson reciting a prayer, part of which ran thus: "Hoddentin eshkin, bi hoddentin ashi" ("Hoddentin child, you hoddentin I offer"), and to learn that it was a personification of hoddentin.

The fact that the myths of the Apache relate that Assanut-li-je spilled hoddentin over the surface of the sky to make the Milky Way may be looked upon as an inchoate form of a calendar, just as the Aztecs transferred to their calendar the reed, rabbit, etc.

So constant is the appearance of hoddentin in ceremonies of a religious nature among the Apache that the expression "hoddentin schlawn" (plenty of hoddentin) has come to mean that a particular performance or place is sacred. Yet, strange to say, this sacred pollen of the tule is gathered without any special ceremony; at least, I noticed none when I saw it gathered, although I should not fail to record that at the time of which I speak the Apache and the Apache-Yuma were returning from an arduous campaign, in which blood had been shed, and everything they did—the bathing in the sweat lodges and the singing of the Apache and the plastering of mud upon their heads by the Apache-Yuma—had a reference to the lustration or purgation necessary under such circumstances. Not only men but women may gather the pollen. When the tule is not within reach our cat-tail rush is used. Thus, the Chiricahua, confined at Fort Pickens, Florida, gathered the pollen of the cat-tail rush, some of which was given me by one of the women who gathered it.

Before making an examination into the meaning to be attached to the use of hoddentin, it is well to determine whether or not such a powder or anything analogous to it is to be found among the tribes adjacent.

THE "KUNQUE" OF THE ZUÑI AND OTHERS.

The term "kunque" as it appears in this chapter is one of convenience only. Each pueblo, or rather each set of pueblos, has its own name in its own language, as, for example, the people of Laguna and Acoma, who employ it in all their ceremonies as freely as do the Zuñi, call it in their tongue "hinawa." In every pueblo which I visited—and I visited them all, from Oraibi of Tusayan, on the extreme west, to

Picuris, on the extreme east; from Taos, in the far north, to Isleta del Sur, in Texas—I came upon this kunque, and generally in such quantities and so openly exposed and so freely used that I was both astonished and gratified; astonished that after centuries of contact with the Caucasian the natives should still adhere with such tenacity to the ideas of a religion supposed to have been extirpated, and gratified to discover a lever which I could employ in prying into the meaning of other usages and ceremonials.

Behind the main door in the houses at Santa Clara, San Ildefonso, Picuris, Laguna, Acoma, San Felipe, Jemez, and other towns, there is a niche containing a bowl or saucer filled with this sacred meal, of which the good housewife is careful to throw a pinch to the sun at early dawn and to the twilight at eventide. In every ceremony among the Pueblos naturally enough, more particularly among those who have been living farthest from the Mexicans, the lavish scattering of sacred meal is the marked feature of the occasion. At the snake dance of the Tusayan, in 1881, the altars were surrounded with baskets of pottery and with flat plaques of reeds, which were heaped high with kunque. When the procession moved out from under the arcade and began to make the round of the sacred stone the air was white with meal, and in my imagination I could see that it was a procession of Druids circling about a " sacred stone " in Ireland previous to the coming of St. Patrick. When the priests threw the snakes down upon the ground it was within a circle traced with kunque, and soon the snakes were covered with the same meal flung upon them by the squaws. There was only one scalp left among the Tusayan in 1881, but there were several among the Zuñi, and one or two each at Acoma and Laguna. In every one of these towns kunque was offered to the scalps.

At the feast of the Little God of Fire among the Zuñi, in 1881, my personal notes relate that " the moment the head of the procession touched the knoll upon which the pueblo is built the mass of people began throwing kunque upon the Little God and those with him as well as on the ground in front of, beside, and behind them. This kunque was contained in sacred basket-shaped bowls of earthenware. The spectators kept the air fairly misty with clouds of the sacred kunque. This procession passed around the boundaries of the pueblo of Zuñi, stopping at eight holes in the ground for the purpose of enacting a ceremonial of consecration suggestive of the 'terminalia' of the Romans. They visited each of the holes, which were 18 inches deep and 12 inches square, with a sandstone slab to serve as a cover. Each hole was filled with kunque and sacrificial plumes. * * * 'Every morning of the year, when the sky is clear, at the rising of Lucero [the morning star], at the crowing of the cock, we throw corn flour [kunque] to the sun. I am never without my bag of kunque; here it is [drawing it from his belt]. Every Zuñi has one. We offer it to the sun for good rain and good crops.'"[1]

---

[1] Interview with Pedro Pino.

Subsequently Pedro went on to describe in detail a phallic dance and ceremony, in which there was a sort of divination. The young maiden who made the lucky guess was richly rewarded, while her less fortunate companions were presented with a handful of kunque, which they kept during the ensuing year. This dance is called "ky'áklu," and is independent of the great phallic dance occurring in the month of December. Pedro also stated that until very recently the Zuñi were in the habit of celebrating a fire dance at Noche Buena (Christmas). There were four piles of wood gathered for the occasion, and upon each the medicine-men threw kunque in profusion. This dance, as Pedro described it, closely resembled one mentioned by Landa in his Cosas de Yucatan. High up on the vertical face of the precipice of Tâaiyalana there is a phallic shrine of the Zuñi to which I climbed with Mr. Frank Cushing. We found that the place had been visited by young brides who were desirous of becoming mothers. The offerings in every case included kunque.

In the account given in the National Tribune, Washington, District of Columbia, May 20, 1886, of the mode of life of the Zuñi woman Wehwa while in the national capital, and while engaged in the kirmes, we read:

She also strewed sacred corn meal along on her way to the theater to bring good luck to her and the other dancers.   *   *   *   She has gone from her comfortable room to pray in the street at daylight every morning, whatever the weather has been.   *   *   *   At such times she strews corn meal all around her until the front-door steps and the sidewalk are much daubed with dough. But this is not the corn meal in common use in the United States, but is sacred meal ground in Zuñi with sacred stones.[1]

So long a time has elapsed since any of the Pueblos have been on the warpath that no man can describe their actual war customs except from the dramatic ceremonial of their dances or from the stories told him by the "old men." The following from an eyewitness will therefore be of interest: "Before the Pueblos reached the heights they were ordered to scale they halted on the way to receive from their chiefs some medicine from the medicine bags which each of them carried about his person. This they rubbed upon their heart, as they said, to make it big and brave, and they also rubbed it upon other parts of their bodies and upon their rifles for the same purpose."[2]

The constant use of kunque by the different Pueblo tribes has been noticed from the first days of European contact. In the relation of Don Antonio de Espejo (1583) we are told that upon the approach of the Spaniards to the town of Zaguato, lying 28 leagues west of Zuñi, "a great multitude of Indians came forth to meete them, and among the rest their Caçiques, with so great demonstration of joy and gladnes,

---

[1] Kunque has added to the cornmeal the meal of two varieties of corn, blue and yellow, a small quantity of pulverized sea shells, and some sand, and when possible a fragment of the blue stone called "chalchihuitl." In grinding the meal on the metates the squaws are stimulated by the medicine-men who keep up a constant singing and drumming.

[2] Simpson, Expedition to the Navajo Country, in Senate Doc. 64, 31st Cong., 1st sess., 1849-'50, p. 95·

that they cast much meale of Maiz upon the ground for the horses to tread upon."[1]

I am under the impression that the ruins of this village are those near the ranch of Mr. Thomas V. Keam, at Keam's Canyon, Arizona, called by the Navajo "Talla-hogandi," meaning "singing house," in reference to the Spanish mission which formerly existed there. This village is, as I have hitherto shown, the ruin of the early pueblo of Awátubi.

In his poem descriptive of the conquest of New Mexico, entitled "Nueva Mejico," Alcala de Henares, 1610, Villagrá uses the following language:[2]

> Passando à Mohoçe, Zibola, y Zuni,
> Por cuias nobles tierras descubrimos,
> Una gran tropa de Indios que venia,
> Con cantidad harina que esparcian,
> Sobre la gente toda muy apriessa,
> Y entrando assi en los pueblos las mugeres
> Dieron en arrojarnos tanta della,
> Que dimos en tomarles los costales,
> De donde resultò tener con ellas,
> Unas carnestolendas bien reñidas.

It is gratifying to observe that the Spanish writer in the remote wilds of America struck upon an important fact in ethnology: that the throwing of "harina" or flour by the people of Tusayan (Mohoçe or Moqui), Cibola, and Zuñi (observe the odd separation of "Zibola" from either Moqui or Zuñi) was identical with the "carnestolendas" of Spain, in which, on Shrove Tuesday, the women and girls cover all the men they meet with flour. The men are not at all backward in returning the compliment, and the streets are at times filled with the farinaceous dust.

"Harina de maiz azul" is used by Mexicans in their religious ceremonies, especially those connected with the water deities.[3] The Peruvians, when they bathed and sacrificed to cure themselves of sickness, "untandose primero con Harina de Maiz, i con otras cosas, con muchas, i diversas ceremonias, i lo mismo hacen en los Baños."[4] The kunque of the Peruvians very closely resembled that of the Zuñi. We read that it was a compound of different-colored maize ground up with sea shells.[5] The Peruvians had a Priapic idol called Hua-can-qui, of which we read: " On offre à cette idole une corbeille ornée de plumes de diverses couleurs et remplie d'herbes odoriférantes; on y met aussi de la *farine de maïs* que l'on renouvelle tous les mois, et les femmes se lavent la

---

[1] Hakluyt, Voyages, vol. 3, p. 470. "Echavan mucha harina de maiz por el suelo para que la pisassen los caballos."—Padre Fray Juan Gonzales de Mendoza, De las Cosas de Chino, etc., Madrid, 1586, p. 172. See also the Relacion of Padre Fray Alonso Fernandez, Historia Eclesiastica de Nuestros Tiempos, Toledo, 1611, pp. 15, 16.

[2] P. 162.

[3] Diego Duran, vol. 2, cap. 49, pp. 506, 507.

[4] Herrera, dec. 5., lib. 4, cap. 5, p. 92.

[5] Padre Christoval de Molina, Fables and Rites of the Yncas, translated by Markham in Hakluyt Soc. Trans , vol. 48. p. 63, London, 1873.

figure avec celle que l'on ôte, en accompagnant cette ablution de plusieurs cérémonies superstitieuses."[1]

The tribes seen on the Rio Colorado in 1540 by Alarcon " carry also certaine little long bagges about an hand broade tyed to their left arme, which serve them also instead of brasers for their bowes, full of the powder of a certaine herbe, whereof they make a certaine beverage.[2] We are at a loss to know what this powder was, unless hoddentin. The Indians came down to receive the son of the sun, as Alarcon led them to believe him to be, in full gala attire, and no doubt neglected nothing that would add to their safety.

" Ils mirent dans leur bouche du maïs et d'autres semences, et les lancèrent vers moi en disant que c'était la manière dont ils faisaient les sacrifices au soleil."[3]

Kohl speaks of seeing inside the medicine wigwam, during the great medicine ceremonies of the Ojibwa, "a snow-white powder."[4] In an address delivered by Dr. W. J. Hoffman before the Anthropological Society of Washington, D. C., May 2, 1888, upon the symbolism of the Midē', Jes'sakkid, and Wâbeno of the Ojibwa of Minnesota, he stated in reply to a question from me that he had not been able to find any of the "snow-white powder" alluded to by Kohl in Kitchi-gami.[5]

In Yucatan, when children were baptized, one of the ceremonies was that the chac, or priest in charge, should give the youngster a pinch of corn meal, which the boy threw in the fire. These chacs were priests of the god who presided over baptism and over hunting.[6]

At the coronation of their kings the Aztecs had a sacred unction, and a holy water, drawn from a sacred spring, and "about his neck is tied a small gourd, containing a certain powder, which is esteemed a strong preservative against disease, sorcery, and treason."[7]

"At the entrance to one of the narrow defiles of the Cordilleras . . . a large mass of rock with small cavities upon its surface, into which the Indians, when about to enter the pass, generally deposit a few glass beads, a handful of meal, or some other propitiatory offering to the 'genius' supposed to preside over the spot and rule the storm."

Again, "on receiving a plate of broth, an Indian, before eating, spills a little upon the ground; he scatters broadcast a few pinches of the meal that is given him, and pours out a libation before raising the wine cup to his lips, as acts of thanksgiving for the blessings he receives."[8]

When Capt. John Smith was captured by the Pamunkey tribe of Vir-

[1] Montesinos, pp. 161, 162, in Ternaux-Compans, vol. 17, Mémoires sur l'ancien Pérou.
[2] Relation of the voyage of Don Fernando Alarcon, in Hakluyt Voyages, vol. 3, p. 508.
[3] Alarcon in Ternaux-Compans, Voy., vol. 9, p. 330. See also in Hakluyt Voyages, vol. 3, p. 516.
[4] Kitchi-gami, London, 1860, p. 51.
[5] See also on the subject Acosta, Hist. Naturelle des Indes, lib. 5, cap. 19, p. 241.
[6] Landa, Cosas de Yucatan, Paris, 1864, page 148.
[7] Bancroft, Native Races, vol. 2, p. 145. See also Clavigero, Hist. of Mexico, Philadelphia, 1817, vol. 2, p. 128.
[8] Smith, Araucanians, 1855, pp. 274–275.

ginia in 1607 he was taken to " a long house," where, on the morning following " a great grim fellow" came skipping in, " all painted over with coale, mingled with oyle. With most strange gestures and passions he began his invocation, and environed the fire with a circle of meale." This priest was followed by six others, who " with their rattles began a song, which ended, the chiefe priest layd downe five wheat cornes." This ceremony was apparently continued during the day and repeated on the following two days. [1] Capt. Smith's reception by the medicine-men of the Virginians is described by Picart.[2] These medicine-men are called " prêtres," and we are informed that they sang "des chants magiques." The grains of wheat ("grains de blé") were "rangez cinq à cinq."

Gomara tells us that in the religious festivals of Nicaragua there were used certain "taleguillas con polvos," but he does not tell what these " polvos" were; he only says that when the priests sacrifice themselves they cured the wounds, "curan las heridas con polvo de herbas ó carbon." [3]

While the Baron de Graffenreid was a prisoner in the hands of the Tuscarora, on the Neuse River, in 1711, the conjurer or high priest (" the priests are generally magicians and even conjure up the devil") "made two white rounds, whether of flour or white sand, I do not know, just in front of us."[4]

Lafitau says of one of the medicine women of America : " Elle commença d'abord par préparer un espace de terrain qu'elle nétoya bien & qu'elle couvrit de farine, ou de cendre très-bien bluttée (je ne me souviens pas exactement laquelle des deux)."[5]

In a description of the ceremonial connected with the first appearance of the catamenia in a Navajo squaw, there is no reference to a use of anything like hoddentın, unless it may be the corn which was ground into meal for a grand feast, presided over by a medicine-man. [6]

When a woman is grinding corn or cooking, and frequently when any of the Navajo, male or female, are eating, a handful of corn meal is put in the fire as an offering (to the sun). [7]

The Pueblos of New Mexico are described as offering sacrifices of food to their idols. " Los Indios del Norte tienan multitud de Idolos, en pequeños Adoratorios, donde los ponen de comer." [8]

Maj. Backus, U. S. Army, describes certain ceremonies which he saw performed by the Navajo at a sacred spring near Fort Defiance, Arizona, which seems to have once been a geyser:

---

[1] Smith, True Travels, Adventures and Observations, Richmond, 1819, vol. 1, p. 161.

[2] Cérémonies et Coûtumes, Amsterdam, 1735, vol. 6, p. 74.

[3] Historia de las Indias, p. 284.

[4] Colonial Records of North Carolina, 1886, vol. 1, p. 930.

[5] Mœurs des Sauvages, Paris, 1724, vol. 1, p. 386.

[6] Personal notes of May 26, 1881; conversation with Chi and Damon at Fort Defiance. Navajo Agency, Arizona.

[7] Ibid.

[8] Barcia, Ensayo Cronologico, p. 160.

I once visited it with three other persons and an Indian doctor, who carried with him five small bags, each containing some vegetable or mineral substance, all differing in color. At the spring each bag was opened and a small quantity of its contents was put into the right hand of each person present. Each visitor, in succession, was then required to kneel down by the spring side, to place his closed hand in the water up to his elbow, and after a brief interval to open his hand and let fall its contents into the spring. The hand was then slowly withdrawn and each one was then permitted to drink and retire. [1]

Columbus in his fourth voyage touched the mainland, going down near Brazil. He says:

In Cariay and the neighboring country there are great enchanters of a very fearful character. They would have given the world to prevent my remaining there an hour. When I arrived they sent me immediately two girls very showily dressed; the eldest could not be more than eleven years of age and the other seven, and both exhibited so much immodesty that more could not be expected from public women. They carried concealed about them a magic powder. [2]

The expedition of La Salle noticed, among the Indians on the Mississippi, the Natchez, and others, "todos los dias, que se detuvieren en aquel Pueblo, ponia la Cacica, encima de la Sepultura de Marle [i. e., a Frenchman who had been drowned], una Cestilla llena de Espigas de Maíz, tostado." [3]

"He showed me, as a special favor, that which gave him his power— a bag with some reddish powder in it. He allowed me to handle it and smell this mysterious stuff, and pointed out two little dolls or images, which, he said, gave him authority over the souls of others; it was for their support that flour and water were placed in small birch-rind saucers in front." [4]

On page 286, narrative of the Jeannette Arctic expedition, Dr. Newcomb says: "One day, soon after New Year's, I was out walking with one of the Indians. Noticing the new moon, he stopped, faced it, and, blowing out his breath, he spoke to it, invoking success in hunting. The moon, he said, was 'Tyunne,' or ruler of deers, bears, seals, and walrus." The ceremony herein described I have no doubt was analogous in every respect to hoddentin-throwing. As the Indians mentioned were undoubtedly Tinneh, my surmise seems all the more reasonable. [5]

Tanner relates that among the Ojibwa the two best hunters of the band had "each a little leather sack of medicine, consisting of certain roots pounded fine and mixed with red paint, to be applied to the little images or figures of the animals we wish to kill." [6]

"In the parish of Walsingham, in Surrey, there is or was a custom which seems to refer to the rites performed in honor of Pomona. Early in the spring the boys go round to the several orchards in the parish

---

[1] Schoolcraft, Ind. Tribes, vol. 4, p. 213.

[2] Columbus Letters, in Hakluyt Soc. Works, London, 1847, vol 2, p. 192.

[3] Barcia, Ensayo Cronologico, p. 279.

[4] The medicine-men of the Swampy Crees, as described in Bishop of Rupert's Land's works, quoted by Henry Youle Hind, Canadian Exploring Expedition, vol. 1, p. 113.

[5] Personal notes, November 22, 1885, at Baker's ranch, summit of the Sierra Ancha, Arizona.

[6] Tanner's Narrative, p. 174.

and whip the apple trees. . . . The good woman gives them some meal."[1]

Among the rustics of Great Britain down to a very recent period there were in use certain "love powders," the composition of which is not known, a small quantity of which had to be sprinkled upon the food of the one beloved.[2]

Attached to the necklace of human fingers before described, captured from one of the chief medicine-men of the Cheyenne Indians, is a bag containing a powder very closely resembling hoddentin, if not hoddentin itself.

It is said that the Asinai made sacrifice to the scalps of their enemies, as did the Zuñi as late as 1881. "Ofrecen á las calaveras pinole molido y de otras cosas comestibles."[3]

Perrot says the Indians of Canada had large medicine bags, which he calls "pindikossan," which, among other things, contained "des racines ou des poudres pour leur servir de médecines."[4]

In an article on the myth of Manibozho, by Squier, in American Historical Magazine Review, 1848, may be found an account of the adventures of two young heroes, one of whom is transferred to the list of gods. He commissioned his comrade to bring him offerings of a white wolf, a polecat, some pounded maize, and eagles' tails.

Laplanders sprinkle cow and calf with flour.[5]

Cameron met an old chief on the shores of Lake Tanganyika, of whom he says: "His forehead and hair were daubed with vermilion, yellow, and white powder, the pollen of flowers."[6]

In the incantations made by the medicine-men of Africa, near the head of the Congo, to preserve his expedition from fire, Cameron saw the sacrifice of a goat and a hen, and among other features a use of powdered bark closely resembling hoddentin: "Scraping the bark off the roots and sticks, they placed it in the wooden bowl and reduced it to powder." The head medicine-man soon after "took up a handful of the powdered bark and blew some toward the sun and the remainder in the opposite direction."[7]

The magic powder, called "uganga," used as the great weapon of divination of the mganga, or medicine-men of some of the African tribes, as mentioned by Speke,[8] must be identical with the powder spoken of by Cameron.

Near the village of Kapéka, Cameron was traveling with a caravan

---

[1] Blount,Tenures of Land and Customs of Manors, London, 1874, p. 355.

[2] Brand, Popular Antiquities, London, 1882, vol. 3, pp. 307 et seq.

[3] Crónica Seráfica, p. 434.

[4] Nicolas Perrot, Mœurs, Coustumes et Relligion des sauvages de l'Amérique Septentrionale (Ed. of Rev. P. J. Tailhan, S. J.,) Leipzig, 1864. Perrot was a coureur de bois, interpreter, and donné of the Jesuit missions among the Ottawa, Sioux, Iowa, etc., from 1665 to 1701.

[5] Leems', Account of Danish Lapland, in Pinkerton's Voyages, London, 1814, vol. 1, p. 484.

[6] Across Africa, London, 1877, vol. 1, p. 277.

[7] Ibid., vol. 2, pp. 118, 120.

[8] Source of the Nile, London, 1863, introd., p. XXI.

in which the principal man was a half-breed Portuguese named Alvez. "On Alvez making his entry he was mobbed by women, who shrieked and yelled in honor of the event and pelted him with flour." This was Alvez's own home and all this was a sign of welcome.[1]

Speke describes a young chief wearing on his forehead "antelope horns, stuffed with magic powder to keep off the evil eye."[2]

After describing an idol, in the form of a man, in a small temple on the Lower Congo, Stanley says: "The people appear to have considerable faith in a whitewash of cassava meal, with which they had sprinkled the fences, posts, and lintels of doors."[3]

"According to Consul Hutchinson (in his interesting work 'Impressions of Western Africa'), the Botikaimon [a medicine-man], previous to the ceremony of coronation, retires into a deep cavern, and there, through the intermediary of a 'rukaruka' (snake demon), consults the demon Maon. He brings back to the king the message he receives, sprinkles him with a yellow powder called 'tsheoka,' and puts upon his head the hat his father wore."[4] In a note, it is stated that: "Tsheoka is a vegetable product, obtained, according to Hutchinson, by collecting a creamy coat that is found on the waters at the mouth of some small rivers, evaporating the water, and forming a chalky mass of the residue."[5] Schultze says[6] that the Congo negroes "appease the hurricane" by "casting meal into the air."

The voudoo ceremonies of the negroes of New Orleans, which would seem to have been transplanted from Africa, include a sprinkling of the congregation with a meal which has been blessed by the head medicine-man or conjurer.

At the feast of Huli, at the vernal equinox (our April fool's day), the Hindu throw a purple powder (abir) upon each other with much sportive pleasantry. A writer in "Asiatick Researches"[7] says they have the idea of representing the return of spring, which the Romans called "purple."

During the month of Phalgoonu, there is a festival in honor of Krishna, when the "Hindus spend the night in singing and dancing and wandering about the streets besmeared with the dolu (a red) powder, in the daytime carrying a quantity of the same powder about with them, which, with much noise and rejoicing, they throw over the different passengers they may meet in their rambles. Music, dancing, fireworks, singing, and many obscenities take place on this occasion."[8]

On pages 434-435 of my work, "Scatalogic Rites of all Nations," are to be found extracts from various authorities in regard to the Hindu

---

[1] Cameron, Across Africa, London, 1877, vol. 2, p. 201.
[2] Source of the Nile, London, 1863, pp. 130, 259.
[3] Dark Continent, vol. 2, p. 260.
[4] Schultze, Fetichism, New York, 1885, p. 53.
[5] Ibid., footnote, page 53.
[6] Ibid., p. 67.
[7] Asiatick Researches, Calcutta, 1805, vol. 8, p. 78.
[8] Coleman, Mythology of the Hindus, London, 1832, p. 44.

feast of Holi or Hulica, in which this statement occurs: "Troops of men and women, wreathed with flowers and drunk with bang, crowd the streets, carrying sacks full of bright-red vegetable powder. With this they assail the passers-by, covering them with clouds of dust, which soon dyes their clothes a startling color."

"Red powder (gulál) is a sign of a bad design of an adulterous character. During the Holi holidays, the Maháráj throws gulál on the breasts of female and male devotees."[1]

" In India, the devotees throw red powder on one another at the festival of the Huli, or vernal equinox. This red powder, the Hindoos say, is the imitation of the pollen of plants, the principle of fructification, the flower of the plant."[2]

The women of the East Indies (Brahmins), on the 18th of January, celebrate a feast in honor of the goddess Parvati: "Leur but est d'obtenir une longue vie pour leurs maris, & qu'elles ne deviennent jamais veuves. Elles font une Image de Parvati avec de la farine de riz & du grain rouge qu'elles y mêlent; elles l'ornent d'habits & de fleurs & après l'avoir ainsi servie pendant neuf jours, elles la portent le dixiéme dans un Palenquin hors de la Ville. Une foule de femmes mariées la suivent, on la jette ensuite dans un des étangs sacrez, où on la laisse, & chacune s'en retourne chez elle."[3]

Speaking of the methods in use among the Lamas for curing disease, Rev. James Gilmour says: "Throwing about small pinches of millet seed is a usual part of such a service."[4]

Dr. W. W. Rockhill described to me a Tibetan festival, which includes a procession of the God of Mercy, in which procession there are masked priests, holding blacksnake whips in their hands, and carrying bags of flour which they throw upon the people.

The use of these sacred powders during so many different religious festivals and ceremonies would seem to resemble closely that made by the Apache of hoddentin and the employment of kunque by the Zuñi and others; and from Asia it would seem that practices very similar in character found their way into Europe. Of the Spanish witches it is related:

When they entered people's houses they threw a powder on the faces of the inmates, who were thrown thereby into so deep a slumber that nothing could wake them, until the witches were gone. . . . . Sometimes they threw these powders on the fruits of the field and produced hail which destroyed them. On these occasions the demon accompanied them in the form of a husbandman, and when they threw the powders they said:

> "Polvos, polvos,
> Pierda se tado,
> Queden los nuestros,
> Y abrasense otros."[5]

---

[1] History of the Sect of the Mahárájahs, quoted by Inman, Ancient Faiths, etc., vol. 1, p. 393.
[2] Higgins, Anacalypsis, vol. 1, p. 261.
[3] Picart, Cérémonies et Coûtumes, etc., vol. 6, part 2, p. 119.
[4] Among the Mongols, London, 1883, p. 179.
[5] Wright, Sorcery and Magic, London, 1851, vol. 1, p. 346.

Higgins says: "The flour of wheat was the sacrifice offered to the Χρης or Ceres in the Εὐχάριστία." [1]

What relation these powders have had to the "carnestolendas" of the Spanish and Portuguese, already alluded to, and the throwing of "confetti" by the Italians, which is a modification, it would be hard to say. Some relation would appear to be suggested.

USE OF POLLEN BY THE ISRAELITES AND EGYPTIANS.

There are some suggestions of a former use of pollen among the Israelites and Egyptians.

Manna, which we are assured was at one time a source of food to the Hebrews, was afterward retained as an offering in the temples. Forlong, however, denies that it ever could have entered into general consumption. He says:

Manna, as food, is an absurdity, but we have the well-known produce of the desert oak or ash—Fraxinus. . . . . An omer of this was precious, and in this quantity, at the spring season, not difficult to get; it was a specially fit tribute to be "laid up" before any Phallic Jah, as it was the pollen of the tree of Jove and of Life, and in this sense the tribe lived spiritually on such "spiritual manna" as this god supplied or was supplied with.[2]

The detestation in which the bean was held by the high-caste people of Egypt does not demonstrate that the bean was not an article of food to a large part of the population, any more than the equal detestation of the occupation of swineherd would prove that none of the poor made use of swine's flesh. The priesthood of Egypt were evidently exerting themselves to stamp out the use of a food once very common among their people, and to supersede it with wheat or some other cereal. They held a man accursed who in passing through a field planted with beans had his clothing soiled with their pollen. Speke must have encountered a survival of this idea when he observed in equatorial Africa, near the sources of the Nile, and among people whose features proclaimed their Abyssinian origin, the very same aversion. He was unable to buy food, simply because he and some of his followers had eaten "the bean called maharagüé." Such a man, the natives believed, "if he tasted the products of their cows, would destroy their cattle."[3]

One other point should be dwelt upon in describing the kunque of the Zuñi, Tusayan, and other Pueblos. It is placed upon one of the sacred flat baskets and packed down in such a manner that it takes the form of one of the old-fashioned elongated cylindro-conical cheeses. It should be noted also that by something more than a coincidence this form was adhered to by the peoples farther to the south when they arranged their sacred meal upon baskets.

At the festival of the god Teutleco the Aztecs made "de harina de

---

[1] Anacalypsis, vol. 2, p. 244.
[2] Rivers of Life, vol. 1, p. 161.
[3] Source of the Nile, London, 1863, pp. 205, 208.

maiz un montecillo muy tupido de la forma de un queso."[1] This closely resembles the corn meal heaps seen at the snake dance of the Tusayan.

The Zuñi, in preparing kunque or sacred meal for their religious festivals, invariably made it in the form of a pyramid resting upon one of their flat baskets. It then bore a striking resemblance to the pyramids or phalli which the Egyptians offered to their deities, and which Forlong thinks must have been "just such Lingham-like sweet-bread as we still see in Indian Sivaic temples."[2] Again, "the orthodox Hislop, in his Two Babylons, tells us that 'bouns,' buns, or bread offered to the gods from the most ancient times were similar to our 'hotcross' buns of Good Friday, that . . .   the buns known by that identical name were used in the worship of the Queen of Heaven, the goddess Easter (Ishtar or Astarti) as early as the days of Kekrops, the founder of Athens, 1500 years B. C."[3]

Forlong[4] quotes Capt. Wilford in Asiatick Researches, vol. 8, p. 365, as follows:

When the people of Syracuse were sacrificing to goddesses, they offered cakes called *mulloi,* shaped like the female organ; and Dulare tells us that the male organ was similarly symbolised in pyramidal cakes at Easter by the pious Christians of Saintogne, near Rochelle, and handed about from house to house; that even in his day the festival of Palm Sunday was called *La Fête des Pinnes,* showing that this fête was held to be on account of both organs, although, of course, principally because the day was sacred to the palm, the ancient tree Phallus. . . .   We may believe that the Jewish cakes and show bread were also emblematic.

Mr. Frank H. Cushing informs me that there is an annual feast among the Zuñi in which are to be seen cakes answering essentially to the preceding description.

HODDENTIN A PREHISTORIC FOOD.

The peculiar manner in which the medicine-men of the Apache use the hoddentin (that is, by putting a pinch upon their own tongues); the fact that men and women make use of it in the same way, as a restorative when exhausted; its appearance in myth in connection with Assanutlije, the goddess who supplied the Apache and Navajo with so many material benefits, all combine to awaken the suspicion that in hoddentin we have stumbled upon a prehistoric food now reserved for sacrificial purposes only. That the underlying idea of sacrifice is a food offered to some god is a proposition in which Herbert Spencer and W. Robertson Smith concur. In my opinion, this definition is incomplete; a perfect sacrifice is that in which a *prehistoric* food is offered to a god, and, although in the family oblations of everyday life we meet with the food of the present generation, it would not be difficult to show that where the whole community unites in a function of exceptional impor-

---

[1] Sahagun, vol. 2, in Kingsborough, vol. 6, p. 29.
[2] Forlong, Rivers of Life, vol. 1, p. 184.
[3] Ibid., pp. 185, 186.
[4] Ibid., p. 186.

tance the propitiation of the deities will be effected by foods whose use has long since faded away from the memory of the laity.

The sacred feast of stewed puppy and wild turnips forms a prominent part of the sun dance of the Sioux, and had its parallel in a collation of boiled puppy (catullus), of which the highest civic and ecclesiastical dignitaries of pagan Rome partook at stated intervals.

The reversion of the Apache to the food of his ancestors—the hoddentin—as a religious offering has its analogue in the unleavened bread and other obsolete farinaceous products which the ceremonial of more enlightened races has preserved from oblivion. Careful consideration of the narrative of Cabeza de Vaca sustains this conclusion. In the western portion of his wanderings we learn that for from thirty to forty days he and his comrades passed through tribes which for one-third of the year had to live on "the powder of straw" (on the powder of bledos), and that afterwards the Spaniards came among people who raised corn. At that time, Vaca, whether we believe that he ascended the Rio Concho or kept on up the Rio Grande, was in a region where he would certainly have encountered the ancestors of our Apache tribe and their brothers the Navajo. The following is Herrera's account of that part of Vaca's wanderings: "Padeciendo mucha hambre en treinta i quatro Jornadas, pasando por una Gente que la tercera parte del Año comen polvos de paja, i los huvieron de comer, por haver llegado en tal ocasion."[1]

This powder (polvo) of paja or grass might at first sight seem to be grass seeds; but why not say "flour," as on other occasions? The phrase is an obscure one, but not more obscure than the description of the whole journey. In the earlier writings of the Spaniards there is ambiguity because the new arrivals endeavored to apply the names of their own plants and animals to all that they saw in the western continent. Neither Castañeda nor Cabeza de Vaca makes mention of hoddentin, but Vaca does say that when he had almost ended his journey: "La côte ne possède pas de maïs; on n'y mange que de la poudre de paille de blette." "Blette" is the same as the Spanish "bledos."[2] "Nous parvînmes chez une peuplade qui, pendant le tiers de l'année, ne vit que de poudre de paille." "We met with a people, who the third part of the yeere eate no other thing save the powder of straw."[3]

Davis, who seems to have followed Herrera, says: "These Indians lived one-third of the year on the powder of a certain straw . . . . . . After leaving this people they again arrived in a country of permanent habitations, where they found an abundance of maize. . . . The inhabitants gave them maize both in grain and flour.[4]

The Tusayan Indians were formerly in the habit of adding a trifle of

[1] Dec. 6, lib. 1, p. 9.

[2] Ternaux-Compans, Voyages, vol. 7, pp. 242, 250.

[3] Relation of Cabeza de Vaca in Purchas, vol. 4, lib. 8, cap. 1, sec. 4, p. 1524.

[4] Conquest of New Mexico, p. 100.

chopped straw to their bread, but more as our own bakers would use bran than as a regular article of diet.

Barcia[1] makes no allusion to anything resembling hoddentin or "polvos de bledos" in his brief account of Vaca's journey. But Buckingham Smith, in his excellent translation of Vaca's narrative, renders "polvos de paja" thus: "It was probably the seed of grass which they ate. I am told by a distinguished explorer that the Indians to the west collect it of different kinds and from the powder make bread, some of which is quite palatable." And for "polvos de bledos": "The only explanation I can offer for these words is little satisfactory. It was the practice of the Indians of both New Spain and New Mexico to beat the ear of young maize, while in the milk, to a thin paste, hang it in festoons in the sun, and, being thus dried, was preserved for winter use."

This explanation is very unsatisfactory. Would not Vaca have known it was corn and have said so? On the contrary, he remarks in that very line in Smith's own translation: "There is no maize on the coast."

The appearance of all kinds of grass seeds in the food of nearly all the aborigines of our southwestern territory is a fact well known, but what is to be demonstrated is the extensive use of the "powder" of the tule or cat-tail rush. Down to our day, the Apache have used not only the seeds of various grasses, but the bulb of the wild hyacinth and the bulb of the tule. The former can be eaten either raw or cooked, but the tule bulb is always roasted between hot stones. The taste of the hyacinth bulb is somewhat like that of raw chestnuts. That of the roasted tule bulb is sweet and not at all disagreeable.[2]

Father Jacob Baegert[3] enumerates among the foods of the Indians of southern California "the roots of the common reed" (i. e., of the tule).

Father Alegre, speaking of the tribes living near the Laguna San Pedro,[4] in latitude 28° north—two hundred leagues north of the City of Mexico—says that they make their bread of the root, which is very frequent in their lakes, and which is like the plant called the "anea" or rush in Spain. "Forman el pan de una raiz muy frecuente en sus lagunas, semejante á las que llaman aneas en España."[5]

The Indians of the Atlantic Slope made bread of the bulb of a plant which Capt. John Smith[6] says "grew like a flag in marshes." It was roasted and made into loaves called "tuckahoe."[7]

Kalm, in his Travels in North America,[8] says of the tuckahoe:

It grows in several swamps and marshes and is commonly plentiful. The hogs greedily dig up its roots with their noses in such places, and the Indians of Carolina likewise gather it in their rambles in the woods, dry it in the sun, grind, and make

[1] Ensayo Cronologico, pp. 12 et seq.
[2] See also on this point Corbusier, in American Antiquarian, November, 1886.
[3] Rau's translation in Smithsonian Ann. Rep., 1863, p. 364.
[4] Probably the Lake of Parras.
[5] Historia de la Compañía de Jesus en Nueva-España, vol. 1, p. 284.
[6] History of Virginia.
[7] See also article by J. Howard Gore, Smithsonian Report, 1881.
[8] Pinkerton, Voyages, London, 1814, vol. 13, p. 468.

bread of it. Whilst the root is fresh it is harsh and acrid, but, being dried, it loses the greater part of its acrimony. To judge by these qualities, the tuckahoe may very likely be the Arum virginianum.

The Shoshoni and Bannock of Idaho and Montana eat the tule bulb.[1]

Something analogous to hoddentin is mentioned by the chronicler of Drake's voyage along the California coast about A. D. 1540. Speaking of the decorations of the chiefs of the Indians seen near where San Francisco now stands, he says another mark of distinction was " a certain downe, which groweth up in the countrey upon an herbe much like our lectuce, which exceeds any other downe in the world for finenesse and beeing layed upon their cawles, by no winds can be removed. Of such estimation is this herbe amongst them that the downe thereof is not lawfull to be worne, but of such persons as are about the king, . . . and the seeds are not used but onely in sacrifice to their gods."[2]

Mr. Cushing informs me that hoddentin is mentioned as a food in the myths of the Zuñi under the name of oneya, from oellu, " food."

In Kamtchatka the people dig and cook the bulbs of the Kamtchatka lily, which seems to be some sort of a tuber very similar to that of the tule.

" Bread is now made of rye, which the Kamtchadals raise and grind for themselves; but previous to the settlement of the country by the Russians the only native substitute for bread was a sort of baked paste, consisting chiefly of the grated tubers of the purple Kamtchatkan lily."[3]

HODDENTIN THE YIAUHTLI OF THE AZTECS.

There would seem to be the best of reason for an identification of hoddentin with the "yiauhtli" which Sahagun and Torquemada tell us was thrown by the Aztecs in the faces of victims preparatory to sacrificing them to the God of Fire, but the explanation given by those authors is not at all satisfactory. The Aztecs did not care much whether the victim suffered or not; he was sprinkled with this sacred powder because he had assumed a sacred character.

Padre Sahagun[4] says that the Aztecs, when about to offer human sacrifice, threw "a powder named 'yiauhtli' on the faces of those whom they were about to sacrifice, that they might become deprived of sensation and not suffer much pain in dying."

In sacrificing slaves to the God of Fire, the Aztec priests " tomaban ciertos polvos de una semilla, llamada Yauhtli, y polvoreaban las caras

---

[1] Personal notes, April 5, 1881.

[2] Drake, World Encompassed, pp. 124–126, quoted by H. H. Bancroft, Native Races, vol. 1, pp. 387–388. (This chaplain stated so many things ignorantly that nothing is more probable than that he attempted to describe, without seeing it, the plant from which the Indians told him that hoddentin (or downe) was obtained. The principal chief or '' king '' would, on such an awe-inspiring occasion as meeting with strange Europeans, naturally want to cover himself and followers with all the hoddentin the country afforded.)

[3] Kennan, Tent Life in Siberia, p. 66.

[4] Quoted by Kingsborough, vol. 6, p. 100.

con ellas, para que perdiesen el sentido, y no sintiesen tanto la muerte cruel, que las daban."[1]

Guautli, generally spelled "yuautli," one of the foods paid to Monte-zuma as tribute, may have been tule pollen. Gallatin says: "I can not discover what is meant by the guautli. It is interpreted as being *semilla de Bledo;* but I am not aware of any other native grain than maize having been, before the introduction of European cereales, an article of food of such general use, as the quantity mentioned seems to indi-cate."[2]

Among the articles which the king of Atzapotzalco compelled the Aztecs to raise for tribute is mentioned "ahuauhtli (que es como bledos)."[3]

"BLEDOS" OF ANCIENT WRITERS—ITS MEANING.

Lafitau[4] gives a description of the Iroquois mode of preparing for the warpath. He says that the Iroquois and Huron called war "n'ondoutagette" and "gaskenragette." "Le terme *Ondouta* signifie le duvet qu'on tire de l'épy des Roseaux de Marais & signifie aussi la plante toute entière, dont ils se servent pour faire les nattes sur quoi ils couchent, de sorte qu'il y a apparence qu'ils avoient affecté ce terme pour la Guerre, parce que chaque Guerrier portoit avec soy sa natte dans ces sortes d'expeditions."

This does not seem to be the correct explanation. Rather, it was because they undoubtedly made some sacrificial meal of this "duvet," or pollen, and used it as much as the Apache do hoddentin, their sacred meal made of the pollen of the tule, which is surely a species of "roseaux de marais."

The great scarcity of corn among the people passed while en route to Cibola is commented upon in an account of Coronado's expedition to Cibola, in Coleccion de Documentos Inéditos, relativos al descu-brimiento, conquista y colonizacion de las posesiones Españolas de América y Oceanía.[5]

We are also informed[6] that the people of Cibola offered to their idols "polbos amarillos de flores."

Castañeda speaks of the people beyond Chichilticale making a bread of the mesquite which kept good for a whole year. He seems to have been well informed regarding the vegetable foods of the tribes passed through by Coronado's expedition.[7]

That the "blettes" or "bledos" did not mean the same as grass is a certainty after we have examined the old writers, who each and all

---

[1] Torquemada, Monarchia Indiana, vol. 2, lib. 10, cap. 22, p. 274.

[2] Gallatin, in Trans. Am. Ethnol. Soc., vol. 1, pp. 117–118.

[3] Vetancurt, Teatro Mexicano, vol. 1, p. 271.

[4] Mœurs des Sauvages, vol. 2, pp. 194, 195.

[5] Madrid, 1870, vol. 14, p. 320.

[6] Ibid.

[7] Ternaux-Compans, Voyages, vol. 9, p. 159.

show that the bledos meant a definite kind of plant, although exactly what this plant was they fail to inform us. It can not be intended for the sunflower, which is mentioned distinctly by a number of writers as an article of diet among the Indians of the Southwest.[1]

TZOALLI.

An examination of the Spanish writers who most carefully transmitted their observations upon the religious ceremonies of the Aztecs and other nations in Mexico and South America brings out two most interesting features in this connection. The first is that there were commemorative feasts of prehistoric foods, and the second that one or more of these foods has played an important part in the religion of tribes farther north. The first of these foods is the " tzoalli," which was the same as " bledos," which latter would seem beyond question to have been hoddentin or yiauhtli. Brasseur de Bourbourg's definition simply states that the tzoalli was a compound of leguminous grains peculiar to Mexico and eaten in different ways: " Le Tzohualli était un composé de graines légumineuses particulières au Mexique, qu'on mangeait de diverses manières." [2]

In the month called Tepeilhuitl the Aztecs made snakes of twigs and covered them with dough of bledos (a kind of grain or hay seed). Upon these they placed figures, representing mountains, but shaped like young children.[3] This month was the thirteenth on the Mexican calendar, which began on our February 1. This would put it October 1, or thereabout.

Squier cites Torquemada's description of the sacrifices called Ecatotontin, offered to the mountains by the Mexicans. In these they made figures of serpents and children and covered them with " dough," named by them tzoalli, composed of the seeds of bledos.[4]

A dramatic representation strongly resembling those described in the two preceding paragraphs was noted among the Tusayan of Arizona by Mr. Taylor, a missionary, in 1881, and has been mentioned at length in The Snake Dance of the Moquis. Clavigero relates that the Mexican priests " all eat a certain kind of gruel which they call *Etzalli*." [5]

Torquemada relates that the Mexicans once each year made an idol or statue of Huitzlipotchli of many grains and the seeds of bledos and other vegetables which they kneaded with the blood of boys who were sacrificed for the purpose. " Juntaban muchos granos y semilla de

---

[1] Among others consult Cronica Seráfica y Apostolica of Espinosa, Mexico, 1746, p. 419, speaking of the Asinai of Texas in 1700: " Siembran tambien cantidad de Gyrasoles que se dan muy corpulentos y la flor muy grande que en el centro tienen la semilla como de piñones y de ella mixturada con el maiz hacen un bollo que es de mucho sabor y sustancia."

[2] Brasseur de Bourbourg, Hist. Nations Civilisées, quoted by Bancroft, Native Races, vol. 3, p. 421.

[3] Sahagun, in book 7, Kingsborough, p. 71.

[4] Squier, Serpent Symbol, p. 193, quoting Torquemada, lib. 7, cap. 8.

[5] History of Mexico, Philadelphia, 1817, vol. 2, p. 79. See the additional note from Clavigero, which would seem to show that this etzalli was related to the espadaña or rush.

Bledos, y otras legumbres, y molianlas con mucha devocion, y recato, y de ellas amasaban, y formaban la dicha Estatua, del tamaño y estatura de un Hombre. El licor, con que se resolbian y desleìan aquellas harinas era sangre de Niños, que para este fin se sacrificaban." [1]

It is remarkable the word "maiz" does not occur in this paragraph. Huitzlipotchli being the God of War, it was natural that the ritual devoted to his service should conserve some, if not all, of the foods, grains, and seeds used by the Mexicans when on the warpath in the earliest days of their history; and that this food should be made into a dough with the blood of children sacrificed as a preliminary to success is also perfectly in accordance with all that we know of the mode of reasoning of this and other primitive peoples. Torquemada goes on to say that this statue was carried in solemn procession to the temple and idol of Huitzlipotchli and there adorned with precious jewels (chalchihuitl), embedded in the soft mass. Afterward it was carried to the temple of the god Paynalton, preceded by a priest carrying a snake in the manner that the priests in Spain carried the cross in the processions of the church. "Con una Culebra mui grande, y gruesa en las manos, tortuosa, y con muchas bueltas, que iba delante, levantada en alto, á manera de Cruz, en nuestras Procesiones." [2] This dough idol, he says, was afterwards broken into "migajas" (crumbs) and distributed among the males only, boys as well as men, and by them eaten after the manner of communion; "este era su manera de comunion." [3] Herrera, speaking of this same idol of Vitzliputzli, as he calls him, says it was made by the young women of the temple, of the flour of bledos and of toasted maize, with honey, and that the eyes were of green, white, or blue beads, and the teeth of grains of corn. After the feast was over, the idol was broken up and distributed to the faithful, "á manera de comunion." "Las Doncellas recogidas en el templo, dos Dias antes de la Fiesta, amasaban harina de Bledos, i de Maiz tostado, con miel, y de la masa hacian un Idolo grande, con los ojos de cuentas grandes, verdes, açules, ò blancas; i por dientes granos de maiz. [4]

H. H. Bancroft speaks of the festival in honor of Huitzilopochtli, "the festival of the wafer or cake." He says: "They made a cake of the meal of bledos, which is called tzoalli," which was afterward divided in a sort of communion. [5] Diego Duran remarks that at this feast the chief priest carried an idol of dough called "tzoally," which is made of the seeds of bledos and corn made into a mass with honey. [6] "Un ydolo de masa, de una masa que llaman tzoally, la cual se hace de semilla de bledos y maiz amasado con miel." This shows that

---

[1] Monarchia Indiana, vol. 2, lib. 6, cap. 38, p. 71.
[2] Ibid., p. 72.
[3] Ibid., p. 73.
[4] Dec. 3, lib. 2, pp. 71, 72.
[5] Native Races, vol. 3, p. 323.
[6] Diego Duran, vol. 3, p. 187.

"bledos" and "maiz" were different things.[1] A few lines farther on Duran tells us that this cake, or bread, was made by the nuns of the temple, "las mozas del recogimiento de este templo," and that they ground up a great quantity of the seed of bledos, which they call huauhtly, together with toasted maize. "Molian mucha cantidad de semilla de bledos que ellos llaman huauhtly juntamente con maiz tostado."[2] He then shows that the "honey" (miel) spoken of by the other writers was the thick juice of the maguey. "Despues de molido, amasabanlo con miel negra de los magueis."

Acosta describes a Mexican feast, held in our month of May, in which appeared an idol called Huitzlipotchli, made of "mays rosty," "semence de blettes," and "amassoient avec du miel."[3]

In the above citations it will be seen that huauhtly or yuauhtli and tzoally were one and the same. We also find some of the earliest if not the very earliest references to the American popped corn.

That the Mexicans should have had such festivals or feasts in honor of their god of battles is no more extraordinary than that in our own country all military reunions make it a point to revert to the "hard tack" issued during the campaigns in Virginia and Tennessee. Many other references to the constant use as a food, or at least as a sacrificial food, of the bledos might be supplied if needed. Thus Diego Duran devotes the twelfth chapter of his third book to an obscure account of a festival among the Tepanecs, in which appeared animal gods made of "masa de semilla de bledos," which were afterwards broken and eaten.

Torquemada speaks of such idols employed in the worship of snakes and mountains.[4] In still another place this authority tells us that similar figures were made and eaten by bride and groom at the Aztec marriage ceremony.[5]

The ceremonial manner in which these seeds were ground recalls the fact that the Zuñi regard the stones used for grinding kunque as sacred and will not employ them for any other purpose.

Idols made of dough much after the fashion of the Aztecs are to be found among the Mongols. Meignan speaks of seeing "an idol, quite open to the sky and to the desert, representing the deity of travelers. It was made of compressed bread, covered over with some bituminous substance, and perched on a horse of the same material, and held in its hand a lance in Don Quixote attitude. Its horrible features were surmounted with a shaggy tuft of natural hair. A great number of offerings of all kinds were scattered on the ground all around. Five or six images, formed also of bread, were bending in an attitude of prayer before the deity."[6]

---

[1] See notes already given from Buckingham Smith's translation of Vaca.

[2] Diego Duran, vol. 3, p. 195.

[3] José Acosta, Hist. des Indes, ed. of Paris, 1600, liv. 5, cap. 24, p. 250.

[4] Monarchia Indiana, lib. 10, cap. 33.

[5] Ibid., lib. 6, cap. 48.

[6] From Paris to Pekin, London, 1885, pp. 312, 313.

Dr. Edwin James, the editor of Tanner's Narrative,[1] cites the " Calica Puran" to show that medicinal images are employed by the people of the East Indies when revenge is sought upon an enemy; " water must be sprinkled on the meal or earthen victim which represents the sacrificer's enemy."

In those parts of India where human sacrifice had been abolished, a substitutive ceremony was practiced " by forming a human figure of flour-paste, or clay, which they carry into the temples, and there cut off its head or mutilate it, in various ways, in presence of the idols."[2]

Gomara describes the festival in honor of the Mexican God of Fire, called " Xocothuecl," when an idol was used made of every kind of seed and was then enwrapped in sacred blankets to keep it from breaking. " Hacian aquella noche un ídolo de toda suerte de semillas, envolvíanlo en mantas benditas, y liábanlo, porque no se deshiciese."[3]

These blessed blankets are also to be seen at the Zuñi feast of the Little God of Fire, which occurs in the month of December. It is a curious thing that the blessed blankets of the Zuñi are decorated with the butterfly, which appeared upon the royal robes of Montezuma.

What other seeds were used in the fabrication of these idols is not very essential to our purpose, but it may be pointed out that one of them was the seed of the " agenjo," which was the " chenopodium" or " artemisia," known to us as the " sagebrush."

Of the Mexicans we learn from a trustworthy author: "Tambien usaban alguna manera de comunion ó recepcion del sacramento, y es que hacian unos idolitos chiquitos de semilla de bledos ó cenizos, ó de otras yerbas, y ellos mismos se los recibian, como cuerpo ó memoria de sus dioses."[4]

Mendieta wrote his Historia Eclesiástica Indiana in 1596, " al tiempo que esto escribo (que es por Abril del año de noventa y seis)"[5] and again,[6] " al tiempo que yo esto escribo."

The Mexicans, in the month of November, had a festival in honor of Tezcatlipuca. " Hacian unos bollos de masa de maíz y semejante de agenjos, aunque son de otra suerte que los de acá, y echábanlos á cocer en ollas con agua sola. Entre tanto que hervian y se cocian los bollos, tañian los muchachos un atabal . . . . y después comíanselos con gran devocion."[7]

Gomara's statement, that while these cakes of maize and wormwood seed were cooking the young men were beating on drums, would find its parallel in any account that might be written of the behavior of the Zuñi, while preparing for their sacred feasts. The squaws grind the

---

[1] New York, 1830, p. 191.
[2] Dubois, People of India, London, 1817, p. 490.
[3] Gomara; Historia de Méjico, p. 445.
[4] Mendieta, Hist. Eclesiástica Ind., p. 108.
[5] Ibid., p. 402.
[6] Ibid., p. 515.
[7] Gomara, Historia de Méjico, p. 446.

meal to be used on these occasions to the accompaniment of singing by the medicine-men and much drumming by a band of assistants selected from among the young men and boys.

Mr. Francis La Flèche, a nearly full-blood Omaha Indian, read before the Anthropological Society of Washington, D. C., in 1888, a paper descriptive of the funeral customs of his people, in which he related that when an Indian was supposed to be threatened with death the medicine-men would go in a lodge sweat-bath with him and sing, and at the same time " pronouncing certain incantations and sprinkling the body of the client with the powder of the artemisia, supposed to be the food of the ghosts."[1]

To say that a certain powder is the food of the ghosts of a tribe is to say indirectly that the same powder was once the food of the tribe's ancestors.

The Peruvians seem to have made use of the same kind of sacrificial cakes kneaded with the blood of the human victim. We are told that in the month of January no strangers were allowed to enter the city of Cuzco, and that there was then a distribution of corn cakes made with the blood of the victim, which were to be eaten as a mark of alliance with the Inca. " Les daban unos Bollos de Maíz, con sangre de el sacrificio, que comian, en señal de confederacion con el Inga."[2]

Balboa says that the Peruvians had a festival intended to signalize the arrival of their young men at manhood, in which occurred a sort of communion consisting of bread kneaded by the young virgins of the sun with the blood of victims. This same kind of communion was also noted at another festival occurring in our month of September of each year. (" Un festin composé de pain pétri par les jeunes vierges du Soleil avec le sang des victimes."[3]) There were other ceremonial usages among the Aztecs, in which the tule rush itself, " espadaña," was employed, as at childbirth, marriage, the festivals in honor of Tlaloc, and in the rough games played by boys. It is possible that from being a prehistoric food the pollen of the tule, or the plant which furnished it, became associated with the idea of sustenance, fertility, reproduction, and therefore very properly formed part of the ritual necessary in weddings or connected with the earliest hours of a child's life, much as rice has been used so freely in other parts of the world.[4]

Among the Aztecs the newly born babe was laid upon fresh green tule rushes, with great ceremony, while its name was given to it.[4]

Gomara says that the mats used in the marriage ceremonies of the Aztecs were made of tules. "Esteras verdes de espadañas."[5]

"They both sat down upon a new and curiously wrought mat, which was spread in the middle of the chamber close to the fire." The marriage bed was made "of mats of rushes, covered with small sheets,

[1] From the account of lecture appearing in the Evening Star, Washington, D. C., May 19 1888.
[2] Herrera, dec. 5, lib. 4, cap. 5, p. 92.
[3] Balboa, Histoire du Pérou, in Ternaux-Compans, Voyages, vol. 15, pp. 124 and 127.
[4] See the explanatory text to the Codex Mendoza, in Kingsborough, vol. 5, p. 90, et seq.
[5] Historia de Méjico, p. 439.

with certain feathers, and a gem of chalchihuitl in the middle of them." [1]

The third festival of Tlaloc was celebrated in the sixth month, which would about correspond to our 6th of June. [2] But there was another festival in honor of the Tlaloc, which seems very hard to understand. A full description is given by Bancroft. [3] To celebrate this it was incumbent upon the priests to cut and carry to the temples bundles of the tule, which were woven into a sacred mat, after which there was a ceremonial procession to a tule swamp in which all bathed.

The Aztecs, like the Apache, had myths showing that they sprang originally from a reed swamp. There was an Aztec god, Napatecutli, who was the god of the tule and of the mat-makers. [4] This rush was also strewn as part of several of their religious ceremonies.

Fosbrooke [5] has this to say about certain ceremonies in connection with the churches in Europe: "At certain seasons the Choir was strewed with hay, at others with sand. On Easter sabbath with ivy-leaves; at other times with rushes." He shows that hay was used at Christmas and the vigil of All Saints, at Pentecost, Athelwold's Day, Assumption of the Blessed Virgin, and Ascension, etc.

The Mexican populace played a game closely resembling our "blind man's buff" in their seventeenth month, which was called Tititl and corresponded to the winter solstice. In this game, called "nechichiquavilo," men and boys ran through the streets hitting every one whom they met with small bags or nets ("taleguillas ó redecillas") filled with tule powder or fine paper ("llenas de flor de las espadañas ó de algunos papeles rotos"). [6]

The same thing is narrated by other early Spanish writers upon Mexico.

In the myths of Guatemala it is related that there were several distinct generations of men. The first were made of wood, without heart or brains, with worm-eaten feet and hands. The second generation was an improvement upon this, and the women are represented as made of tule. "Las mugeres fueron hechas de corazon de espadaña." [7]

Picart, enumerating the tree gods of the Romans, says that they had deified "les Roseaux pour les Rivieres." [8]

GENERAL USE OF THE POWDER AMONG INDIANS.

This very general dissemination among the Indians of the American continent of the sacred use of the powder of the tule, of images, idols, or sacrificial cakes made of such prehistoric foods, certainly suggests

[1] Clavigero, History of Mexico, Philadelphia, 1817, vol. 2, p. 101.
[2] "They strewed the temple in a curious way with rushes."—Ibid., p. 78.
[3] Native Races, vol. 3, pp. 334-343.
[4] Sahagun, in Kingsborough, vol. 7, p. 16.
[5] British Monachism, London, 1817, p. 289.
[6] Kingsborough, vol. 7, p. 83, from Sahagun.
[7] Ximenez, Guatemala, Translated by Scherzer, p. 13.
[8] Cérémonies et Coûtumes, etc., vol. 1, p. 27.

that the Apache and the Aztecs, among whom they seem to have been most freely used on ceremonial occasions, were invaders in the country they respectively occupied, comparatively recent in their arrival among the contiguous tribes like the Zuñi and Tusayan who on corresponding occasions offered to their gods a cultivated food like corn. The Tlascaltec were known in Mexico as the "bread people," possibly because they had been acquainted with the cultivation of the cereals long before the Aztecs. Similarly, there was a differentiation of the Apache from the sedentary Pueblos. The Apache were known to all the villages of the Pueblos as a "corn-buying tribe," as will presently be shown. It is true that in isolated cases and in widely separated sections the Apache have for nearly two centuries been a corn-planting people, because we find accounts in the Spanish chronicles of the discovery and destruction by their military expeditions of "trojes" or magazines of Apache corn near the San Francisco (or Verde) River, in the present Territory of Arizona, as early as the middle of the last century. But the general practice of the tribe was to purchase its bread or meal from the Pueblos at such times as hostilities were not an obstacle to free trade. There was this difference to be noted between the Apache and the Aztecs: The latter had been long enough in the valley of Anahuac to learn and adopt many new foods, as we learn from Duran, who relates that at their festivals in honor of Tezcatlipoca, or those made in pursuance of some vow, the woman cooked an astonishing variety of bread, just as, at the festivals of the Zuñi, Tusayan, and other Pueblos in our own time, thirty different kinds of preparations of corn may be found.[1] I was personally informed by old Indians in the pueblos along the Rio Grande that they had been in the habit of trading with the Apache and Comanche of the Staked Plains of Texas until within very recent years; in fact, I remember seeing such a party of Pueblos on its return from Texas in 1869, as it reached Fort Craig, New Mexico, where I was then stationed. I bought a buffalo robe from them. The principal article of sale on the side of the Pueblos was cornmeal. The Zuñi also carried on this mixed trade and hunting, as I was informed by the old chief Pedro Pino and others. The Tusayan denied that they had ever traded with the Apache so far to the east as the buffalo country, but asserted that the Comanche had once sent a large body of their people over to Walpi to trade with the Tusayan, among whom they remained for two years. There was one buffalo robe among the Tusayan at their snake dance in 1881, possibly obtained from the Ute to the north of them.

The trade carried on by the "buffalo" Indians with the Pueblos was noticed by Don Juan de Oñate as early as 1599. He describes them as "dressed in skins, which they also carried into the settled provinces to sell, and brought back in return cornmeal."[2]

---

[1] "Tanta diferencia de manjares y de géneros de pan que era cosa estraña."—Diego Duran, vol. 3 cap. 4, p. 219.

[2] Davis, Conquest of New Mexico, p. 273.

Gregg[1] speaks of the "Comancheros" or Mexicans and Pueblos who ventured out on the plains to trade with the Comanche, the principal article of traffic being bread. Whipple[2] refers to this trade as carried on with all the nomadic tribes of the Llano Estacado, one of which we know to have been the eastern division of the Apache. The principal article bartered with the wild tribes was flour, i. e., cornmeal.

In another place he tells us of "Pueblo Indians from Santo Domingo, with flour and bread to barter with the Kái-ò-wàs and Comanches for buffalo robes and horses."[3] Again, Mexicans were seen with flour, bread, and tobacco, "bound for Comancne land to trade. We had no previous idea of the extent of this Indian trade."[4] Only one other reference to this intertribal commerce will be introduced.

Vetancurt[5] mentions that the Franciscan friars, between 1630 and 1680, had erected a magnificent "temple" to "Our Lady of the Angels of Porciúncula," and that the walls were so thick that offices were established in their concavities. On each side of this temple, which was erected in the pueblo of Pecos (situated at or near the head of the Pecos River, about 30 miles southeast of Santa Fé, New Mexico, on the eastern rim of the Llano Estacado), were three towers. At the foot of the hill was a plain about one league in circumference, to which the Apache resorted for trade. These were the Apache living on the plains of Texas. They brought with them buffalo robes, deer skins and other things to exchange for corn. They came with their dog-trains loaded, and there were more than five hundred traders arriving each year.

Observe that here we have the first and only reference to the use of dog trains by the Apache who in every other case make their women carry all plunder in baskets on their backs. In this same extract from Vetancurt there is a valuable remark about Quivira: "Este es el paso para los reinos de la Quivira."

ANALOGUES OF HODDENTIN.

In the citation from the Spanish poet Villagra, already given, the suggestion occurs that some relationship existed between the powder scattered so freely during the Spanish "carnestolendas" and the "kunque" thrown by the people of Tusayan upon the Spaniards and their horses when the Spaniards first entered that country. This analogy is a very striking one, even though the Spaniards have long since lost all idea of the meaning of the practice which they still follow. It is to be noted, however, that one of the occasions when this flour is most freely

---

[1] Commerce of the Prairies, vol. 2, p. 54.

[2] Pacific R. R. Report, 1856, vol. 3, pt. 1, p. 34.

[3] Ibid., p. 34.

[4] Ibid., p. 38.

[5] Los Apaches traian pieles de cíbolas, gamuzas y otras cosas, á hacer cambio por maíz." "Venian con sus recuas de perros cargados mas de quinientos mercaderes cada año."—Teatro Mexicano, vol. 3, p. 323.

used is the Eve of All Saints (Hallowe'en), when the ghosts or ancestors of the community were to be the recipients of every attention.[1]

In the East, the use of the reddish or purple powder called the "gulal" is widely prevalent, but it is used at the feast of Huli, which occurs at the time of the vernal equinox.

There seems to have been used in Japan in very ancient days a powder identical with the hoddentin, and, like it, credited with the power to cure and rejuvenate.

In the mythical period, from the most ancient times to about B. C. 200, being the period of the so-called pure Japanese "medicine," it is related that Ona-muchi-no-mikoko gave these directions to a hare which had been flayed by a crocodile: "Go quickly now to the river mouth, wash thy body with fresh water, then take the pollen of the sedges and spread it about, and roll about upon it; whereupon thy body will certainly be restored to its original state."[2]

There is no indication that in the above case the "pollen of the sedges" had ever occupied a place in the list of foods. It would appear that its magical effects were strictly dependent upon the fact that it was recognized as the reproductive agent in the life of the plant.

No allusion has yet been made to the hoddentin of the Navajo, who are the brothers of the Apache. Surgeon Matthews[3] has referred to it under the name of tqa-di-tin', or ta-di-tin', "the pollen, especially the pollen of corn."

This appears to me to be a very interesting case of a compromise between the religious ideas of two entirely different systems or sects. The Navajo, as now known to us, are the offspring of the original Apache or Tinneh invaders and the refugees from the Rio Grande and Zuñi Pueblos, who fled to the fierce and cruel Apache to seek safety from the fiercer and more cruel Spanish.

The Apache, we have shown, offer up in sacrifice their traditional food, the pollen of the tule. The Zuñi, as we have also shown, offer up their traditional food, the meal of corn, to which there have since been added sea shells and other components with a symbolical significance. The Navajo, the progeny of both, naturally seek to effect a combination or compromise of the two systems and make use of the pollen of the corn. Kohl narrates an Ojibwa legend to the effect that their god Menaboju, returning from the warpath, painted his face with "pleasant yellow stripes . . . of the yellow foam that covers the water in spring," and he adds that this is "probably the yellow pollen that falls fromt he pine." He quotes[4] another legend of the magic red

---

[1] In burlesque survivals the use of flour prevails not only all over Latin Europe, but all such portions of America as are now or have been under Spanish or Portuguese domination. The breaking of egg-shells over the heads of gentlemen upon entering a Mexican ball room is one manifestation of it Formerly the shell was filled with flour.

[2] Dr. W. Norton Whitney. Notes from the History of Medical Progress in Japan, Yokohama, 1885, p. 248.

[3] The prayer of a Navajo Shaman, in American Anthropologist, vol. 1, No. 2, 1888, p. 169.

[4] Kitchi-gami, pp. 416, 423, 424.

powder for curing diseases once given by the snake spirit of the waters to an Ojibwa.

Godfrey Higgins[1] has this to say of the use of pollen by the ancients which he recognizes as connected with the principle of fertility:

Αρωμα, the sweet smell, means also a flower, that is Pushpa or Pushto. This was the language of the followers of the Phasah or the Lamb—it was the language of the Flower, of the Natzir, of the Flos-floris of Flora, of the Arouma, and of the flour of Ceres, or the Eucharistia. It was the language of the pollen, the pollen of plants, the principle of generation, of the Pole or Phallus.

Again he says:

Buddha was a flower, because as flour or pollen he was the principle of fructification or generation. He was flour because flour was the fine or valuable part of the plant of Ceres, or wheat, the pollen which, I am told, in this plant, and in this plant alone, renews itself when destroyed. When the flour, pollen, is killed, it grows again several times. This is a very beautiful type or symbol of the resurrection. On this account the flour of wheat was the sacrifice offered to the Χρης or Ceres in the Ευχαριστια. In this pollen we have the name of pall or pallium and of Pallas, in the first language meaning *wisdom*. . . . When the devotee ate the bread he ate the pollen, and thus ate the body of the God of generation; hence might come transubstantiation.

Lupton,[2] in 1660, describes a "powder of the flowers [pollen?] of elder, gathered on a midsummer day," which was taken to restore lost youth. Brand, it may be as well to say, traces back the custom of throwing flour into the faces of women and others on the streets at Shrovetide, in Minorca and elsewhere, to the time of the Romans.[3]

In writing the description of the Snake Dance of the Moquis of Arizona, I ventured to advance the surmise that the corn flour with which the sacred snakes were covered, and with which the air was whitened, would be found upon investigation to be closely related to the crithomancy or divination by grains of the cereals, as practiced among the ancient Greeks. Crithomancy, strictly speaking, meant a divination by grains of corn. The expression which I should have employed was alphitomancy, a divination " by meal, flower, or branne."[4] But both methods of divination have been noticed among the aborigines of America.

In Peru the medicine-men were divided into classes, as were those of ancient Egypt. These medicine-men "made the various means of divination specialities." Some of them predicted by "the shapes of grains of maize taken at random."[5] In Guatemala grains of corn or of chile were used indiscriminately, and in Guazacualco the medicine-women used grains of frijoles or black beans. In Guatemala they had what they called "ahquij." " Este modo de adivinar se llama ahquij, malol-

---

[1] Anacalypsis, London, 1836, vol. 2, pp. 242–244.

[2] Brand, Pop. Antiq., vol. 3, p. 285.

[3] Ibid., vol. 1, p. 69.

[4] Ibid., vol. 3, pp. 329 et seq.

[5] Brinton, Myths of the New World, New York, 1868, pp. 278, 279.

tzitè, malol-ixim, esto es: el que adivina por el sol, ó por granos de maiz ó chile." [1]

In Guazacuàlco the medicine-women "hechaban suertes con granos de Frisoles, a manera de Dados, i hacian sus invocaciones, porque eran Hechiceros: i si el Dado decia bien, proseguian en la cura, diciendo que sanaria: i si mal, no bolvian al enfermo." [2]

Herrera in the preceding paragraph recognizes the close similarity between this sacred ceremony of casting lots or divining, and the more orthodox method of gambling, pure and simple, which has in every case been derived from a sacred origin.

"Les Hachus [one class of Peruvian priests] consultaient l'avenir au moyen de grains de maïs ou des excréments des animaux." [3]

The Mexicans " para saber si los enfermos habian de morir, ó sanar de la enfermedad que tenian, echaban un puñado de maiz lo mas grueso que podian haber, y lanzábanlo siete ó ocho veces, como lanzan los dados los que los juegan, y si algun grano quedaba enhiesto, decian que era señal de muerte." [4]

Father Brebœuf relates that at the Huron feast of the dead, which occurred every 8 or 10 years and which he saw at Ossossane, " a few grains of Indian corn were thrown by the women upon the sacred relics." [5]

THE DOWN OF BIRDS IN CEREMONIAL OBSERVANCES.

No exhaustive and accurate examination of the subject of hoddentin could be made without bringing the investigator face to face with the curious analogue of " down " throwing and sprinkling which seemingly obtains with tribes which at some period of their history have been compelled to rely upon birds as a main component of their diet. Examples of this are to be met with on both sides of the Pacific as well as in remote Australia, and were the matter more fully examined there is no doubt that some other identifications might be made in very unexpected quarters. The down used by the Tchuktchi on occasions of ceremony had a suggestion of religion about it. [6] " On leaving the shore, they sung and danced. One who stood at the head of the boat was employed in plucking out the feathers of a bird's skin and blowing them in the air."

In Langsdorff's Travels [7] we learn that some of the dancers of the Koluschan of Sitka have their heads powdered with the small down feathers of the white-headed eagle and ornamented with ermine; also, that the hair and bodies of the Indians at the mission of Saint Joseph, New California, were powdered with down feathers. [8]

[1] Ximenez, Guatemala, p. 177.

[2] Herrera, dec. 4, lib. 9, cap. 8, p. 188.

[3] Balboa, Hist. du Pérou, in Ternaux-Compans, Voy., vol. 15, p. 29.

[4] Mendieta, Hist. Eclesiástica Ind., p. 110.

[5] Henry Youle Hind, Assiniboine and Saskatchewan Exped., vol. 2, pp. 165, 166.

[6] Lisiansky, Voyage Round the World, London, 1814, pp. 153, 221, 223.

[7] London, 1814, pt. 2, pl. III, p. 113.

[8] Ibid., pl. IV, pp. 194, 195.

The Indians from the North Pacific coast seen visiting the mission of San Francisco, by Kotzebue in 1816, "had their long disordered hair covered with down." [1]

Bancroft says of the Nootka of the northwest coast of British America: "the hair is powdered plentifully with white feathers, which are regarded as the crowning ornament for manly dignity in all these regions." [2]

The bird's down used by the Haida of British North America in their dances seems very closely related to hoddentin. They not only put it upon their own persons, but "delight to communicate it to their partners in bowing," and also "blow it into the air at regular intervals through a painted tube." They also scattered down as a sign of welcome to the first European navigators. [3]

In all these dances, ceremonial visits, and receptions of strangers the religious element can be discerned more or less plainly. The Indians west of the Mississippi with whom Father Hennepin was a prisoner in 1680, and who appear to have been a branch of the Sioux (Issati or Santee and Nadouessan), had a grand dance to signalize the killing of a bear. On this occasion, which was participated in by the "principaux chefs et guerriers," we learn that there was this to be noted in their dress: "ayant même leurs cheveux frottez d'huile d'ours & parsemez de plumes, rouges & blanches & les têtes chargées de duvet d'oiseaux." [4]

" Swan's and bustard's down " was used by the Accancess [i. e., the Arkansas of the Siouan stock] in their religious ceremonies. [5]

Of the war dress of the members of the Five Nations we learn from an early writer: "Their heads [previously denuded of all hair except that of the crown] are painted red down to the eye-brows and sprinkled over with white down." [6]

The Indians of Virginia at their war dances painted themselves to make them more terrible: " Pour se rendre plus terriblee, ils sément des plumes, du duvet, ou du poil de quelque bête sur la peinture toute fraiche." [7] Down was also used by the medicine-men of the Carib. [8] The down of birds was used in much the same way by the tribes of Cumaná, a district of South America not far from the mouth of the Orinoco, in the present territory of Venezuela; [9] by the Tupinambis, of Brazil, who covered the bodies of their victims with it; [10] by the Chirib-

---

[1] Voyage, vol. 1, p. 282.

[2] Native Races, vol. 1, p. 179.

[3] Ibid., vol. 1, pp. 170, 171.

[4] Père Louis Hennepin, Voyage, etc., Amsterdam, 1714, pp. 339-240. Ibid., translated by B. F. French, in Historical Collections of Louisiana, pt. 1, 1846.

[5] Joutel's Journal, in Historical Collections of Louisiana, tr. by B. F. French, pp. 181, 1846.

[6] Maj. Rogers, Account of North America, in Knox's Voyages, vol. 2, London, 1767, p. 167.

[7] Picart, Cérémonies et Coûtumes Religieuses, etc., Amsterdam, 1735, vol. 6, p. 77.

[8] Ibid., p. 89.

[9] John De Laet, lib. 18, cap. 4; Gomara, Hist. de las Indias, p. 203; Padre Gumilla, Orinoco, pp. 68, 96.

[10] Hans Staden, in Ternaux-Compans, Voyages, vol. 3, pp. 269, 299.

chi, of South America,[1] and by the tribes of the Isthmus of Darien.[2] This down has also been used by some of the Australians in their sacred dances.[3] "The hair, or rather the wool upon their heads, was very abundantly powdered with white powder. . . . They powder not only their heads, but their beards too."[4]

In China "there is a widespread superstition that the feathers of birds, after undergoing certain incantations, are thrown up into the air, and being carried away by the wind work blight and destruction wherever they alight."

The down of birds seems not to have been unknown in Europe. To this day it is poured upon the heads of the bride and groom in weddings among the Russian peasantry.[5]

This leads up to the inquiry whether or not the application of tar and feathers to the person may not at an early period have been an act of religious significance, perverted into a ridiculous and infamous punishment by a conquering and unrelenting hostile sect. The subject certainly seems to have awakened the curiosity of the learned Buckle, whose remarks may as well be given.

Richard, during his stay in Normandy (1189), made some singular laws for regulating the conduct of the pilgrims in their passage by sea. "A robber, convicted of theft, shall be shaved in the manner of a champion; and boiling pitch poured upon his head, and the feathers of a pillow shaken over his head to distinguish him; and be landed at the first port where the ships shall stop."[6]

The circumstances mentioned in the text respecting tarring and feathering is a fine subject for comment by the searchers into popular antiquities.[7]

HAIR POWDER.

Speaking of the "duvet" or down, with which many American savage tribes deck themselves, Picart observes very justly: "Cet ornement est bizare, mais dans le fond l'est il beaucoup plus que cette poudre d'or dont les Anciens, se poudroient la tête, ou que cette poudre composée d'amidon avec laquelle nos petits maitres modernes affectent de blanchir leurs cheveux ou leurs perruques?"[8]

Picart does not say, and perhaps it would not be wise for us to surmise, that these modes of powdering had a religious origin.

The custom of powdering the hair seems to be a savage "survival;" at least, it is still to be found among the Friendly Islanders, among

---

[1] Peter Martyr, in Hakluyt's Voyages, vol. 5, p. 460.

[2] Bancroft, Nat. Races of the Pacific Slope, vol. 1, p. 750.

[3] Smyth, Aborigines of Victoria, vol. 1, p. 73; vol. 2, p. 302. See also Carteret's description of the natives of the Queen Charlotte Islands, visited by him in 1767.

[4] Hawkesworth, Voyages, vol. 1, p. 379.

[5] Perry S. Heath, A Hoosier in Russia, New York, 1888, p. 114.

[6] Fosbrooke, British Monachism, p. 442.

[7] See works cited in Buckle's Common place Book, vol. 2, of "Works," London, 1872, p. 47.

[8] Picart, Cérémonies et Coûtumes Religieuses, vol. 6, p. 20.

whom it was observed by Forster.[1]   These islanders used a white lime powder, also one of blue and another of orange made of turmeric.

The Sandwich Islanders plastered their hair over "with a kind of lime made from burnt shells,"[2] and Dillon speaks of the Friendly Islanders using lime, as Forster has already informed us.[3]   The Hottentots made a lavish use of the medicinal powder of the buchu, which they plastered on their heads, threw to their sacred animals, and used liberally at their funerals.[4]   Kolben dispels all doubt by saying: "These powderings are religious formalities."   He also alludes to the use, in much the same manner, of ashes by the same people.[5]

The use of ashes also occurs among the Zuñi, the Apache (at times), and the Abipone of Paraguay.   Ashes are also "thrown in the way of a whirlwind to appease it."[6]

In the Witches' Sabbath, in Germany, "it was said that the witches burned a he goat, and divided its ashes among themselves."[7]

In all the above cases, as well as in that of the use of ashes in the Christian churches, it is possible that the origin of the custom might be traced back either to a desire to share in the burnt offering or else in that of preserving some of the incinerated dust of the dead friend or relative for whom the tribe or clan was in mourning.   Ashes in the Christian church were not confined to Lent alone; they "were worn four times a year, as in the beginning of Lent."[8]

Tuphramancy or divination by ashes was one of the methods of forecast in use among the priests of pagan Rome.[9]

In Northumberland the custom prevailed of making bonfires on the hills on St. Peter's day.   "They made encroachments, on these occasions, upon the bonfires of the neighbouring towns, of which they took away some of the ashes by force: This they called 'carrying off the flower (probably the flour) of the wake.'[10]   Moresin thinks this a vestige of the ancient Cerealia."

The mourning at Iddah, in Guinea, consists in smearing the forehead "with wood ashes and clay water, which is allowed to dry on.   They likewise powder their hair with wood ashes."[11]

---

[1] Voyage Round the World, London, 1777, pp. 462, 463.

[2] Archibald Campbell, Voyage Round the World, N. Y., 1819, p. 136.

[3] Voyage of La Pérouse, London, 1829, vol. 2, p. 275.

[4] Peter Kolben's Voyage to the Cape of Good Hope, in Knox's Voyage and Travels, London, 1767, vol. 2, pp. 391, 395, 406, 407.

[5] Ibid., p. 406.

[6] Spencer, Desc. Sociology, art. "Abipones."

[7] Gubernatis, Zoological Mythology, London, 1872, vol. 1, p. 423.

[8] Fosbrooke, British Monachism, p. 83.

[9] Gaule, Mag-astromancers Posed and Puzzel'd, p. 165, quoted in Brand, Popular Antiquities, vol. 3, pp. 329 et seq.

[10] Brand, Popular Antiquities, vol. 1, pp. 337, 338.

[11] Laird and Oldfield's Expedition into the Interior of Africa, quoted in Buckle's Common place Book, p. 466.

DUST FROM CHURCHES—ITS USE.

The last ceremonial powder to be described is dust from the ground, as among some of the Australians who smear their heads with pipe-clay as a sign of mourning.[1]

The French writers mention among the ceremonies of the Natchez one in which the Great Sun "gathered dust, which he threw back over his head, and turned successively to the four quarters of the world in repeating the same act of throwing dust."[2]

Mention is made of "an old woman who acted as beadle" of a church, who "once brought to the bedside of a dying person some of the sweepings from the floor of the altar, to ease and shorten a very lingering death."[3]

Altar dust was a very ancient remedy for disease. Frommann says that, of the four tablets found in a temple of Esculapius, one bore this inscription: "Lucio affecto lateris dolore; veniret et ex ara tollerit cinerem et una cum vino comisceret et poneret supra latus; et convaluit," etc.[4]

It seems then that the mediæval use of altar dust traces back to the Roman use of altar ashes.

So hard is it to eradicate from the minds of savages ideas which have become ingrafted upon their nature that we need not be surprised to read in the Jesuit relations of affairs in Canada (1696–1702) that, at the Mission of Saint Francis, where the Indians venerated the memory of a saintly woman of their own race, Catheraine Tagikoo-ita, "pour guérir les malades que les rémèdes ordinaires ne soulagent point, on avale dans l'eau ou dans un bouillon un peu de la poussière de son tombeau."

A few persons are to be found who endeavor to collect the dust from the feet of one hundred thousand Brahmins. One way of collecting this dust is by spreading a cloth before the door of a house where a great multitude of Brahmins are assembled at a feast, and, as each Brahmin comes out, he shakes the dust from his feet as he treads upon this cloth. Many miraculous cures are declared to have been performed upon persons using this dust.[5]

A widow among the Armenian devil-worshipers is required "to strew dust on her head and to smear her face with clay."[6]

CLAY-EATING.

The eating of clay would appear to have once prevailed all over the world. In places the custom has degenerated into ceremonial or is to

---

[1] Smyth, Aborigines of Victoria, vol. 2, p. 273.

[2] Gayarre, Louisiana, 1851, p. 308.

[3] Notes and Queries, 4th ser., vol. 8, p. 505.

[4] Tractatus de Fascinatione, Nuremberg, 1675, 197.

[5] Southey, quoting Ward, in Buckle's Common place Book, London, 1849, 2d ser., p. 521.

[6] North American, October 27, 1888.

be found only in myths. The Aztec devotee picked up a pinch of clay in the temple of Tezcatlipoca and ate it with the greatest reverence.[1]

Sahagun is quoted by Squier[2] as saying that the Mexicans swore by the sun and "by our sovereign mother, the Earth," and ate a piece of earth.

But the use of clay by the Mexicans was not merely a matter of ceremony; clay seems to have been an edible in quite common use.

Edible earth was sold openly in the markets of Mexico; " y aun tierra," says Gomara in the list of foods given by him.[3]

The eating of clay was forbidden to Mexican women during pregnancy.

Diego Duran describes the ceremonial eating of clay in the temples of Mexico; "Llegó el dedo al suelo, y cogiendo tierra en él lo metió en la boca; á la cual ceremonia llamaban comer tierra santa."[4]   And again he says that in their sacrifices the Mexican nobles ate earth from the feet of the idols.   " Comian tierra de la que estaba á los pies del Ydolo."[5] But the Mexicans did not limit themselves to a ceremonial clay-eating alone.   Thomas Gage relates that " they ate a kind of earth, for at one season in the yeer they had nets of mayle, with the which they raked up a certaine dust that is bred upon the water of the Lake of Mexico, and that is kneaded together like unto oas of the sea."[6]

Diego Duran[7] mentions the ceremonial clay-eating at the feast of Tezcatlipoca agreeing with the note already taken from Kingsborough.

There is reference to clay-eating in one of the myths given in the Popol-Vuh.   The Quiche deities Hunahpu and Xbalanqué, desiring to overcome the god Cabrakan, fed him upon roasted birds, but they took care to rub one of the birds with "tizate" and to put white powder around it.   The circle of white powder was, no doubt, a circle of hoddentin or something analogous thereto, intended to prevent any baleful influence being exercised by Cabrakan.   " Mais ils frottèrent l'un des oiseaux avec du *tizate* et lui mirent de la poussière blanche à l'entour."[8]

In a footnote the word " tizate" is explained to be a very friable whitish earth, used in polishing metals, making cement, etc.:   " Terre blanchâtre fort friable, et dont ils se servent pour polir les métaux, faire du ciment, etc."

Cabeza de Vaca says that the Indians of Florida ate clay—"de la terre."[9]   He says also[10] that the natives offered him many mesquite beans, which they ate mixed with earth—" mele avec de la terre."[11]

---

[1] Kingsborough, vol. 5, p. 198.

[2] Serpent Symbols, p. 55.

[3] Hist. de Méjico p. 348.

[4] Lib. 2, cap. 47, p. 490.

[5] Lib. 1, cap. 18, p. 208.

[6] New Survey of the West Indies, London, 1648, p. 51.

[7] Op. cit., vol. 3, cap. 4.

[8] Popol-Vuh (Brasseur de Bourbourg), p. 65.

[9] Ternaux-Compans, Voy., vol. 7, p. 143.

[10] Ibid., p. 202.

[11] Purchas, vol. 4, lib. 8, cap. 1, p. 1519; also, Davis, Conquest of New Mexico, p. 84.

The Jaguaces of Florida ate earth (tierra).[1]

At the trial of Vasco Pocallo de Figueroa, in Santiago de Cuba, in 1522, " for cruelty to the natives," he sought to make it appear that the Indians ate clay as a means of suicide: "el abuso de los Indios en comer tierra . . . seguian matandose de intento comiendo tierra."[2]

The Muiscas had in their language the word "jipetera," a "disease from eating dirt."[3] Whether the word " dirt" as here employed means filth, or earth and clay, is not plain; it probably means clay and earth.

Venegas asserts that the Indians of California ate earth. The traditions of the Indians of San Juan Capistrano, California, and vicinity show that "they had fed upon a kind of clay," which they "often used upon their heads by way of ornament."[4]

The Tatu Indians of California mix "red earth into their acorn bread . . . to make the bread sweet and make it go further."[5]

Long[6] relates that when the young warrior of the Oto or Omaha tribes goes out on his first fast he "rubs his person over with a whitish clay," but he does not state that he ate it.

Sir John Franklin[7] relates that the banks of the Mackenzie River in British North America contain layers of a kind of unctuous mud, probably similar to that found near the Orinoco, which the Tinneh Indians "use occasionally as food during seasons of famine, and even at other times chew as an amusement. . . . It has a milky taste and the flavour is not disagreeable."

Father de Smet[8] says of the Athapascan: "Many wandering families of the Carrier tribe . . . have their teeth worn to the gums by the earth and sand they swallow with their nourishment." This does not seem to have been intentionally eaten.

"Some of the Siberian tribes, when they travel, carry a small bag of their native earth, the taste of which they suppose will preserve them from all the evils of a foreign sky."[9]

We are informed that the Tunguses of Siberia eat a clay called " rock marrow," which they mix with marrow. "Near the Ural Mountains, powdered gypsum, commonly called 'rock meal,' is sometimes mixed with bread, but its effects are pernicious."[10]

"The Jukabiri of northeastern Siberia have an earth of sweetish and rather astringent taste," to which they " ascribe a variety of sanatory properties."[11]

---

[1] Gomara, Hist. de las Indias, p. 182.

[2] Buckingham Smith, Coleccion de Varios Documentos para la Historia de Florida, London, 1857, vol. 1, p. 46.

[3] Bollaert, Researches in South America, London, 1860, p. 63.

[4] Boscana, Chinigchinich, pp. 245, 253.

[5] Powers, Contrib. to N. A. Ethnol., vol. 3, p. 140.

[6] Long's Expedition, vol. 1, p. 240.

[7] Second Expedition to the Polar Sea, p. 19.

[8] Oregon Missions, p. 192.

[9] Gmelin, quoted by Southey, in Common place Book, 1st ser., London, 1849, p. 239.

[10] Malte-Brun, Univ. Geog., Philadelphia, 1827, vol. 1, lib. 37, p. 483.

[11] Von Wrangel, Polar Expedition, New York, 1842, p. 188.

There is nothing in the records relating to Victoria respecting the use of any earth for the purpose of appeasing hunger, but Grey mentions that one kind of earth, pounded and mixed with the root of the *Mene* (a species of Hæmadorum), is eaten by the natives of West Australia.[1]

The Apache and Navajo branches of the Athapascan family are not unacquainted with the use of clay as a comestible, although among the former it is now scarcely ever used and among the latter used only as a condiment to relieve the bitterness of the taste of the wild potato; in the same manner it is known to both the Zuñi and Tusayan.

Wallace says that eating dirt was "a very common and destructive habit among Indians and half-breeds in the houses of the whites.[2]

"Los apassionados à comer tierra son los Indios Otomacos."[3]

"The earth which is eaten by the Ottomacs [of the Rio Orinoco] is fat and unctuous."[4]

Waitz[5] cites Heusinger as saying that the Ottomacs of the Rio Orinoco eat large quantities of a fatty clay.

Clay was eaten by the Brazilians generally.[6]

The Romans had a dish called "alica" or "frumenta," made of the grain zea mixed with chalk from the hills at Puteoli, near Naples.[7]

According to the myths of the Cingalese, their Brahmins once "fed on it [earth] for the space of 60,000 years."[8]

PREHISTORIC FOODS USED IN COVENANTS.

It has been shown that the Apache, on several occasions, as when going out to meet strangers, entering into solemn agreements, etc., made use of the hoddentin. A similar use of food, generally prehistoric, can be noted in other regions of the world.

It was a kind of superstitious trial used among the Saxons to purge themselves of any accusation by taking a piece of barley bread and eating it with solemn oaths and execrations that it might prove poisonous or their last morsel if what they asserted or denied was not true.[9] Those pieces of bread were first execrated by the priest, from which he infers that at a still earlier day sacramental bread may have been used for the same purpose.

At Rome, in the time of Cicero and Horace, a master who suspected that his slaves had robbed him conducted them before a priest. They were each obliged to eat a cake over which the priest had "pronounced some magical words (*carmine infectum*)."[10]

---

[1] Smyth, Aborigines of Victoria, vol. 1, p. xxxiv.
[2] Travels on the Amazon, p, 311.
[3] Gumilla, Orinoco, Madrid, 1741, p. 102; the Guamas, also, ibid., pp. 102 and 108.
[4] Malte-Brun, Univ. Geog., Phila., 1827, vol. 3, lib. 87, p. 323.
[5] Anthropology, vol. 1, p. 116.
[6] Spencer. Desc. Sociology.
[7] Pliny, Nat. History, lib. 18, cap. 29.
[8] Asiatick Researches, Calcutta, 1801, vol. 7, p. 440.
[9] Blount, Tenures of Land and Customs of Manors, London, 1874, p. 2233.
[10] Salverte, Philosophy of Magic, vol. 2, p. 140.

The people living on the coast of Coramandel have an ordeal consisting in the chewing of unboiled rice. No harm will attach to him who tells the truth, but the perjurer is threatened with condign punishment in this world and in that to come.[1] Bread is bitten when the Ostaaks of Siberia take a solemn oath, such as one of fealty to the Czar.[2]

SACRED BREADS AND CAKES.

Since the employment of hoddentin, or tule pollen, as a sacred commemorative food would seem to have been fairly demonstrated, before closing this section I wish to add a few paragraphs upon the very general existence of ritualistic farinaceous foods in all parts of the world. They can be detected most frequently in the ceremonial reversion to a grain or seed which has passed or is passing out of everyday use in some particular form given to the cake or bread or some circumstance of time, place, and mode of manufacture and consumption which stamps it as a "survival." So deeply impressed was Grimm[3] with the wide horizon spreading around the consideration of this topic that he observed: "Our knowledge of heathen antiquities will gain both by the study of these drinking usages which have lasted into later times and also of the shapes given to *baked meats,* which either retained the actual forms of ancient idols or were accompanied by sacrificial observances. A history of German cakes and bread rolls might contain some unexpected disclosures. . . . Even the shape of cakes is a reminiscence of the sacrifices of heathenism."

The first bread or cake to be mentioned in this part of the subject is the pancake, still so frequently used on the evening of Shrove Tuesday. In antiquity it can be traced back before the Reformation, before the Crusades were dreamed of, before the Barbarians had subverted Rome, before Rome itself had fairly taken shape.

There seems to have been a very decided religious significance in the preparation of pancakes on Shrove Tuesday. In Leicestershire, "On Shrove Tuesday a bell rings at noon, which is meant as a signal for the people to begin frying their pancakes."[4]

" The Norman *Crispellæ* (Du Cange) are evidently taken from the *Fornacalia,* on the 18th of February, in memory of the method of making bread, before the Goddess *Fornax* invented ovens."[5]

Under "Crispellæ," Du Cange says: "Rustici apud Normannos vocant Crespes, ova pauca mixta cum farina, et in sartagine frixa," and says that they are "ex herba, farina et oleo."[6] These same Crispellæ are to be seen on the Rio Grande during Christmas week.

In the Greek Church and throughout Russia there is to the present time a " pancake feast" at Shrovetide.[7]

---

[1] Voyage of Capt. Amasa Delano, Boston, 1847, p. 230. Compare with the ordeal of Scotch conspirators, who ate a fragment of barley bread together.

[2] Gauthier de la Peyronie, Voyages de Pallas, Paris, 1793, vol. 4, p. 75.

[3] Teutonic Mythology, vol. 1, p. 63.

[4] Macaulay quoted in Brand, Pop. Ant., vol. 1, p. 85.

[5] Fosbrooke, British Monachism, p. 83.

[6] Du Cange, Glossarium, articles " Crispellæ " and " Crespellæ."

[7] Brand, Pop. Ant., vol. 1, p. 88.

At one time a custom prevailed of going about from one friend's house to another, masked, and committing every conceivable prank. "Then the people feasted on blinnies—a pancake similar to the English crumpet."[1]

In the pancake we have most probably the earliest form of farinaceous food known to the nations which derived their civilization from the basin of the Mediterranean. Among these nations wheat has been in use from a time far beyond the remotest historical period, and to account for its introduction myth has been invoked; but this wheat was cooked without leaven, or was fried in a pan, after the style of the tortilla still used in Spanish-speaking countries, or of the pancake common among ourselves. Pliny[2] says that there were no bakers known in Rome until nearly six hundred years after the foundation of the city, in the days of the war with Persia; but he perhaps meant the public bakers authorized by law. The use of wheat and the art of baking bread, as we understand it to-day, were practically unknown to the nations of northern Europe until within the recent historical period.[3]

---

[1] Heath, A Hoosier in Russia, p. 109.

[2] Nat. Hist., lib. 18, cap. 28.

[3] Wheat, which is now the bread corn of twelve European nations and is fast supplanting maize in America and several inferior grains in India, was no doubt widely grown in the prehistoric world. The Chinese cultivated it 2700 B. C. as a gift direct from Heaven; the Egyptians attributed its origin to Isis and the Greeks to Ceres. A classic account of the distribution of wheat over the primeval world shows that Ceres, having taught her favorite Triptolemus agriculture and the art of bread-making, gave him her chariot, a celestial vehicle which he used in useful travels for the purpose of distributing corn to all nations.

Ancient monuments show that the cultivation of wheat had been established in Egypt before the invasion of the shepherds, and there is evidence that more productive varieties of wheat have taken the place of one, at least, of the ancient sorts. Innumerable varieties exist of common wheat. Colonel Le Couteur, of Jersey, cultivated 150 varieties; Mr. Darwin mentions a French gentleman who had collected 322 varieties, and the great firm of French seed merchants, Vilmorin-Andrieux et Cie, cultivate about twice as many in their trial ground near Paris. In their recent work on Les meilleurs blés M. Henry L. de Vilmorin has described sixty-eight varieties of best wheat, which he has classed into seven groups, though these groups can hardly be called distinct species, since M. Henry L. de Vilmorin has crossbred three of them, *Triticum vulgare, Triticum turgidum* and *Triticum durum*, and has found the offspring fertile.

Three small-grained varieties of common wheat were cultivated by the first lake dwellers of Switzerland (time of Trojan war), as well as by the less ancient lake dwellers of western Switzerland and of Italy, by the people of Hungary in the stone age, and by the Egyptians, on evidence of a brick of a pyramid in which a grain was embedded and to which the date of 3359 B. C. has been assigned.

The existence of names for wheat in the most ancient languages confirms this evidence of the antiquity of its culture in all the more temperate parts of Europe, Asia, and Africa, but it seems improbable that wheat has ever been found growing persistently in a wild state, although the fact has often been asserted by poets, travelers, and historians. In the Odyssey, for example, we are told that wheat grew in Sicily without the aid of man, but a blind poet could not have seen this himself, and a botanical fact can hardly be accepted from a writer whose own existence has been contested. Diodorus repeats the tradition that Osiris found wheat and barley growing promiscuously in Palestine, but neither this nor other discoveries of persistent wild wheat seem to us to be credible, seeing that wheat does not appear to be endowed with a power of persistency except under culture.—Edinburgh Review.

The origin of baking precedes the period of history and is involved in the obscurity of the early ages of the human race. Excavations made in Switzerland gave evidence that the art of making bread was practiced by our prehistoric ancestors as early as the stone period. From the shape of loaves it is thought that no ovens were used at that time, but the dough was rolled into small round cakes and laid on hot stones, being covered with glowing ashes. Bread is mentioned in the book of Genesis, where Abraham, wishing to entertain three angels, offered to "fetch a morsel of bread." Baking is again referred to where Sarah has instructions to "make ready quickly three measures of fine meal, knead it and make cakes upon the hearth." Lot entertained two angels by giving them unleavened

Nothing would be more in consonance with the mode of reasoning of a primitive people than that, at certain designated festivals, there should be a recurrence to the earlier forms of food, a reversion to an earlier mode of life, as a sort of propitiation of the gods or goddesses who had cared for the nation in its infancy and to secure the continuance of their beneficent offices. Primitive man was never so certain of the power of the gods of the era of his own greatest development that he could rely upon it implicitly and exclusively and ignore the deities who had helped him to stand upon his feet. Hence, the recurrence to pancakes, to unleavened breads of all kinds, among various peoples. This view of the subject was made plain to me while among the Zuñi Indians. Mr. Frank H. Cushing showed me that the women, when baking the "loaves" of bread, were always careful to place in the adobe ovens a tortilla with each batch of the newer kind, and no doubt for the reason just given.

UNLEAVENED BREAD.

The unleavened bread of the earliest period of Jewish history has come down to our own times in the Feast of Unleavened Bread, still observed by the Hebrews in all parts of the world, in the bread used in the eucharistic sacrifice by so large a portion of the Christian world, and apparently in some of the usages connected with the half-understood fast known as the " Ember Days." Brand quotes from an old work in regard to the Ember Days: "They were so called 'because that our elder fathers wolde on these days ete no brede but cakes made under ashes.'" [1]

The sacred cake or " draona " of the Parsi " is a small round pancake or wafer of unleavened bread, about the size of the palm of the hand. It is made of wheaten flour and water, with a little clarified butter, and is flexible." [2] A variety of the "draona," called a " frasast," is marked with the finger nail and set aside for the guardian spirits of the departed. [3]

Cakes and salt were used in religious rites by the ancients. The Jews probably adopted their appropriation from the Egyptians. [4] " Dur-

---

bread. The mere mention of unleavened bread shows that there were two kinds of bread made even at that time.

The art of baking was carried on to a high perfection among the Egyptians, who are said to have baked cakes in many fantastic shapes, using several kinds of flour. The Romans took up the art of baking, and public bakeries were numerous on the streets of Rome. In England the business of the baker was considered to be one so closely affecting the interests of the public that in 1266 an act of Parliament was passed regulating the price to be charged for bread. This regulation continued in operation until 1822 in London and until 1836 in the rest of the country. The art of making bread has not yet reached some countries in Europe and Asia. In the rural parts of Sweden no bread is made, but rye cakes are baked twice a year and are as hard as flint. It is less than a century ago that bread was used in Scotland, the Scotch people of every class living on barley bannocks and oaten cakes.—Chicago News.

[1] Pop. Antiq., vol. 1, p. 96.

[2] Shâyast lâ-Shâyast, par. 32, note 6, pp. 283, 284 (Max Müller's ed., Oxford, 1880).

[3] Ibid., p. 315, note 3.

[4] "And if thou bring an oblation of a meat offering baken in the oven, it shall be unleavened cakes of fine flour " (Levit., II, 4); "With all thine offerings thou shalt offer salt " (Ibid., 13)—Brand, Pop. Ant., vol. 2, p. 82.

ing all the Passover week—14th to 21st Nisan, i. e., during this week's moon—Shemites fast, only eating unleavened bread, and most diligently—not without reason—cleansing their houses." "And especially had all leavened matter to be removed, for the new leavener had now arisen, and prayers with curses were offered up against any portions which might have escaped observation. The law of their fierce Jahveh was that, whoever during all this festival tasted leavened bread, 'that soul should be cut off,' which Godwyn mollifies by urging that this only meant the offender should die without children; which was still a pretty considerable punishment for eating a piece of bread!"[1]

"The great day of Pentecost is the 6th of Sivan, or, say, the 22d of May, 1874. From the first barley *two loaves* were then made, 'the offering of which was the distinguishing rite of the day of Pentecost.'"[2]

On St. Bridget's Eve every farmer's wife in Ireland makes a cake, called *bairinbreac;* the neighbors are invited, the madder of ale and the pipe go round, and the evening concludes with mirth and festivity.[3] Vallencey identifies this as the same kind of offering that was made to Ceres, and to "the queen of heaven, to whom the Jewish women burnt incense, poured out drink offerings, and made cakes for her with their own hands."[4]

THE HOT CROSS BUNS OF GOOD FRIDAY.

The belief prevailed that these would not mold like ordinary bread.[5]

"In several counties [in England] a small loaf of bread is annually baked on the morning of Good Friday and then put by till the same anniversary in the ensuing year. This bread is not intended to be eaten, but to be used as a medicine, and the mode of administering it is by grating a small portion of it into water and forming a sort of panada. It is believed to be good for many disorders, but particularly for a diarrhœa, for which it is considered a sovereign remedy. Some years ago a cottager lamented that her poor neighbour must certainly die of this complaint, because she had already given her two doses of Good Friday bread without any benefit. No information could be obtained from the doctress respecting her nostrum, but that she had heard old folks say that it was a good thing and that she always made it."[6]

Brand quotes a writer in the Gentleman's Magazine who shows that they were "formerly, at least, unleavened," p. 156. They "are constantly marked with the form of the cross." "It is an old belief that the observance of the custom of eating buns on Good Friday protects the house from fire, and several other virtues are attributed to these buns," p. 156. "Hutchinson, in his History of Northumberland, follow-

---

[1] Forlong, Rivers of Life, vol. 1, p. 441.

[2] Ibid., p. 447.

[3] Brand, Pop. Antiq., vol. 1, pp. 345, 346, quoting Gen. Vallencey's Essay on the Antiquity of the Irish Language.

[4] Ibid., p. 345.

[5] Ibid., p. 154.

[6] Ibid., pp. 155, 156.

ing Bryant's Analysis, derives the Good Friday bun from the sacred cakes which were offered at the Arkite Temples, styled Boun, and presented every seventh day," p. 155. A very interesting' dissertation upon these sacred cakes as used by the Greeks, Egyptians, and Jews in the time of their idolatry, is to be found in Brand's work, pp. 155–156.[1]

Practices analogous to those referred to are to be noted among the Pueblo Indians. They offer not only the kunque, but bread also in their sacrifices.

In the sacred rabbit hunt of the Zuñi, which occurs four times a year and is carried on for the purpose of procuring meat for the sacred eagles confined in cages, a great fire was made on the crest of a hill, into which were thrown piles of bread crusts and in the smoke of which the boomerangs or rabbit sticks were held while the hunter recited in an audible tone and with downcast head the prayers prescribed for the occasion. One of the early Spanish writers informs us that the women of the pueblo of Santo Domingo, on the Rio Grande, offered bread on bended knees to their idols and then preserved it for the remainder of the year, and the house which did not have a supply of such blessed bread was regarded as unfortunate and exposed to danger. [2]

A prehistoric farinaceous food of the Romans survives in our bride-cake or wedding cake. It is well understood that among the Romans there were three kinds of marriage: that called "coemptio," that called "concubitu" or "usu," and the highest form of all, known as "confarratio," from the fact that bride and groom ate together of a kind of cake or bread made of the prehistoric flour, the "far." We have preserved the custom of having bridecake, which is still served with many superstitious ceremonies: "it must be cut by the bride herself; it must be broken in pieces (formerly these pieces were cast over the heads of the bridesmaids), and, after being passed through a wedding ring a certain number of times, it must be placed under the pillow of the anxious maiden to serve as a basis for her dreams." [3]

Exactly what this prehistoric food was it is now an impossibility to determine with exactness. Torquemada shows that long after the Romans had obtained the use of wheat they persisted in the sacrificial use of the "nola isla," "farro," and "escanda," forms of wild grain once roasted and ground and made into bread by their forefathers.[4] A similar usage prevailed among the Greeks. Pliny speaks of "the bearded red wheat, named in Latin 'far,'" and tells us that rye was called "secale" or "farrago."[5] The radical "far" is still to be found all over

---

[1] See also "Buns" in Inman's Ancient Faiths.

[2] "Ofrecian el pan al idolo, hincados de rodillas. Bendezianlo los sacerdotes, y repartian como pan bendito, con lo qual se acabaua la fiesta. Guardauan aquel pan todo el año, teniendo por desdichada, y sugeta a muchos peligros la casa que sin el estaua."—Padre Fray Alonso Fernandez (Dominican). Historia Eclesiastica de Nuestros Tiempos, Toledo, 1611, p. 16.

[3] Brand, Popular Antiquities, vol. 2, pp. 100 et seq., quoting Blount, Moffet, and Moresin.

[4] Torquemada, Monarchia Indiana, vol. 2, lib. 7, cap. 9, p. 100.

[5] Nat. Hist., lib. xviii, caps 10 et seq. and 39.

Europe in the word for flour, "farina," "farine," or "harina," while it is also possible that it may be detected in the ever-to-be-honored name of Farragut. [1]

In the eight marriage rites described by Baudhâyana, the initiatory oblation in the fourth (that in which the father gives his daughter away) consists of "parched grain." This rite is one of the four which are lawful for a Brahman. The parched grain to be used would seem to be either sesamum or barley, although this is not clear. Vasish*tha* says, chapter 27, concerning secret penances: "He who . . . uses barley (for his food) becomes pure." [2]

The pages of Brand [3] are filled with references to various forms of cake which seem properly to be included under this chapter. In England there formerly prevailed the custom of preparing "soul cakes" for distribution among visitors to the family on that day and to bands of waifs or singers, who expected them as a dole for praying and singing in the interests of the souls of the dead friends and relatives of the family. On the island of St. Kilda the soul cake was "a large cake in the form of a triangle, furrowed round, and which was to be all eaten that night." [4] In Lancashire and Hertfordshire the cake was made of oatmeal, but in many other parts it was a "seed cake" [5] and in Warwickshire, "at the end of barley and bean seed time, there is a custom there to give the plowmen *froise*, a species of thick pancake." [6] "All-soul cakes" were distributed at time of All Souls' Day.

In England and Scotland the old custom [7] was to have a funeral feast, which all friends and relations were expected to attend. Wine, currant cake, meat, and other refreshments, varying according to the fortune of the family, were served liberally. The bread given out was called "arvil-bread." There is no special reason for believing that this could be called a hoddentin custom, except that the writer himself calls attention to the fact that in the earlier times the bread was in the form of "wafers." [8]

The Romans had a college of priests called the "Fratres Arvales," nine, or, as some say, twelve in number, to whose care were committed the sacrifices in honor of Ceres at the old limits of the city, to propitiate that goddess and induce her to bestow fertility upon the fields. These

---

[1] "Var (from the Hebrew word *var, frumentum*) Grain. It not only means a particular kind of grain, between wheat and barley, less nourishing than the former, but more so than the latter, according to Vossius; but it means bread corn, grain of any kind. Ætius gives this application to any kind of frumentaceous grain, decorticated, cleansed from the husks, and afterwards bruised and dried." London Medical Dictionary, Bartholomew Parr, M. D., Philadelphia, 1820, article "Far".

"*Ador* or *Athor* was the most sacred wheat, without beard, offered at adoration of gods. In Latin *Adorea* was a present of such after a victory, and *Ad-oro* is 'I adore,' from *oro*, 'I pray to.'"—Forlong, Rivers of Life, vol. 1, p. 473, footnote, speaking of both Greeks and Romans.

[2] Sacred Books of the East, edition of Max Müller, vol. 14, pp. 131, 205.

[3] Brand, Popular Antiquities, vol. 1, pp. 391 et seq., article "Allhallow even."

[4] Ibid., p. 391.

[5] Ibid., p. 392.

[6] Ibid., p. 393.

[7] Ibid., vol. 2, pp. 237 et seq.

[8] Ibid., p. 244.

ceremonies, which are believed by the editor of Bohn's Strabo to survive in the Rogation Day processions of the Roman Catholic Church, recall the notes already taken upon the subject of the Arval bread of the Scotch.[1] The sacrifices themselves were designated "Ambarva" and "Ambarvalia."

In Scotland and England it was customary for bands of singers to go from door to door on New Year's Eve, singing and receiving reward. In the latter country "cheese and oaten cakes, which are called *farls*, are distributed on this occasion among the cryers." In the former country "there was a custom of distributing sweet cakes and a particular kind of sugared bread."[2]

A fine kind of wheat bread called "wassail-bread" formed an important feature of the entertainment on New Year's Day in old England.[3]

Among love divinations may be reckoned the dumb cake, so called because it was to be made without speaking, and afterwards the parties were to go backward up the stairs to bed and put the cake under their pillows, when they were to dream of their lovers. [4]

References to the beal-tine ceremonies of Ireland and Scotland, in which oatmeal gruel figured as a dish, or cakes made of oatmeal and carraway seeds, may be found in Brand, Pop. Antiq., vol. 1, p. 226; in Blount, Tenures of Land and Customs of Manors, London, 1874, p. 131; and in Pennant's Tour in Scotland, in Pinkerton's Voyages, vol. 3, p. 49. In "A Charm for Bewitched Land" we find the mode of making a cake or loaf with holy water.

The mince pie and plum pudding of Christmas are evidently ancient preparations, and it is not unlikely that the shape of the former, which, prior to the Reformation, was that of a child's cradle, had a reminiscence of the sacrifice of babies at the time of the winter solstice. Grimm has taught that where human sacrifice had been abolished the figure of a coffin or a cradle was still used as a symbol.

There is a wide field of information to be gleaned in the investigation of the subject of bean foods at certain periods or festivals of the year, and upon this point I have some notes and memoranda, but, as my present remarks are limited to prehistoric *farinaceous* foods, I do not wish to add to the bulk of the present chapter.[5]

"Kostia—boiled rice and plums—is the only thing partaken of on Christmas Eve." [6]

---

[1] Strabo, Geography, Bohn's edition, London, 1854, vol. 1, pp. 341, 342, footnote.

[2] Brand, Popular Antiquities, vol. 1, p. 460.

[3] Ibid., p. 7.

[4] Strutt, Sports and Pastimes, pp. 3, 180. On the same page: "Dumb cake, a species of dreaming bread prepared by unmarried females with ingredients traditionally suggested in witching doggerel. When baked, it is cut into three divisions; a part of each to be eaten and the remainder put under the pillow. When the clock strikes twelve, each votary must go to bed backwards and keep a profound silence, whatever may appear."

[5] A writer in the Gentleman's Magazine for July, 1783, inquires: "May not the *minced pye*, a compound of the choicest productions of the East, have in view the offerings made by the wise men who came from afar to worship, bringing *spices*, etc." Quoted in Brand, Pop. Ant., vol. 1, p. 526. The mince pie was before the Reformation made in the form of a crib, to represent the manger in which the holy child lay in the stable. Ibid., p. 178.

[6] Heath, A Hoosier in Russia, p. 109.

GALENA.

At times one may find in the "medicine" of the more prominent and influential of the chiefs and medicine-men of the Apache little sacks which, when opened, are found to contain pounded galena; this they tell me is a "great medicine," fully equal to hoddentin, but more difficult to obtain. It is used precisely as hoddentin is used; that is, both as a face paint and as a powder to be thrown to the sun or other elements to be propitiated. The Apache are reluctant to part with it, and from living Apache I have never obtained more than one small sack of it.

No one seems to understand the reason for its employment. Mr. William M. Beebe has suggested that perhaps the fact that galena always crystallizes in cubes, and that it would thus seem to have a mysterious connection with the cardinal points to which all nomadic peoples pay great attention as being invested with the power of keeping wanderers from going astray, would not be without influence upon the minds of the medicine-men, who are quick to detect and to profit by all false analogies. The conjecture appears to me to be a most plausible one, but I can submit it only as a conjecture, for no explanation of the kind was received from any of the Indians. All that I can say is that whenever procurable it was always used by the Apache on occasions of unusual importance and solemnity and presented as a round disk painted in the center of the forehead.

The significance of all these markings of the face among savage and half-civilized nations is a subject deserving of the most careful research; like the sectarial marks of the Hindus, all, or nearly all, the marks made upon the faces of American Indians have a meaning beyond the ornamental or the grotesque.

Galena was observed in use among the tribes seen by Cabeza de Vaca. "Ils nous donnèrent beaucoup de bourses, contenant des sachets de marcassites et d'antimoine en poudre." ("Taleguillas de margaxita y de alcohol molido.")[1] This word "margaxita" means iron pyrites. The Encyclopædia Britannica says that the Peruvians used it for "amulets;" so also did the Apache. What Vaca took for antimony was pounded galena no doubt. He was by this time in or near the Rocky Mountains.[2]

On the northwest coast of America we read of the natives: "One, however, as he came near, took out from his bosom some iron or lead-colored micaceous earth and drew marks with it across his cheeks in the shape of two pears, stuffed his nostrils with grass, and thrust thin pieces of bone through the cartilage of his nose."[3]

It is more than probable that some of the face-painting with "black earth," "ground charcoal," etc., to which reference is made by the early writers, may have been galena, which substance makes a deep-black

---

[1] Alvar Nuñez Cabeça de Vaca, in Ternaux-Compans, Voy., vol. 7, p. 220.

[2] See also Davis, Conquest of New Mexico, p. 90.

[3] William Coxe, Russian Discoveries between Asia and America, London, 1803, p. 57, quoting Steller.

mark. The natives would be likely to make use of their most sacred powder upon first meeting with mysterious strangers like Vaca and his companions. So, when the expedition of La Salle reached the mouth of the Ohio, in 1680, the Indians are described as fasting and making superstitious sacrifices; among other things, they marked themselves with "black earth" and with "ground charcoal." "Se daban con Tierra Negra o Carbon molido."[1]

From an expression in Burton, I am led to suspect that the application of kohl or antimony to the eyes of Arabian beauty is not altogether for ornament. "There are many kinds of kohl used in medicine and magic."[2]

Corbusier says of the Apache-Yuma: "Galena and burnt mescal are used on their faces, the former to denote anger or as war paint, being spread all over the face, except the chin and nose, which are painted red."[3]

In Coleman's Mythology of the Hindus, London, 1832, page 165, may be found a brief chapter upon the subject of the sectarial marks of the Hindus. With these we may fairly compare the marks which the Apache, on ceremonial occasions, make upon cheeks and forehead. The adherents of the Brahminical sects, before entering a temple, must mark themselves upon the forehead with the tiluk. Among the Vishnuites, this is a longitudinal vermilion line. The Seevites use several parallel lines in saffron.[4] Maurice adds that the Hindus place the tiluk upon their idols in twelve places.[5] "Among the Kaffir the warriors are rendered invulnerable by means of a black cross on their foreheads and black stripes on the cheeks, both painted by the Inyanga, or fetich priest."[6]

A piece of galena weighing $7\frac{1}{2}$ pounds was found in a mound near Naples, Illinois.[7] Occasionally with the bones of the dead are noticed small cubes of galena; and in our collection is a ball of this ore, weighing a pound and two ounces, which was taken from a mound, and which probably did service, enveloped in raw hide, as some form of weapon.[8] Galena was much prized by the former inhabitants of North America. "The frequent occurrence of galena on the altars of the sacrificial mounds proves, at any rate, that the ancient inhabitants attributed a peculiar value to it, deeming it worthy to be offered as a sacrificial gift."[9] See also Squier and Davis.[10]

[1] Barcia, Ensayo Cronologico, Madrid, 1723.

[2] Arabian Nights, Burton's edition, vol. 8, p. 10, footnote.

[3] American Antiquarian, September, 1886, p. 281.

[4] Maurice, Indian Antiquities, London, 1801, vol. 5, pp. 82 and 83.

[5] Ibid., vol. 5, p. 85.

[6] Schultze, Fetichism, N. Y., 1885, p. 32.

[7] Paper by Dr. John G. Henderson on "Aboriginal remains near Naples, Ill.," Smith. Rept., 1882.

[8] J. F. Snyder, "Indian remains in Cass County, Illinois," Smith. Rept., 1881, p. 575.

[9] Rau, in Sm. Rept., 1872, p. 356.

[10] "Ancient monuments of the Mississippi Valley," in Smithsonian Contributions, vol. 1, p. 160.

CHAPTER III.

THE IZZE-KLOTH OR MEDICINE CORD OF THE APACHE.

There is probably no more mysterious or interesting portion of the religious or " medicinal " equipment of the Apache Indian, whether he be medicine-man or simply a member of the laity, than the " izze-kloth" or medicine cord, illustrations of which accompany this text. Less, perhaps, is known concerning it than any other article upon which he relies in his distress.

I regret very much to say that I am unable to afford the slightest clew to the meaning of any of the parts or appendages of the cords which I have seen or which I have procured. Some excuse for this is to be found in the fact that the Apache look upon these cords as so sacred that strangers are not allowed to see them, much less handle them or talk about them. I made particular effort to cultivate the most friendly and, when possible, intimate relations with such of the Apache and other medicine-men as seemed to offer the best chance for obtaining information in regard to this and other matters, but I am compelled to say with no success at all.

Fig. 7.—Single-strand medicine cord (Zuñi).

I did advance so far in my schemes that Na-a-cha, a prominent medicine-man of the Tonto Apache, promised to let me have his cord, but as an eruption of hostility on the part of the tribe called me away from the San Carlos Agency, the opportunity was lost. Ramon, one of the principal medicine-men of the Chiricahua Apache, made me the same promise concerning the cord which he wore and which figures in these plates. It was, unfortunately, sent me by mail, and, although the best in the series and really one of the best I have ever been fortunate enough to see on either living or dead, it was not accompanied by a description of the symbolism of the different articles attached. Ramon also gave me the head-dress which he wore in the spirit or ghost dance, and explained everything thereon, and I am satisfied that he would also, while in the same frame of mind, have given me all the information in his power in regard to the sacred or medicine cord as well, had I been near him.

There are some things belonging to these cords which I understand from having had them explained at other times, but there are others about which I am in extreme doubt and ignorance. There are four specimens of medicine cords represented and it is worth while to observe that they were used as one, two, three, and four strand cords, but whether this fact means that they belonged to medicine-men or to warriors of different degrees I did not learn nor do I venture to conjecture.

The single-strand medicine cord with the thirteen olivella shells belonged to a Zuñi chief, one of the priests of the sacred order of the bow, upon whose wrist it was worn as a sign of his exalted rank in the tribe. I obtained it as a proof of his sincerest friendship and with injunctions to say nothing about it to his own people, but no explanation was made at the moment of the signification of the wristlet or cord itself or of the reason for using the olivella shells of that particular number or for placing them as they were placed.

One of the four-strand cords was obtained from Ramon and is the most beautiful and the most valuable of the lot. Ramon called my attention to the important fact that it was com-

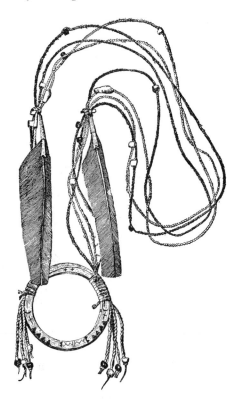

Fig. 8.—Four-strand medicine cord (Apache).

posed of four strands and that originally each had been stained a different color. These colors were probably yellow, blue, white, and black, although the only ones still discernible at this time are the yellow and the blue.

The three-strand cord was sent to me at Washington by my old friend, Al. Seiber, a scout who has been living among the Apache for twenty-five years. No explanation accompanied it and it was probably procured from the body of some dead warrior during one of the innumerable scouts and skirmishes which Seiber has had with this warlike race during his long term of service against them. The two strand cord was obtained by myself so long ago that the circumstances connected with it have escaped my memory. These cords, in their perfection, are decorated with beads and shells strung along at intervals, with pieces of the sacred green chalchihuitl, which has had such a

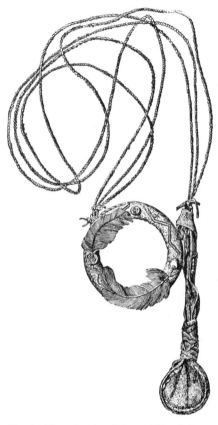

mysterious ascendancy over the minds of the American Indians— Aztec, Peruvian, Quiche, as well as the more savage tribes, like the Apache and Navajo; with petrified wood, rock crystal, eagle down, claws of the hawk or eaglet, claws of the bear, rattle of the rattlesnake, buckskin bags of hoddentin, circles of buckskin in which are inclosed pieces of twigs and branches of trees which have been struck by lightning, small fragments of the abalone shell from the Pacific coast, and much other sacred paraphernalia of a similar kind.

That the use of these cords was reserved for the most sacred and important occasions, I soon learned; they were not to be seen on occasions of no moment, but the dances for war, medicine, and summoning the spirits at once brought them out, and every medicine-man of any consequence would appear with one hanging from his right shoulder over his left hip.

FIG. 9.—Three-strand medicine cord (Apache).

Only the chief medicine-men can make them, and after being made and before being assumed by the new owner they must be sprinkled, Ramon told me, with "heap hoddentin," a term meaning that there is a great deal of attendant ceremony of a religious character.

These cords will protect a man while on the warpath, and many of the Apache believe firmly that a bullet will have no effect upon the warrior wearing one of them. This is not their only virtue by any means; the wearer can tell who has stolen ponies or other property from him or from his friends, can help the crops, and cure the sick. If the circle attached to one of these cords (see Fig. 8) is placed upon the head it will at once relieve any ache, while the cross attached to another (see Fig. 11) prevents the wearer from going astray, no matter where he may be; in other words, it has some connection with cross-trails and the four cardinal points to which the Apache pay the strictest attention. The Apache assured me that these cords were not mnemonic and that the beads, feathers, knots, etc., attached to them were not for the purpose of recalling to mind some duty to be performed or prayer to be recited.

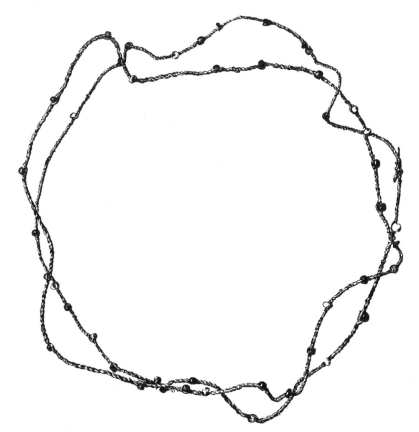

Fig. 10.—Two-strand medicine cord (Apache).

I was at first inclined to associate these cords with the quipus of the Peruvians, and also with the wampum of the aborigines of the Atlantic coast, and investigation only confirms this first suspicion. It is true that both the wampum and the quipu seem to have advanced from their primitive position as "medicine" and attained, ethnologically speaking, the higher plane of a medium for facilitating exchange or disseminating information, and for that reason their incorporation in this chapter might be objected to by the hypercritical; but a careful perusal of all the notes upon the subject can not fail to convince the reader that the use of just such medicine cords prevailed all over the world, under one form or another, and has survived to our own times.

First, let me say a word about rosaries, the invention of which has been attributed to St. Dominick, in Spain, and to St. Bridget, in Ireland. Neither of these saints had anything to do with the invention or introduction of the rosary, although each in his or her own province may have adapted to new and better uses a cord already in general service among all the peoples of Europe. The rosary, as such, was in general use in parts of the world long before the time of Christ. Again, the

Fig. 11.—Four-strand medicine cord (Apache).

cords of the various religious orders were looked upon as medicine cords and employed in that manner by the ignorant peasantry.

In this chapter I will insert notes showing the use of such cords by other tribes, and follow with descriptions of the uses to which the cords of St. Francis and others were put, and with references to the rosaries of different races or different creeds; finally, I will remark upon the superstitions connected with cords, belts, and strings, knotted or unknotted, made of serpent skin, human skin, or human hair. The strangest thing about it all is that observers have, with scarcely an exception, contented themselves with noting the existence of such cords without making the slightest effort to determine why they were used.

There are certain cords with medicine bags attached to be seen in the figures of medicine men in the drawings of the sacred altars given by Matthews in his account of the Navajo medicine-men.

Cushing also has noted the existence of such cords in Zuñi, and there is no doubt that some at least of the so-called "fishing lines" found in the Rio Verde cliff dwellings in Arizona were used for the same purposes.

Describing the tribes met on the Rio Colorado, in 1540–1541, Alarcon says: "Likewise on the brawne of their armes they weare a streit string, which they wind so often about that it becommeth as broad as one's hand."[1] It must be remembered that the Indians thought that Alarcon was a god, that they offered sacrifice to him, and that they wore all the "medicine" they possessed.

In 1680, the Pueblos, under the leadership of Popé, of the pueblo of San Juan, were successful in their attempt to throw off the Spanish yoke. He made them believe that he was in league with the spirits, and "that they directed him to make a rope of the palm leaf and tie in it a number of knots to represent the number of days before the rebellion was to take place; that he must send this rope to all the Pueblos in the kingdom, when each should signify its approval of, and union with, the conspiracy by untying one of the knots."[2]

I suspect that this may have been an izze-kloth. We know nothing about this rebellion excepting what has been derived through Spanish sources; the conquerors despised the natives, and, with a very few notable exceptions among the Franciscans, made no effort to study their peculiarities. The discontent of the natives was aggravated by this fact; they saw their idols pulled down, their ceremonial chambers closed, their dances prohibited, and numbers of their people tried and executed for witchcraft.[3] Fray Geronimo de Zarate Salmeron was a striking example of the good to be effected by missionaries who are not above studying their people; he acquired a complete mastery of the language of the pueblo of Jemez, "and preached to the inhabitants in their native tongue." He is represented as exercising great influence over the people of Jemez, Sia, Santa Ana, and Acoma. In this rebellion of 1680 the Pueblos expected to be joined by the Apache.[4]

The izze-kloth of the Apache seems to have had its prototype in the sacred string of beans with which Tecumseh's brother, the Shawnee prophet, traveled among the Indian tribes, inciting them to war. Every young warrior who agreed to go upon the warpath touched this "sacred string of beans" in token of his solemn pledge.[5]

Tanner says in the narrative of his captivity among the Ojibwa: "He [the medicine-man] then gave me a small hoop of wood to wear on my

---

[1] Relation of the Voyage of Don Fernando Alarcon, in Hakluyt's Voyages, vol. 3, p. 508.

[2] Davis, Conquest of New Mexico, p. 288.

[3] Davis, ibid., pp. 280, 284, 285.

[4] Ibid., pp. 277, 292.

[5] Catlin, North American Indians. London, 1845, vol. 2, p. 117.

head like a cap. On one-half of this hoop was marked the figure of a snake, whose office, as the chief told me, was to take care of the water."[1] The "small hoop of wood" of which Tanner speaks, to be worn on the head, seems to be analogous to the small hoop attached to the izze-kloth, to be worn or applied in cases of headache (Fig. 8).   Reference to something very much like the izze-kloth is made by Harmon as in use among the Carriers of British North America. He says: "The lads, as soon as they come to the age of puberty, tie cords, wound with swan's-down, around each leg a little below the knee, which they wear during one year, and then they are considered as men."[2] Catlin speaks of "mystery-beads" in use among the Mandan.[3] "The negro suspends all about his person cords with most complicated knots."[4]

The female inhabitants of Alaska, Unalaska, and the Fox Islands were represented by the Russian explorers of 1768 (Captain Krenitzin) to "wear chequered strings around the arms and legs."[5] These cords bear a striking resemblance to the "wresting cords" of the peasantry of Europe. Some of the Australians preserve the hair of a dead man. "It is spun into a cord and fastened around the head of a warrior."[6] "A cord of opossum hair around the neck, the ends drooping down on the back and fastened to the belt," is one of the parts of the costume assumed by those attaining manhood in the initiation ceremonies of the Australians.[7] Again, on pages 72 and 74, he calls it "the belt of manhood." "The use of amulets was common among the Greeks and Romans, whose amulets were principally formed of gems, crowns of pearls, necklaces of coral, shells, etc."[8]

When I first saw the medicine cords of the Apache, it occurred to me that perhaps in some way they might be an inheritance from the Franciscans, who, two centuries ago, had endeavored to plant missions among the Apache, and did succeed in doing something for the Navajo part of the tribe. I therefore examined the most convenient authorities and learned that the cord of S. François, like the cord of St. Augustine and the cord of St. Monica, was itself a medicine cord, representing a descent from a condition of thought perfectly parallel to that which has given birth to the izze-kloth. Thus Picart tells us: "On appelle Cordon de S. François la grosse corde qui sert de ceinture aux Religieux qui vivent sous la Regle de ce Saint. . . . Cette corde ceint le corps du Moine, & pend à peu prés jusqu'aux pieds. Elle lui sert de discipline, & pour cet effet, elle est armée de distance en distance de fort gros nœuds. . . .   La Corde de S. François a souvent gueri les malades, facilité les accouchemens, fortifié la santé, procuré lignée & fait

---

[1] Tanner's Narrative, p. 188.
[2] Journal, p. 289.
[3] North American Indians, London, 1845, vol. 1, p. 135.
[4] Schultze, Fetichism, New York, 1885, p. 32, quoting Bastian.
[5] Coxe, Russian Discoveries between America and Asia, London, 1803, p. 254.
[6] Smyth, Aborigines of Victoria, vol. 1, pp. xxix, 112.
[7] Ibid., vol. 1, p. 68.
[8] Pettigrew, Medical Superstitions, Philadelphia, 1844, pp. 67, 72, 74.

une infinité d'autres miracles édifians."[1]   This author says of the girdle of St. Augustine " Elle est de cuir," and adds that the Augustin-
ians have a book which treats of the origin of their order, in which
occur these words: " Il est probable que nos premiers Peres, qui vivoient
sous la Loi de nature, étant habillés de peau devoient porter une
Ceinture de même étoffe."[2]   This last assumption is perfectly plausible.
For my part it has always seemed to me that monasticism is of very
ancient origin, antedating Christianity and representing the most conservative element in the religious part of human nature.   It clings
obstinately to primitive ideas with which would naturally be associated
primitive costume.   The girdle of St. Monica had five knots.   " The
monks [of the Levant] use a girdle with twelve knots, to shew that they
are followers of the twelve apostles."[3]   Among the "sovereign remedies
for the headache" is mentioned " the belt of St. Guthlac."[4]   Buckle
refers to the fact that English women in labor wore " blessed girdles."
He thinks that they may have been Thomas Aquinas's girdles.[5]

> And good Saynt Frances gyrdle,
> With the hamlet of a hyrdle,
> Are wholsom for the pyppe.[6]

Some older charms are to be found in Bale's Interlude concerning the
Laws of Nature, Moses, and Christ, 4to, 1562.   Idolatry says:

> For lampes and for bottes
> Take me Saynt Wilfride's knottes.[7]

The " girdle of St. Bridget," mentioned by Mooney[8] and by other
writers, through which the sick were passed by their friends, was
simply a " survival" of the " Cunni Diaboli" still to be found in the
East Indies.   This " girdle of St. Bridget" was made of straw and in
the form of a collar.

The custom prevailing in Catholic countries of being buried in the
habits of the monastic orders, of which we know that the cord was a
prominent feature, especially in those of St. Francis or St. Dominick,
is alluded to by Brand.[9]   This custom seems to have been founded
upon a prior superstitious use of magical cords which were, till a comparatively recent period, buried with the dead.   The Roman Catholic
church anathematized those " qui s'imaginent faire plaisir aux morts ou
leur mettant entre les mains, ou en jettant sur leurs fosses, ou dans
leurs tombeaux de petites cordes nouées de plusieurs nœuds, & d'autres

[1] Cérémonies et Coûtumes Religieuses, Amsterdam, 1739, vol. 2, pp. 28, 29.

[2] Ibid., p. 29.

[3] Higgins, Anacalypsis, vol. 2, book 2, p. 77.

[4] Pettigrew, Medical Superstitions, Philadelphia, 1844, p. 61.   See also Black, Folk-Medicine, p. 93.

[5] Citations, Common place Book, p. 395, London, 1872.

[6] Brand, Popular Antiquities, vol. 3, pp. 310, 311.

[7] Brand, Popular Antiquities, vol. 3, p. 310.

[8] Holiday Customs of Ireland, pp. 381 et seq.

[9] Popular Antiquities, vol. 3, p. 325.

semblables, ce qui est expressement condamné par le Synode de Ferrare en 1612."[1]   Evidently the desire was to be buried with cords or amulets which in life they dared not wear.

We may infer that cords and other articles of monastic raiment can be traced back to a most remote ancestry by reading the views of Godfrey Higgins, in Anacalypsis, to the effect that there was a tradition maintained among the Carmelites that their order had been established by the prophet Elisha and that Jesus Christ himself had been one of its members. Massingberd, speaking of the first arrival of the Carmelites in England (about A. D. 1215), says: "They professed to be newly arrived in Italy, driven out by the Saracens from the Holy Land, where they had remained on Mount Carmel from the time of Elisha the prophet. They assert that 'the sons of the prophets' had continued on Mount Carmel as a poor brotherhood till the time of Christ, soon after which they were miraculously converted, and that the Virgin Mary joined their order and gave them a precious vestment called a scapular."[2]

ANALOGUES TO BE FOUND AMONG THE AZTECS, PERUVIANS, AND OTHERS.

According to the different authorities cited below, it will be seen that the Aztec priests were in the habit of consulting Fate by casting upon the ground a handful of cords tied together; if the cords remained bunched together, the sign was that the patient was to die, but if they stretched out, then it was apparent that the patient was soon to stretch out his legs and recover.   Mendieta says: "Tenian unos cordeles, hecho de ellos un manojo como llavero donde las mujeres traen colgadas las llaves, lanzábanlos en el suelo, y si quedaban revueltos, decian que era señal de muerte.   Y si alguno ó algunos salian extendidos, teníanlo por señal de vida, diciendo: que ya comenzaba el enfermo á extender los piés y las manos."[3]   Diego Duran speaks of the Mexican priests casting lots with knotted cords, "con nudillos de hilo echaban suertes."[4]   When the army of Cortes advanced into the interior of Mexico, his soldiers found a forest of pine in which the trees were interlaced with certain cords and papers which the wizards had placed there, telling the Tlascaltecs that they would restrain the advance of the strangers and deprive them of all strength:

Hallaron un Pinar mui espeso, lleno de hilos i papeles, que enredaban los Arboles, i atravesaban el camino, de que mucho se rieron los Castellanos; i dixeron graciosos donaires, quando luego supieron que los Hechiceros havian dado à entender à los Tlascaltecas que con aquellos hilos, i papeles havian de tener à los Castellanos, i quitarles sus fuerças.[5]

---

[1] Picart, Cérémonies et Coûtumes, etc., vol. 10, p. 56.
[2] Massingberd, The English Reformation, London, 1857, p. 105.
[3] Mendieta, p. 110.
[4] Vol. 3, cap. 5, p. 234.
[5] Herrera, dec. 2, lib. 6, p. 141.

Padre Sahagun speaks of the Aztec priests who cast lots with little cords knotted together: "Que hechan suertes con unas cordezuelas que atan unas con otros que llaman Mecatlapouhque." [1] Some such method of divining by casting cords must have existed among the Lettons, as we are informed by Grimm. [2] "Among the Lettons, the bride on her way to church, must throw a bunch of colored threads and a coin into every ditch and pond she sees." [3]

In the religious ceremonies of the Peruvians vague mention is made of "a very long cable," "woven in four colours, black, white, red, and yellow." [4] The Inca wore a "llautu." "This was a red fringe in the fashion of a border, which he wore across his forehead from one temple to the other. The prince, who was heir apparent, wore a yellow fringe, which was smaller than that of his father." [5] In another place, Garcilaso says: "It was of many colours, about a finger in width and a little less in thickness. They twisted this fringe three or four times around the head and let it hang after the manner of a garland." [6] "The Ynca made them believe that they were granted by order of the Sun, according to the merits of each tribe, and for this reason they valued them exceedingly." [7] The investiture was attended with imposing ceremonies. "When the Grounds of the Sun were to be tilled [by the Peruvians], the principal men went about the task wearing white cords stretched across the shoulders after the manner of ministers of the altar" [8] is the vague description to be gathered from Herrera.

Knotted cords were in use among the Carib; "ce qui revient aux Quippos des Péruviens." [9] The accompanying citation from Montfaucon would seem to show that among the Romans were to be found sacred baldrics in use by the war priests; such baldrics are to be seen also among the American aborigines, and correspond very closely to the medicine cords. Montfaucon describes the Saliens, who among the Romans were the priests of Mars, the god of war; these priests in the month of March had a festival which was probably nothing but a war dance, as that month would be most favorable in that climate for getting ready to attack their neighbors and enemies. He says that these Saliens "sont vêtus de robes de diverses couleurs, ceints de baudriers d'airain." These would seem to have been a sort of medicine cord with plates of brass affixed which would rattle when shaken by the dancer. [10]

[1] Kingsborough, vol. 7, chap. 4.

[2] Teutonic Mythology, vol. 3, p. 1233.

[3] Ibid.

[4] Fables and Rites of the Incas, Padre Christoval de Molina (Cuzco, 1570–1584), transl. by Clements R. Markham, Hakluyt Society trans., vol. 48, London, 1873, p. 48.

[5] The common people wore a black "llautu." See Garcilaso, Comentarios, Markham's transl., Hak. Soc., vol. 41, pp. 88, 89.

[6] Ibid., p. 85.

[7] Ibid., p. 89.

[8] "Quando vàn à sembrar las Tierras del Sol, vàn solos los Principales à trabajar, i vàn con insignias blancas, i en las espaldas unos Cordones tendidos blancos, à modo de Ministros del Altar."—Herrera, dec. 5, lib. 4, cap. 6, pp. 94–95.

[9] Picart, Cerémonies et Coûtumes, etc., Amsterdam, 1735, vol. 6, p. 92.

[10] Montfaucon, L'antiquité expliquée, tome 2, pt. 1, p. 33.

Captain Cook found that the men of the tribes seen in Australia wore "bracelets of small cord, wound two or three times about the upper part of their arm.[1]

"Whilst their [the Congo natives'] children are young, these people bind them about with certain superstitious cords made by the wizards, who, likewise, teach them to utter a kind of spell while they are binding them."[2] Father Merolla adds that sometimes as many as four of these cords are worn.

Bosman remarks upon the negroes of the Gold Coast as follows: "The child is no sooner born than the priest (here called Feticheer or Consoe) is sent for, who binds a parcel of ropes and coral and other trash about the head, body, arms, and legs of the infant; after which he exorcises, according to their accustomed manner, by which they believe it is armed against all sickness and ill accidents."[3]

In the picture of a native of Uzinza, Speke shows us a man wearing a cord from the right shoulder to the left hip.[4]

In the picture of Lunga Mândi's son, in Cameron's Across Africa,[5] that young chief is represented as wearing a cord across his body from his right shoulder to the left side.

On the Lower Congo, at Stanley Pool, Stanley met a young chief: "From his shoulders depended a long cloth of check pattern, while over one shoulder was a belt, to which was attached a queer medley of small gourds containing snuff and various charms, which he called his Inkisi."[6] This no doubt was a medicine cord. "According to the custom, which seems to belong to all Africa, as a sign of grief the Dinka wear a cord round the neck."[7] "The Mateb, or baptismal cord, is *de rigueur*, and worn when nothing else is. It formed the only clothing of the young at Seramba, but was frequently added to with amulets, sure safeguards against sorcery."[8] The Abyssinian Christians wear a blue cord as a sign of having been baptized, and "baptism and the blue cord are, in the Abyssinian mind, inseparable."[9] "The cord,[10] or mateb, without which nobody can be really said in Abyssinia to be respectable."[11] It further resembles the Apache medicine cord, inasmuch as it is "a blue cord around the neck."[12] The baptismal cords are made of "blue floss silk."[13]

THE MAGIC WIND KNOTTED CORDS OF THE LAPPS AND OTHERS.

"The navigators of the sixteenth and seventeenth centuries have related many wonderful stories about the magic of the *Finns* or *Finno*

---

[1] Hawkesworth, Voyages, vol. 3, p. 229.
[2] Voyage to Congo, in Pinkerton's Voyages, vol. 16, p. 237.
[3] Pinkerton, Voyages, vol. 16, p. 388.
[4] Speke, Source of the Nile, London, 1863, p. 125.
[5] London, 1877. vol. 2, p. 131.
[6] Stanley, Through the Dark Continent, vol. 2, p. 330.
[7] Schweinfurth, Heart of Africa, London, 1873, vol. 1, p. 154.
[8] Winstanley, Abyssinia, vol. 2, p. 68.
[9] This cord is worn about the neck. Ibid., p. 257.
[10] Ibid., vol. 1, p. 235.
[11] Ibid., vol. 2, p. 132.
[12] Ibid, p. 165.
[13] Ibid, p. 292.

Lappes, who sold wind contained in a cord with three knots. If the first were untied, the wind became favourable, if the second, still more so, but, if the third were loosed, a tempest was the inevitable conse-quence."[1] The selling of wind knots was ascribed not only to the Laps and Finns, but to the inhabitants of Greenland also.[2] "The northern shipmasters are such dupes to the delusions of these impos-tors that they often purchase of them a magic cord which contains a number of knots, by opening of which, according to the magician's di-rections, they expect to gain any wind they want."[3] "They [Lapland witches] further confessed, that while they fastened three knots on a linen towel in the name of the devil, and had spit on them, &c., they called the name of him they doomed to destruction." They also claimed that, "by some fatal contrivance they could bring on men dis-orders," . . . as "by spitting three times on a knife and anoint-ing the victims with that spittle."[4]

Scheffer describes the Laplanders as having a cord tied with knots for the raising of the wind; Brand says the same of the Finlanders, of Norway, of the priestesses of the island of Sena, on the coast of Gaul, in the time of the Emperor Claudius, the "witches" of the Isle of Man, etc.[5]

Macbeth, speaking to the witches, says:

> Though you untie the winds, and let them fight
> Against the churches; though the yesty waves
> Confound and swallow navigation up.[6]

ROSARIES AND OTHER MNEMONIC CORDS.

The rosary being confessedly an aid to memory, it will be proper to include it in a chapter descriptive of the different forms of mnemonic cords which have been noticed in various parts of the world. The use of the rosary is not confined to Roman Catholics; it is in service among Mahometans, Tibetans, and Persians.[7] Picart mentions "chaplets" among the Chinese and Japanese which very strongly suggest the izze-kloth.[8]

Father Grébillon, in his account of Tartary, alludes several times to the importance attached by the Chinese and Tartars to the privilege of being allowed to touch the "string of beads" worn by certain Lamas met on the journey, which corresponds very closely to the rosaries of the Roman Catholics.[9]

---

[1] Malte-Brun, Universal Geography, vol. 4, p. 259, Phila., 1832.

[2] Grimm, Teutonic Mythology, vol. 2, p. 640.

[3] Nightingale, quoted in Madden, Shrines and Sepulchres, vol. 1, pp. 557, 558.

[4] Leems, Account of Danish Lapland, in Pinkerton, Voyages, London, 1808, vol. 1, p. 471.

[5] Brand, Popular Antiquities, vol. 3, p. 5. See also John Scheffer, Lapland, Oxford, 1674, p. 58.

[6] Act IV, scene 1.

[7] Benjamin, Persia, London, 1877, p. 99.

[8] Cérémonies et Coûtumes, vol. 7, p. 320.

[9] Du Halde, History of China, London, 1736, vol. 4, pp. 244, 245, and elsewhere.

" Mr. Astle informs us that the first Chinese letters were knots on cords." [1]

Speaking of the ancient Japanese, the Chinese chronicles relate: "They have no writing, but merely cut certain marks upon wood and make knots in cord." [2] In the very earliest myths of the Chinese we read of "knotted cords, which they used instead of characters, and to instruct their children." [3] Malte-Brun calls attention to the fact that " the hieroglyphics and little cords in use amongst the ancient Chinese recal in a striking manner the figured writing of the Mexicans and the Quipos of Peru." [4] " Each combination [of the quipu] had, however, a fixed ideographic value in a certain branch of knowledge, and thus the *quipu* differed essentially from the Catholic rosary, the Jewish phylactery, or the knotted strings of the natives of North America and Siberia, to all of which it has at times been compared." [5]

E. B. Tylor differs in opinion from Brinton. According to Tylor, " the quipu is a near relation of the rosary and the wampum-string." [6]

The use of knotted cords by natives of the Caroline Islands, as a means of preserving a record of time, is noted by Kotzebue in several places. For instance: " Kadu kept his journal by moons, for which he made a knot in a string." [7]

During the years of my service with the late Maj. Gen. Crook in the Southwest, I was surprised to discover that the Apache scouts kept records of the time of their absence on campaign. There were several methods in vogue, the best being that of colored beads, which were strung on a string, six white ones to represent the days of the week and one black or other color to stand for Sundays. This method gave rise to some confusion, because the Indians had been told that there were four weeks, or Sundays (" Domingos"), in each " Luna," or moon, and yet they soon found that their own method of determining time by the appearance of the crescent moon was much the more satisfactory. Among the Zuñi I have seen little tally sticks with the marks for the days and months incised on the narrow edges, and among the Apache another method of indicating the flight of time by marking on a piece of paper along a horizontal line a number of circles or of straight lines across the horizontal datum line to represent the full days which had passed, a heavy straight line for each Sunday, and a small crescent for the beginning of each month.

Farther to the south, in the Mexican state of Sonora, I was shown, some twenty years ago, a piece of buckskin, upon which certain Opata or Yaqui Indians—I forget exactly which tribe, but it matters very

[1] Higgins, Anacalypsis, vol. 2, p. 218.
[2] Vining, An Inglorious Columbus, p. 635.
[3] Du Halde, History of China, London, 1736, vol. 1, p. 270.
[4] Univ. Geog., vol. 3, book 75, p. 144, Phila., 1832.
[5] Brinton, Myths of the New World, N. Y., 1868, p. 15.
[6] Early History of Mankind, London, 1870, p. 156.
[7] Voyages, vol. 3, p. 102.

little, as they are both industrious and honest—had kept account of the days of their labor. There was a horizontal datum line, as before, with complete circles to indicate full days and half circles to indicate half days, a long heavy black line for Sundays and holidays, and a crescent moon for each new month. These accounts had to be drawn up by the overseer or superintendent of the rancho at which the Indians were employed before the latter left for home each night.

THE SACRED CORDS OF THE PARSIS AND BRAHMANS.

I have already apologized for my own ignorance in regard to the origin and symbolical signification of the izze-kloth of the Apache, and I have now to do the same thing for the writers who have referred to the use by the religious of India of the sacred cords with which, under various names, the young man of the Parsis or Brahmans is invested upon attaining the requisite age. No two accounts seem to agree and, as I have never been in India and cannot presume to decide where so many differ, it is best that I should lay before my readers the exact language of the authorities which seem to be entitled to greatest consideration.

"A sacred thread girdle (kûstîk), should it be made of silk, is not proper; the hair of a hairy goat and a hairy camel is proper, and from other hairy creatures it is proper among the lowly." [1]

Every Parsi wears "a triple coil" of a "white cotton girdle," which serves to remind him of the "three precepts of his morality—'good thoughts,' 'good words,' 'good deeds.'" [2]

Williams describes the sacred girdle of the Pārsīs as made "of seventy-two interwoven woollen threads, to denote the seventy-two chapters of the Yaśna, but has the appearance of a long flat cord of pure white wool, which is wound round the body in three coils." The Pārsī must take off this kustī five times daily and replace it with appropriate prayers. It must be wound round the body three times and tied in two peculiar knots, the secret of which is known only to the Pārsīs. [3]

According to Picart, the "sudra," or sacred cord of the Pārsīs, has four knots, each of which represents a precept. [4]

Marco Polo, in speaking of the Brahmans of India, says: "They are known by a cotton thread, which they wear over the shoulders, tied under the arm, crossing the breast." [5]

Picart described the sacred cord of the Brahmans, which he calls the Dsandhem, as made in three colors, each color of nine threads of cotton, which only the Brahmans have the right to make. It is to be worn after the manner of a scarf from the left shoulder to the right side. It must be worn through life, and, as it will wear out, new ones are provided at

---

[1] Shâyast lâ-Shâyast, cap. 4, pp. 285, 286. In Sacred Books of the East, Max Müller's edition, vol. 5.
[2] Monier Williams, Modern India, p. 56.
[3] Ibid., pp. 179, 180.
[4] Cérémonies et Coûtumes, vol. 7, p. 28.
[5] Marco Polo, Travels, in Pinkerton's Voyages, vol. 7, p. 163.

a feast during the month of August.[1] The Brahman "about the age of seven or nine . . . is invested with 'the triple cord,' and a badge which hangs from his left shoulder."[2]

The Upavita or sacred cord, wound round the shoulders of the Brahmans, is mentioned in the Hibbert Lectures on the Origin and Growth of Religion. "Primarily, the sacred cord was the distinguishing mark of caste among the Aryan inhabitants. It consisted for the Brahmans of three cotton threads; for the Kshatriyas or warriors of three hempen threads; and for the Vaisyas or artisans and tradesmen of woollen threads."[3]

"All coiling roots and fantastic shrubs represent the serpent and are recognized as such all over India. In Bengal we find at the present day the fantastically growing Euphorbia antiquorum regularly wor-shipped, as the representative of the serpent god. The sacred thread, worn alike by Hindoo and Zoroastrian, is the symbol of that old faith; the Brahman twines it round his body and occasionally around the neck of the sacred bull, the Lingam, and its altar. . . . . With the orthodox, the serpent thread should reach down to its closely allied faith, although this Ophite thread idea is now no more known to Hindoos than the origin of arks, altars, candles, spires, and our church fleur-de-lis to Jews and Christians."[4]

General Forlong alludes to the thigh as the symbol of phallic worship. "The serpent on head denoted Holiness, Wisdom, and Power, as it does when placed on gods and great ones of the East still; but the Hindoo and Zoroastrian very early adopted a symbolic thread instead of the ophite deity, and the throwing of this over the head is also a very sacred rite, which consecrates the man-child to his God; this I should perhaps have earlier described, and will do so now. The adoption of the Poita or sacred thread, called also the *Zenar*, and from the most ancient pre-historic times by these two great Bactro-Aryan families, points to a period when both had the same faith, and that faith the Serpent. The Investiture is the Confirmation or second birth of the Hindoo boy; until which he can not, of course, be married. After the worship of the heavenly stone—the Sāligrāma, the youth or child takes a branch of the Vilwa tree in his right hand, and a mystic cloth-bag in the left, when a Poita is formed of three fibres of the Sooroo tree (for the first cord must always be made of the *genuine living fibres* of an orthodox tree), and this is hung to the boy's left shoulder; he then raises the Vilwa branch over his right shoulder, and so stands for some time, *a complete figure* of the old faiths in Tree and Serpent, until the priest offers up various prayers and incantations to Soorya, Savitri or Sot, the Eternal God. The Sooroo-Poita is then removed as not durable enough, and the permanent thread is put over the neck. It also is formed of three threads, each 96 cubits or 48 yards long, folded and twisted together until only so long that, when thrown over the left shoulder, it extends half-way down the right thigh, or a little less; for the object appears to be to unite the Caput, Sol, or Seat of intellect with that of passion, and so form a perfect man.[5]

All Parsis wear the sacred thread of serpent and phallic extraction, and the investiture of this is a solemn and essential rite with both sects [i. e., the Hindus and

[1] Picart, Cérémonies et Coûtumes, etc., vol. 6, pt. 2, p. 99.

[2] Malte-Brun, Univ. Geog., vol. 2, lib. 50, p. 235, Philadelphia, 1832.

[3] Dr. J. L. August Von Eye, The history of culture, in Iconographic Encyc., Philadelphia, 1886, vol. 2, p. 169.

[4] Forlong, Rivers of Life, vol. 1, p. 120.

[5] Ibid., pp. 240–241.

Parsis], showing their joint Aryan origin in high Asia, for the thread is of the very highest antiquity. The Parsi does not, however, wear his thread across the shoulder, and knows nothing of the all-but-forgotten origin of its required length. He wears it next to his skin, tied carefully round the waist, and used to tie it round his right arm, as is still the custom with some classes of Brahmins who have lost purity of caste by intermarriage with lower classes.[1]

At the baptism or investiture of the thread, which takes the place of the Christian confirmation ceremony, but between the ages of 7 and 9, Fire and Water are the great sanctifying elements, and are the *essentials*. The fire is kindled from the droppings of the sacred cow, then sprinkled over with holy water and blessed; and when so consecrated by the priest it is called " Holy Fire."[2]

"The *Brahmans*, the *Rajas*, and the *Merchants*, distinguish themselves from the various casts of Sudras by a narrow belt of thread, which they always wear suspended from the left shoulder to the opposite haunch like a sash."[3] But, as Dubois speaks of the division of all the tribes into "Right-hand and Left-hand," a distinction which Coleman[4] explains as consisting in doing exactly contrariwise of each other, it is not a very violent assumption to imagine that both the present and a former method of wearing the izze-kloth, akin to that now followed by the Apache, may once have obtained in India. The sectaries of the two Hands are bitterly antagonistic and often indulge in fierce quarrels, ending in bloodshed.[5]

" All the Brahmans wear a Cord over the shoulder, consisting of three black twists of cotton, each of them formed of several smaller threads. . . . The three threads are not twisted together, but separate from one another, and hang from the left shoulder to the right haunch. When a Brahman marries, he mounts nine threads instead of three." Children were invested with these sacred cords at the age of from 7 to 9. The cords had to be made and put on with much ceremony, and only Brahmans could make them. According to Dubois, the material was cotton; he does not allude to buckskin.[6]

Coleman[7] gives a detailed description of the manner in which the sacred thread of the Brahmans is made:

The sacred thread must be made by a Brahman. It consists of three strings, each ninety-six hands (forty-eight yards), which are twisted together: it is then folded into three and again twisted; these are a second time folded into the same number and tied at each end in knots. It is worn over the left shoulder (next the skin, extending half way down the right thigh), by the Brahmans, Ketries and Vaisya castes. The first are usually invested with it at eight years of age, the second at eleven, and the Vaisya at twelve. . . . The Hindus of the Sutra caste do not receive the poita.

The ceremony of investiture comprehends prayer, sacrifice, fasting, etc., and the wearing of a preliminary poita " of three threads, made of the fibers of the *suru*, to which a piece of deer's skin is fastened."[8] This piece of buckskin was added no doubt in order to let the neophyte

[1] Forlong, Rivers of Life, vol. 1, p. 328.
[2] Ibid., p. 323.
[3] Dubois, People of India, p. 9.
[4] Mythology of the Hindus.
[5] Mythology of the Hindus, pp. 9, 10, 11.
[6] Ibid., p. 92.
[7] Ibid., p. 155.
[8] Ibid., pp. 135, 154, 155.

know that once buckskin formed an important part of the garment.
The Brahmans use three cords, while the Apache employ four; on this
subject we shall have more to learn when we take up the subject of
numbers.

Maurice says that the "sacred cord of India," which he calls the
zennar, is "a cord of three threads in memory and honor of the three
great deities of Hindostan."[1] It "can be woven by no profane hand; the
Brahmin alone can twine the hallowed threads that compose it and it
is done by him with the utmost solemnity, and with the addition of
many mystic rites."[2] It corresponds closely to the izze-kloth; the Apache
do not want people to touch these cords. The zennar "being put
upon the left shoulder passes to the right side and hangs down as low
as the fingers can reach."[3]   The izze-kloth of the Apache, when possible, is made of twisted antelope skin; they have no cord of hemp;
but when the zennar is "put on for the first time, it is accompanied
with a piece of the skin of an antelope, three fingers in breadth, but
shorter than the zennar."[4]

On p. 128 of Vining's An Inglorious Columbus, there is a figure of
worshipers offering gifts to Buddha; from Buddha's left shoulder to
his right hip there passes what appears to be a cord, much like the
izze-kloth of the Apache.

Examples of the use of such cords are to be found elsewhere.

In the conjuration of one of the shamans, "They took a small line
made of deers' skins of four fathoms long, and with a small knot the
priest made it fast about his neck and under his left arm, and gave it
unto two men standing on both sides of him, which held the ends together."[5] It is difficult to say whether this was a cord used on the
present occasion only or worn constantly by the shaman. In either
case the cord was "medicine."

Hagennaar relates that he "saw men wearing ropes with knots in
them, flung over their shoulders, whose eyes turned round in their
heads, and who were called Jammaboos, signifying as much as conjurors or exorcists."[6]

The Mahometans believe that at the day of judgment Jesus Christ
and Mahomet are to meet outside of Jerusalem holding a tightly-
stretched cord between them upon which all souls must walk. This
may or may not preserve a trace of a former use of such a cord in their
"medicine," but it is well to refer to it.[7]

---

[1] Maurice, Indian Antiquities, London, 1801, vol. 5, p. 205.

[2] Ibid., vol. 4, p. 375, where a description of the mode of weaving and twining is given.

[3] Ibid., p. 376.

[4] Ibid., vol. 5, p. 206.

[5] Notes of Richard Johnson, Voyages of Sir Hugh Willoughby and others to the northern part of
Russia and Siberia, Pinkerton's Voyages, vol. 1, p. 63.

[6] Caron's account of Japan in Pinkerton's Voyages, vol. 7, p. 631.

[7] Rev. Father Dandini's Voyage to Mount Libanus, in Pinkerton's Voyages, vol. 10, p. 286.

The sacred thread and garment which were worn by all the perfect among the Cathari, and the use of which by both Zends and Brahmans shows that its origin is to be traced back to a pre-historic period.[1]

"No religious rite can be performed by a (child) before he has been girt with the sacred girdle, since he is on a level with a Sûdra before his (new) birth from the Veda."[2]

In explaining the rules of external purification—that is, purification in which water is the medium—Baudhâyana says:[3]

The sacrificial thread (shall be made) of Kusa grass, or cotton, (and consist) of thrice three strings.

(It shall hang down) to the navel.

(In putting it on) he shall raise the right arm, lower the left, and lower the head.

The contrary (is done at sacrifices) to the manes.

(If the thread is) suspended around the neck (it is called) nivîta.

(If it is) suspended below (the navel, it is called) adhopavîta.

A former use of sacred cords would seem to be suggested in the constant appearance of the belief in the mystical properties and the power for good or evil of the knots which constitute the characteristic appendage of these cords. This belief has been confined to no race or people; it springs up in the literature of the whole world and survives with a pertinacity which is remarkable among the peasantry of Europe and among many in both America and Europe who would not hesitate to express resentment were they to be included among the illiterate.

The powers of these knots were recognized especially in strengthening or defeating love, as aiding women in labor, and in other ways which prove them to be cousins-german to the magic knots with which the medicine-men of the Lapps and other nations along the shores of the Baltic were supposed to be able to raise or allay the tempest. "One of the torments with which witchcraft worried men was the Knot by which a man was withheld so that he could not work his will with a woman. It was called in the Latin of the times Nodus and Obligamentum, and appears in the glossaries, translated by the Saxons into lyb, drug." "To make a 'ligatura' is pronounced 'detestable' by Theodorus, Archbishop of Canterbury, in 668. The knot is still known in France, and Nouer l'aiguillette is a resort of ill-will." Then is given the adventure of Hrut, prince of Iceland, and his bride Gunnhilld, princess of Norway, by whom a "knot" was duly tied to preserve his fidelity during his absence.[4] "Traces of this philosophy are to be found elsewhere," (references are given from Pliny and Galens in regard to "nod").[5] "A knot among the ancient northern nations seems to have been the symbol of love, faith, and friendship, pointing out the indissoluble tie of affection and duty. Thus the ancient Runic inscriptions, as we gather from Hickes's Thesaurus, are in the form of a knot. Hence,

---

[1] Henry Charles Lea, History of the Inquisition in the Middle Ages, vol. 1, p. 92, New York, 1888.

[2] Müller, Sacred Books of the East, vol. 14, Vasishtha, cap. 2, par 6.

[3] Ibid., Baudhâyana, prasna 1, adhyâya 5, kandikâ 8, pars. 5–10, p. 165.

[4] Saxon Leechdoms, vol. 1, pp. xli–xliii.

[5] Ibid., p. xliii.

among the northern English and Scots, who still retain, in a great measure, the language and manners of the ancient Danes, that curious kind of a knot, a mutual present between the lover and his mistress, which, being considered as the emblem of plighted fidelity, is therefore called a true-love knot: a name which is not derived, as one would naturally suppose it to be, from the words 'true' and 'love,' but formed from the Danish verb *Trulofa, fidem do*, I plight my troth, or faith. . . . Hence, evidently, the bride favors or the top-knots at marriages, which have been considered as emblems of the ties of duty and affection between the bride and her spouse, have been derived." [1]

Sir Thomas Browne, in his Vulgar Errors, [2] says "the true-lover's knot is much magnified, and still retained in presents of love among us; which, though in all points it doth not make out, had, perhaps, its original from Nodus Herculanus, or that which was called Hercules, his knot resembling the snaky complications in the caduceus or rod of Hermes and in which form the zone or woolen girdle of the bride was fastened, as Turnebus observes in his Adversaria." Brand shows [3] that the true-lover's knot had to be tied three times. Another species of knot divination is given in the Connoisseur, No. 56: " Whenever I go to lye in a strange bed, I always tye my garter nine times round the bed-post, and knit nine knots in it, and say to myself: ' this knot I knit, this knot I tye, to see my love as he goes by,' etc. There was also a suggestion of color symbolism in the true-lover's knot, blue being generally accepted as the most appropriate tint. I find among the illiterate Mexican population of the lower Rio Grande a firm belief in the power possessed by a lock of hair tied into knots to retain a maiden's affections.

" I find it stated that headache may be alleviated by tying a woman's fillet round the head. [4] To arrest incontinence of urine, the extremities of the generative organs should be tied with a thread of linen or papyrus, and a binding passed round the middle of the thigh. [5] It is quite surprising how much more speedily wounds will heal if they are bound up and tied with a Hercules' knot; indeed, it is said that if the girdle which we wear every day is tied with a knot of this description, it will be productive of certain beneficial effects, Hercules having been the first to discover the fact." [6] " Healing girdles were already known to Marcellus." [7]

" In our times 'tis a common thing, saith Erastus in his book *de Lamiis*, for witches to take upon them the making of these philters, to force men and women to love and hate whom they will; to cause tempests, diseases, &c., by charms, spels, characters, knots." [8]

---

[1] Brand, Popular Antiquities, vol. 2, pp. 108, 109.
[2] Browne, Religio Medici, p. 392.
[3] Brand, op. cit., p. 110.
[4] Pliny, Nat. Hist., lib. 28, cap. 22.
[5] Ibid., lib. 28, cap. 17.
[6] Ibid.
[7] Grimm, Teutonic Mythology, vol. 3, p. 1169.
[8] Burton, Anatomy of Melancholy, London, 1827, vol. 1, p. 91; vol. 2, pp. 288, 290.

Burton [1] alludes to the "inchanted girdle of Venus, in which, saith Natales Comes, . . . all witchcraft to enforce love was contained."

The first general council of Milan, in 1565, prohibited the use of what were called phylacteries, ligatures, and reliquaries (of heathen origin) which people all over Europe were in the habit of wearing at neck or on arms or knees. [2]

" King James [3] enumerates thus: 'Such kinde of charmes as . . . staying married folkes to have naturally adoe with each other, by knitting so many knots upon a point at the time of their marriage.'" [4]

"Tying the point was another fascination, illustrations of which may be found in Reginald Scott's Discourse Concerning Devils and Spirits, p. 71; in the Fifteen Comforts of Marriage, p. 225; and in the British Apollo, vol. 2, No. 35, 1709. In the old play of The Witch of Edmonton, 1658 Young Banks says, ' Ungirt, unbless'd, says the proverb.'" [5]

Frommann speaks of the frequent appearance of knots in witchcraft, but, beyond alluding to the " Nodus Cassioticus" of a certain people near Pelusia, who seem, like the Laplanders, to have made a business of fabricating and selling magic knots, he adds nothing to our stock of information on the subject. He seems to regard the knot of Hercules and the Gordian knot as magical knots. [6]

Bogle mentions the adoration of the Grand Lama (Teshu Lama). The Lama's servants " put a bit of silk with a knot upon it, tied, or supposed to be tied, with the Lama's own hands, about the necks of the votaries." [7]

A girdle of Venus, " possessing qualities not to be described," was enumerated among the articles exhibited at a rustic wedding in England. [8]

In 1519, Torralva, the Spanish magician, was given by his guardian spirit, Zequiel, a " stick full of knots," with the injunction, " shut your eyes and fear nothing; take this in your hand, and no harm will happen to you." [9] Here the idea evidently was that the power resided in the knots.

"Immediately before the celebration of the marriage ceremony [in Perthshire, Scotland] every knot about the bride and bridegroom (garters, shoe-strings, strings of petticoats, &c.), is carefully loosened." [10]

"The precaution of loosening every knot about the new-joined pair is strictly observed [in Scotland], for fear of the penalty denounced in the former volumes. It must be remarked that the custom is observed even in France, *nouer l'aiguillette* being a common phrase for disappointments of this nature." [11]

---

[1] Burton, Anatomy of Melancholy, London, 1827, vol. 1, p. 91; vol. 2, p. 290.
[2] Picart, Cérémonies et Coûtumes, etc., vol. 10, pp. 69–73.
[3] Dæmonology, p. 100.
[4] Brand, Pop. Ant., vol. 3, p. 299.
[5] Ibid., p. 170.
[6] Frommann, Tractatus de Fascinatione, Nuremberg, 1675, p. 731.
[7] Markham, Bogle's mission to Tibet, London, 1876, p. 85.
[8] Brand, Pop. Ant., vol. 2, p. 149.
[9] Thomas Wright, Sorcery and Magic, London, 1851, vol. 2, p. 10.
[10] Brand, Pop. Ant., vol. 2, p. 143.
[11] Pennant, in Pinkerton, Voyages, vol. 3, p. 382.

In some parts of Germany " a bride will tie a string of flax around her left leg, in the belief that she will thereby enjoy the full blessing of the married state." [1]

"There was formerly a custom in the north of England, which will be thought to have bordered very closely upon indecency . . . for the young men present at a wedding to strive, immediately after the ceremony, who could first pluck off the bride's garters from her legs. This was done before the very altar . . . I have sometimes thought this a fragment of the ancient ceremony of loosening the virgin zone, or girdle, a custom that needs no explanation." "It is the custom in Normandy for the bride to bestow her garter on some young man as a favour, or sometimes it is taken from her . . . I am of opinion that the origin of the Order of the Garter is to be traced to this nuptial custom, anciently common to both court and country." [2]

Grimm quotes from Hincmar of Rheims to show the antiquity of the use for both good and bad purposes of "ligatures," " cum filulis colorum multiplicium." [3]

To undo the effects of a " ligature," the following was in high repute: "Si quem voles per noctem cum fœmina coire non posse, pistillum coronatum sub lecto illius pone." [4] But a pestle crowned with flowers could be nothing more or less than a phallus, and, therefore, an offering to the god Priapus.

" Owing to a supposed connection which the witches knew between the relations of husband and wife and the mysterious knots, the bridegroom, formerly in Scotland and to the present day in Ireland, presents himself occasionally, and in rural districts, before the clergyman, with all knots and fastenings on his dress loosened, and the bride, immediately after the ceremony is performed, retires to be undressed, and so rid of her knots." [5]

USE OF CORDS AND KNOTS AND GIRDLES IN PARTURITION.

Folk medicine in all regions is still relying upon the potency of mystical cords and girdles to facilitate labor. The following are a few of the many examples which might be presented:

Delivery was facilitated if the man by whom the woman has conceived unties his girdle, and, after tying it round her, unties it, saying: "I have tied it and I will untie it," and then takes his departure. [6]

"Henry, in his History of Britain, vol. 1, p. 459, tells us that ' amongst the ancient Britons, when a birth was attended with any difficulty, they put certain girdles made for that purpose about the women in labour which they imagined gave immediate and effectual relief. Such girdles were kept with care till very lately in many families in the Highlands

---

[1] Hoffman, quoting Friend, in Jour. Am. Folk Lore, 1888, p. 134.

[2] Brand, Pop. Ant., vol. 2, pp. 127 et seq.

[3] Grimm, Teutonic Mythology, vol. 3, p. 1174. He also speaks of the "nouer l'aiguillette, ibid., p. 1175.

[4] Saxon Leechdoms, vol. 1, p. xliv.

[5] Black, Folk-Medicine, London, 1883, pp. 185, 186.

[6] Pliny, Nat. Hist., lib. 28, cap. 9.

of Scotland. They were impressed with several mystical figures; and the ceremony of binding them about the woman's waist was accompanied with words and gestures, which showed the custom to have been of great antiquity, and to have come originally from the Druids.'"[1]

"But my girdle shall serve as a riding *knit*, and a fig for all the witches in Christendom."[2] The use of girdles in labor must be ancient.

"Ut mulier concipiat, homo vir si solvat semicinctum suum et eam præcingat."[3] "Certum est quod partum mirabiliter facilirent, sive instar cinguli circumdentur corpori." These girdles were believed to aid labor and cure dropsy and urinary troubles.[4]

"The following customs of childbirth are noticed in the Traité des Superstitions of M. Thiers, vol. 1, p. 320: 'Lors qu'une femme est preste d'accoucher, prendre *sa ceinture*, aller à l'Eglise, *lier la cloche avec cette ceinture* et la faire sonner trois coups afin que cette femme accouche heureusement. Martin de Arles, Archidiacre de Pampelonne (Tract. de Superstition) asseure que cette superstition est fort en usage dans tout son pays.'"[5]

In the next two examples there is to be found corroboration of the views advanced by Forlong that these cords (granting that the principle upon which they all rest is the same) had originally some relation to ophic rites. Brand adds from Levinus Lemnius: "Let the woman that travels with her child (is in her labour) be girded with the skin that a serpent or a snake casts off, and then she will quickly be delivered."[6] A serpent's skin was tied as a belt about a woman in childbirth. "Inde puerperæ circa collum aut corporem apposito, victoriam in puerperii conflictu habuerunt, citissimeque liberatæ fuerunt."[7]

The following examples, illustrative of the foregoing, are taken from Flemming: The skins of human corpses were drawn off, preferably by cobblers, tanned, and made into girdles, called "Cingula" or Chirothecæ, which were bound on the left thigh of a woman in labor to expedite delivery. The efficacy of these was highly extolled, although some writers recommended a recourse to tiger's skin for the purposes indicated. This "caro humano" was euphemistically styled "mummy" or "mumia" by Von Helmont and others of the early pharmacists, when treating of it as an internal medicament.

There was a "Cingulum ex corio humano" bound round patients during epileptic attacks, convulsions, childbirth, etc., and another kind of belt described as "ex cute humana conficiunt," and used in contraction of the nerves and rheumatism of the joints,[8] also bound round the body in cramp.[9]

---

[1] Brand, Pop. Ant., vol. 2, p. 67.

[2] Ibid., p. 170.

[3] Sextus Placitus, De Medicamentis ex Animalibus, Lyons, 1537, pages not numbered, article "de Puello et Puellæ Virgine."

[4] Etmüller, Opera Omnia, Lyons, 1690, vol. 2, p. 279, Schroderii Dilucidati Zoologia.

[5] Brand, Pop. Ant., vol. 2, p. 68, footnote.

[6] Ibid., p. 67.

[7] Paracelsus, Chirurgia Minora, in Opera Omnia, Geneva, 1662, vol. 2, p. 70.

[8] Ibid., p. 174.

[9] Beckherius, Medicus Microcosmus, London, 1660, p. 174.

"The *girdle* was an essential article of dress, and early ages ascribe to it other magic influences: e. g., Thôr's divine strength lay in his girdle."[1] In speaking of the belief in lycantrophy he says: "The common belief among us is that the transformation is effected by *tying a strap round the body;* this girth is only three fingers broad, and is cut out of human skin."[2] Scrofulous tumors were cured by tying them with a linen thread which had choked a viper to death.[3] "Filum rubrum seraceum [silk] cum quo strangulata fuit vipera si circumdatur collo angina laborantes, eundem curare dicitur propter idem strangulationis et suffocationis."[4]

"Quidam commendant tanquam specificum, ad Anginam filum purpureum cum quo strangulata fuit vipera, si collo circumdetur."[5]

"MEDIDAS," "MEASURING CORDS," "WRESTING THREADS," ETC.

Black says:[6] "On the banks of the Ale and the Teviot the women have still a custom of wearing round their necks blue woollen threads or cords till they wean their children, doing this for the purpose of averting ephemeral fevers. These cords are handed down from mother to daughter, and esteemed in proportion to their antiquity. Probably these cords had originally received some blessing."

Black's surmise is well founded. These cords were, no doubt, the same as the "medidas" or measurements of the holy images of Spain and other parts of Continental Europe. "The ribands or serpent symbols [of Our Lady of Montserrat] are of silk, and exactly the span of the Virgin's head, and on them is printed ' *medida de la cabeza de Nuestra Señora Maria Santísima de Montserrat,*' i. e., exact head measurement of Our Lady of Montserrat."[7]

These same "medidas" may be found in full vogue in the outlying districts of Mexico to-day. Twenty years ago I saw them at the "funcion" of San Francisco, in the little town of Magdalena, in Sonora. I watched carefully to see exactly what the women did and observed that the statue of St. Francis (which, for greater convenience, was exposed outside of the church, where the devout could reach it without disturbing the congregation within) was measured from head to foot with pieces of ribbon, which were then wrapped up and packed away. In reply to my queries, I learned that the "medida" of the head was a specific for headache, that of the waist for all troubles in the abdominal region, those of the legs, arms, and other parts for the ailments peculiar to each of them respectively. This was in a community almost, if not absolutely, Roman Catholic; but in the thoroughly Protestant neighborhood of Carlisle, Pa., the same superstition exists

---

[1] Grimm, Teutonic Mythology, vol. 3, p. 1094, footnote.
[2] Ibid., p. 1096.
[3] Pliny, Nat. Hist., lib. 30, cap. 12.
[4] Etmüller, Opera Omnia, Lyons, 1690, vol. 2, pp. 282, 283, Schroderii Dilucidati Zoologia.
[5] Ibid., p. 278a.
[6] Black, Folk-Medicine, London, 1883, p. 113.
[7] Forlong, Rivers of Life, London, 1883, vol. 2, p. 313.

in full vigor, as I know personally. Three years ago my second child was suffering from the troubles incident to retarded dentition and had to be taken to the mountains at Holly Springs, within sight of Carlisle. I was begged and implored by the women living in the place to have the child taken to " a wise woman" to be "measured," and was assured that some of the most intelligent people in that part of the country were firm believers in the superstition. When I declined to lend countenance to such nonsense I was looked upon as a brutal and unnatural parent, caring little for the welfare of his offspring.

"In John Bale's Comedye concernynge thre Lawes, 1538 . . . Hypocrysy is introduced, mentioning the following charms against barrenness:

> And as for Lyons, there is the length of our Lorde
> In a great pyller. She that will with a coorde
> Be fast bound to it, and *take soche chaunce as fall*
> Shall sure have chylde, for within it is hollowe all." [1]

When a person in Shetland has received a sprain " it is customary to apply to an individual practiced in casting the 'wrested thread.' This is a thread spun from black wool, on which are cast nine knots, and tied round a sprained leg or arm." It is applied by the medicine-man with the usual amount of gibberish and incantation.[2] These "wresting or wrested threads" are also to be found among Germans, Norwegians, Swedes, and Flemings.[3]

Grimm quotes from Chambers's Fireside Stories, Edinburgh, 1842, p. 37: " During the time the operator is putting the thread round the afflicted limb he says, but *in such a tone of voice as not to be heard by the bystanders,* nor even by the person operated upon: " The *Lord* rade, and the foal slade; he lighted, and he righted, set joint to joint, bone to bone, and sinew to sinew. Heal in the Holy Ghost's name!"[4]

" Eily McGarvey, a Donegal wise woman, employs a green thread in her work. She measures her patient three times round the waist with a ribbon, to the outer edge of which is fastened a green thread. . . . She next hands the patient nine leaves of ' heart fever grass,' or dandelion, gathered by herself, directing him to eat three leaves on successive mornings."[5]

Miss Edna Dean Proctor, the poet, told me, June 9, 1887, that some years ago, while visiting relations in Illinois, she met a woman who, having been ill for a long time, had despaired of recovery, and in hope of amelioration had consulted a man pretending to occult powers, who prescribed that she wear next the skin a certain knotted red cord which he gave her.

On a previous page the views of Forlong have been presented, showing that there were reasons for believing that the sacred cords of the

[1] Brand, Pop. Ant., vol. 2, p. 69.
[2] Notes and Queries, 1st series, vol. 4, p. 500.
[3] See also Black, Folk-Medicine, London, 1883, p. 79.
[4] Grimm, Teutonic Mythology, vol. 3, p. 1233.
[5] Black, Folk-Medicine, London, 1883, p. 114.

East Indies could be traced back to an ophic origin, and it has also been shown that, until the present day, among the peasantry of Europe, there has obtained the practice of making girdles of snake skin which have been employed for the cure of disease and as an assistance in childbirth. The snake itself, while still alive, as has been shown, is applied to the person of the patient by the medicine-men of the American Indians.

In connection with the remarks taken from Forlong's Rivers of Life on this subject, I should like to call attention to the fact that the long knotted blacksnake whip of the wagoners of Europe and America, which, when not in use, is worn across the body from shoulder to hip, has been identified as related to snake worship.

There is another view to take of the origin of these sacred cords which it is fair to submit before passing final judgment. The izze-kloth may have been in early times a cord for tying captives who were taken in war, and as these captives were offered up in sacrifice to the gods of war and others they were looked upon as sacred, and all used in connection with them would gradually take on a sacred character. The same kind of cords seem to have been used in the chase. This would explain a great deal of the superstition connected with the whole subject of "hangman's rope" bringing luck, curing disease, and averting trouble of all sorts, a superstition more widely disseminated and going back to more ancient times than most people would imagine. One of the tribes of New Granada, "quando iban à la Guerra llevaban Cordeles para atar à los Presos."[1] This recalls that the Apache themselves used to throw lariats from ambush upon travelers, and that the Thugs who served the goddess Bhowani, in India, strangled with cords, afterwards with handkerchiefs. The Spaniards in Peru, under Jorge Robledo, going toward the Rio Magdalena, in 1542, found a large body of savages "que llevaban Cordeles, para atar à los Castellanos, i sus Pedernales, para despedaçarlos, i Ollas para cocerlos."[2] The Australians carried to war a cord, called "Nerum," about 2 feet 6 inches long, made of kangaroo hair, used for strangling an enemy.[3]

The easiest method of taking the hyena "is for the hunter to tie his girdle with seven knots, and to make as many knots in the whip with which he guides his horse."[4] Maj. W. Cornwallis Harris[5] describes a search made for a lost camel. A man was detailed to search for the animal and provided with the following charm to aid him in his search: "The rope with which the legs of the lost animal had been fettered was rolled betwixt his (the Ras el Káfilah's) hands, and sundry cabalistic words having been muttered whilst the Devil was dislodged

---

[1] Herrera, dec. 6, lib. 8, cap. 1, p. 171.
[2] Ibid., dec. 7, lib. 4, cap. 5, p. 70.
[3] Smyth, Aborigines of Victoria, vol. 1, p. 351. See also previous references to the use of such cords by the Australians.
[4] Pliny, Nat. Hist., lib. 28, cap. 27.
[5] Highlands of Æthiopia, vol. 1, p. 247.

by the process of spitting upon the cord at the termination of each spell, it was finally delivered over to the Dankáli about to be sent on the quest." Stanley describes the "lords of the cord" at the court of Mtesa, king of Uganda, but they seem to be provost officers and executioners merely.[1] "In cases of quartan fever they take a fragment of a nail from a cross, or else a piece of a halter that has been used for crucifixion, and after wrapping it in wool, attach it to the patient's neck, taking care, the moment he has recovered, to conceal it in some hole to which the light of the sun can not penetrate."[2] There is a widespread and deeply rooted belief that a rope which has hanged a man, either as a felon or suicide, possesses talismanic powers.[3] Jean Baptiste Thiers[4] says: "Il y a des gens assez fous pour s'imaginer qu'ils seront heureux au jeu . . . pourvu qu'ils ayent sur eux un morceau de corde de pendu." Brand says: "I remember once to have seen, at Newcastle upon Tyne, after a person executed had been cut down, men climb upon the gallows and contend for that part of the rope which remained, and which they wished to preserve for some lucky purpose or other. I have lately made the important discovery that it is reckoned a cure for the headache."[5] "A halter with which one had been hanged was regarded within recent times in England as a cure for headache if tied round the head."[6]

In the long list of articles employed by the ancients for the purpose of developing affection or hatred between persons of opposite sex, Burton mentions "funis strangulati hominis."[7] "A remarkable superstition still prevails among the lowest of our vulgar, that a man may lawfully sell his wife to another, provided he deliver her over with a halter about her neck. It is painful to observe that instances of this frequently occur in our newspapers."[8] While discussing this branch of the subject, it might be well to peruse what has already been inserted under the head of the uses to which were put the threads which had strangled vipers and other serpents.

UNCLASSIFIED SUPERSTITIONS UPON THIS SUBJECT.

In conclusion, I wish to present some of the instances occurring in my studies which apparently have a claim to be included in a treatise upon the subject of sacred cords and knots. These examples are presented without comment, as they are, to all intents and purposes, "survivals," which have long ago lost their true significance. Attention is invited to the fact that the very same use seems to be made by the

---

[1] Through the Dark Continent, vol. 1, p. 398.

[2] Pliny, Nat, Hist.,lib. 28, cap. 11.

[3] Notes and Queries, 4th series, vol. 5, pp. 295, 390.

[4] Traité des Superstitions, tome 1, chap. 3, paragraph 3.

[5] Pop. Ant., vol. 3, p. 276.

[6] Black, Folk-Medicine, p. 109.

[7] Anatomy of Melancholy, vol. 2, pp. 288, 290.

[8] Brand, Pop. Ant., vol. 2 p. 107.

Irish of hair cords as we have already seen has been made by the Australians.

The Jewish garment with knots at the corners would appear to have been a prehistoric garment preserved in religious ceremonial; it would seem to be very much like the short blanket cloak, with tufts or knots at the four corners, still made by and in use among the Zuñi, Navajo, Tusayan, and Rio Grande Pueblos. But magic knots were by no means unknown to Jews, Assyrians, or other nations of Syria and Mesopotamia.

"In Memorable Things noted in the Description of the World, we read: About children's necks the wild Irish hung the beginning of St. John's Gospel, a crooked nail of a horseshoe, or a piece of a wolve's skin, and both the sucking child and nurse were girt with girdles finely plaited with woman's hair."[1]

Gainsford, in his Glory of England, speaking of the Irish, p. 150, says: "They use *incantations* and *spells*, wearing *girdles of woman's haire*, and *locks of their lover's*."

Camden, in his Ancient and Modern Manners of the Irish, says that "they are observed to present their lovers with bracelets of women's hair, whether in reference to Venus' cestus or not, I know not."[2] This idea of a resemblance between the girdle of Venus and the use of the maiden's hair may be worth consideration; on the same page Brand quotes from Beaumont and Fletcher:

> Bracelets of our lovers' hair,
> Which they on our arms shall twist,

and garters of the women were generally worn by lovers.[3]

"Chaque habit qu'ils [the Jews] portent doit avoir quatre pands, & à chacun un cordon pendant en forme de houppe, qu'ils nomment Zizit. Ce cordon est ordinairement de huit fils de laine filée exprès pour cela, avec cinq nœuds chacun, qui occupent la moitié de la longueur. Ce qui n'est pas noué étant éfilé acheve de faire une espece de houppe, qu'ils se fassent, dit la Loi, des cordons aux pands de leurs habits."[4]

The following is from Black:[5]

When Marduk [Assyrian god] wishes to comfort a dying man his father Hea says: "Go—

> Take a woman's linen kerchief!
> Bind it round thy left hand: loose it from the left hand!
> Knot it with seven knots: do so twice:
> Sprinkle it with bright wine:
> Bind it round the head of the sick man:
> Bind it round his hands and feet, like manacles and fetters.
> Sit round on his bed:
> Sprinkle holy water over him.
> He shall hear the voice of Hea.
> Davkina shall protect him!
> And Marduk, Eldest Son of heaven, shall find him a happy habitation."

---

[1] Brand, Pop. Ant., vol. 2, p. 78.
[2] Ibid., p. 91.
[3] Ibid., p. 93.
[4] Picart, Cérémonies et Coûtumes, etc., vol. 1, p. 41.
[5] Folk-Medicine, London, 1883, pp. 185, 186.

A variant of the same formula is to be found in François Lenormant's Chaldean Magic.[1] Lenormant speaks of the Chaldean use of "magic knots, the efficacy of which was so firmly believed in even up to the middle ages."

Again, he says that magic cords, with knots, were " still very common among the Nabathean sorcerers of the Lower Euphrates," in the fourteenth century, and in his opinion the use of these was derived from the ancient Chaldeans. In still another place he speaks of the "magic knots" used by Finnish conjurors in curing diseases.

" The Jewish phylactery was tied in a knot, but more generally knots are found in use to bring about some enchantment or disenchantment. Thus in an ancient Babylonian charm we have—

'Merodach, the son of Hea, the prince, with his holy hands cuts the knots.

That is to say, he takes off the evil influence of the knots. So, too, witches sought in Scotland to compass evil by tying knots. Witches, it was thought, could supply themselves with the milk of any neighbor's cows if they had a small quantity of hair from the tail of each of the animals. The hair they would twist into a rope and then a knot would be tied on the rope for every cow which had contributed hair. Under the clothes of a witch who was burned at St. Andrews, in 1572, was discovered 'a white claith, like a collore craig, with stringis, wheron was mony knottis vpon the stringis of the said collore craig.' When this was taken from her, with a prescience then wrongly interpreted, she said: 'Now I have no hope of myself.' 'Belyke scho thought,' runs the cotemporary account, 'scho suld not have died, that being vpon her,' but probably she meant that to be discovered with such an article in her possession was equivalent to the sentence of death. So lately as the beginning of the last century, two persons were sentenced to capital punishment for stealing a charm of knots, made by a woman as a device against the welfare of Spalding of Ashintilly."[2]

"Charmed belts are commonly worn in Lancashire for the cure of rheumatism. Elsewhere, a cord round the loins is worn to ward off toothache. Is it possible that there is any connection between this belt and the cord which in Burmah is hung round the neck of a possessed person while he is being thrashed to drive out the spirit which troubles him? Theoretically the thrashing is given to the spirit, and not to the man, but to prevent the spirit escaping too soon a charmed cord is hung round the possessed person's neck. When the spirit has been sufficiently humbled and has declared its name it may be allowed to escape, if the doctor does not prefer to trample on the patient's stomach till he fancies he has killed the demon."[3]

" The numerous notices in the folklore of all countries of magic stones, holy girdles, and other nurses' specials, attest the common sympathy of the human race."[4]

[1] P. 41.
[2] Black, Folk-Medicine, p. 186.
[3] Ibid., (after Tylor) pp. 176, 177.
[4] Ibid,, p. 178.

This is from Brand:[1] "Devonshire cure for warts. Take a piece of twine, tie in it as many knots as you have warts, touch each wart with a knot, and then throw the twine behind your back into some place where it may soon decay—a pond or a hole in the earth; but tell no one what you have done. When the twine is decayed your warts will disappear without any pain or trouble, being in fact charmed away."

"In our time, the anodyne necklace, which consists of beads turned out of the root of the white Bryony, and which is hung round the necks of infants, in order to assist their teething, and to ward off the convulsions sometimes incident to that process, is an amulet."[2]

"Rowan, ash, and red thread," a Scotch rhyme goes, "keep the devils frae their speed."[3]

For the cure of scrofula, grass was selected. From one, two, or three stems, as many as nine joints must be removed, which must then be wrapped in black wool, with the grease in it. The person who gathers them must do so fasting, and must then go, in the same state, to the patient's house while he is from home. When the patient comes in, the other must say to him three times, "I come fasting to bring a remedy to a fasting man," and must then attach the amulet to his person, repeating the same ceremony three consecutive days.[4]

Forlong says: "On the 2d [of May], fearing evil spirits and witches, Scotch farmers used to tie red thread upon their wives as well as their cows, saying these prevented miscarriages and preserved the milk."[5]

In Scotland "they hope to preserve the milk of their cows, and their wives from miscarriage, by tying threads about them."[6]

Brand gives a remedy for epilepsy: "If, in the month of October, a little before the full moon, you pluck a twig of the elder, and cut the cane that is betwixt two of its knees, or knots, in nine pieces, and these pieces, being bound in a piece of linnen, be in a thread so hung about the neck that they touch the spoon of the heart, or the sword-formed cartilage."[7]

Black says:[8] "To cure warts a common remedy is to tie as many knots on a hair as there are warts and throw the hair away. Six knots of elderwood are used in a Yorkshire incantation to ascertain if beasts are dying from witchcraft. Marcellus commended for sore eyes that a man should tie as many knots in unwrought flax as there are letters in his name, pronouncing each letter as he worked; this he was to tie round his neck. In the Orkneys, the blue thread was used for an evil purpose because such a colour savored of Popery and priests; in the northern counties it was used because a remembrance of its once pre-

---

[1] Pop. Ant., vol. 3, p. 276.
[2] Salverte, Philosophy of Magic, vol. 1, p. 195.
[3] Black, Folk-Medicine, London, 1883, p. 197.
[4] Pliny, Nat. Hist., lib. 24, cap. 118.
[5] Forlong, Rivers of Life, vol. 1, p. 451.
[6] Pennant, quoted by Brand, Popular Antiquities, vol. 3, p. 54.
[7] Ibid., p. 285.
[8] Folk-Medicine, London, 1883, pp. 185, 186.

eminent value still survived in the minds of those who wore it, unconsciously, though still actively, influencing their thoughts. In perhaps the same way we respect the virtue of red threads, because, as Conway puts it, 'red is sacred in one direction as symbolising the blood of Christ.' "[1]

"To cure ague [Hampshire, England] string nine or eleven snails on a thread, the patient saying, as each is threaded, 'Here I leave my ague.' When all are threaded they should be frizzled over a fire, and as the snails disappear so will the ague."[2]

Dr. Joseph Lanzoni scoffed at the idea that a red-silk thread could avail in erysipelas; "Neque filum sericum chermisinum parti affectæ circumligatum erysipelata fugat." The word "chermesinum" is not given in Ainsworth's Latin-English Dictionary, but it so closely resembles the Spanish "carmesi" that I have made bold to render it as "red" or "scarlet."[3]

"Red thread is symbolical of lightning," and is consequently laid on churns in Ireland "to prevent the milk from being bewitched and yielding no butter." "In Aberdeenshire it is a common practice with the housewife to tie a piece of red worsted thread round the cows' tails before turning them out for the first time in the season to grass. It secured the cattle from the evil-eye, elf-shots, and other dangers."[4] "It [blue] is the sky color and the Druid's sacred colour.[5] "In 1635, a man in the Orkney Islands was, we are led to believe, utterly ruined by nine knots cast on a blue thread and given to his sister."

"In a curious old book, 12mo., 1554, entitled A Short Description of Antichrist, is this passage: 'I note all their Popishe traditions of confirmacion of yonge children with oynting of oyle and creame, and with *a ragge knitte about the necke of the younge babe.*' "[6]

A New England charm for an obstinate ague. "The patient in this case is to take a string made of woolen yarn, of three colors, and to go by himself to an apple-tree; there he is to tie his left hand loosely with the right to the tree by the tri-colored string, then to slip his hand out of the knot and run into the house without looking behind him."[7]

The dust "in which a hawk has bathed itself, tied up in a linen cloth with a red string, and attached to the body,"[8] was one of the remedies for fevers. Another cure for fever: "Some inclose a caterpillar in a piece of linen, with a thread passed three times round it, and tie as many knots, repeating at each knot why it is that the patient performs that operation."[9]

"To prevent nose-bleeding people are told to this day to wear a skein of scarlet silk thread round the neck, tied with nine knots down the front; if the patient is a man, the silk being put on and the knots tied

[1] Folk-Medicine, London, 1883, p. 113.
[2] Ibid., p. 57.
[3] Ephemeridum Physico-medicarum, Leipzig, 1694, vol. 1, p. 49.
[4] Black, Folk-Medicine, p. 112.
[5] Black, Folk-Medicine, p. 112.
[6] Brand, Pop. Ant., vol. 2, p. 86.
[7] Black, Folk-Medicine, p. 38.
[8] Pliny, Nat. Hist., lib. 30, cap. 30.
[9] Ibid.

by a woman; and if the patient is a woman, then these good services being rendered by a man." [1]

A cord with nine knots in it, tied round the neck of a child suffering from whooping cough, was esteemed a sovereign remedy in Worcester, England, half a century ago.

Again, references will be found to the superstitious use of "liga tures" down to a comparatively recent period, and " I remember it was a custom in the north of England for boys that swam to wear an eel's skin about their naked leg to prevent the cramp." [2]

THE MEDICINE HAT.

The medicine hat of the old and blind Apache medicine-man, Nan-ta-do-tash, was an antique affair of buckskin, much begrimed with soot and soiled by long use. Nevertheless, it gave life and strength to him who wore it, enabled the owner to peer into the future, to tell who had stolen ponies from other people, to foresee the approach of an enemy, and to aid in the cure of the sick. This was its owner's own statement in conversation with me, but it would seem that the power residing in the helmet or hat was not very permanent, because when the old man discovered from his wife that I had made a rude drawing of it he became extremely excited and said that such a delineation would destroy all the life of the hat. His fears were allayed by presents of money and tobacco, as well as by some cakes and other food. As a measure of precaution, he insisted upon sprinkling pinches of hoddentin over myself, the hat, and the drawing of it, at the same time muttering various half-articulate prayers. He returned a month afterwards and demanded the sum of $30 for damage done to the hat by the drawing, since which time it has ceased to " work " when needed.

This same old man gave me an explanation of all the symbolism depicted upon the hat and a great deal of valuable information in regard to the profession of medicine-men, their specialization, the prayers they recited, etc. The material of the hat, as already stated, was buckskin. How that was obtained I can not assert positively, but from an incident occurring under my personal observation in the Sierra Madre in Mexico in 1883, where our Indian scouts and the medicine-men with them surrounded a nearly grown fawn and tried to capture it alive, as well as from other circumstances too long to be here inserted, I am of the opinion that the buckskin to be used for sacred purposes among the Apache must, whenever possible, be that of a strangled animal, as is the case, according to Dr. Matthews, among the Navajo.

The body of Nan-ta-do-tash's cap (Fig. 6, p. 53) was unpainted, but the figures upon it were in two colors, a brownish yellow and an earthy blue, resembling a dirty Prussian blue. The ornamentation was of the downy feathers and black-tipped plumes of the eagle, pieces of abalone shell, and chalchihuitl, and a snake's rattle on the apex.

---

[1] Black, Folk-Medicine, p. 111.
[2] Brand, Pop. Ant., vol. 3, pp. 288, 324.

Nan-ta-do-tash explained that the characters on the medicine hat meant: A, clouds; B, rainbow; C, hail; E, morning star; F, the God of Wind, with his lungs; G, the black "kan"; H, great stars or suns.

"Kan" is the name given to their principal gods. The appearance of the kan himself and of the tail of the hat suggest the centipede, an important animal god of the Apache. The old man said that the figures represented the powers to which he appealed for aid in his "medicine" and the kan upon whom he called for help. There were other doctors with other medicines, but he used none but those of which he was going to speak to me.

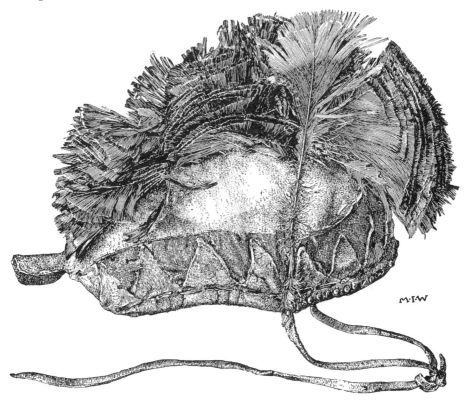

Fig. 12.—Apache war bonnet.

When an Apache or other medicine-man is in full regalia he ceases to be a man, but becomes, or tries to make his followers believe that he has become, the power he represents. I once heard this asserted in a very striking way while I was with a party of Apache young men who had led me to one of the sacred caves of their people, in which we came across a great quantity of ritualistic paraphernalia of all sorts.

"We used to stand down here," they said, "and look up to the top of the mountain and see the kan come down." This is precisely what the people living farther to the south told the early Spanish missionaries.

The Mexicans were wont to cry out "Here come our gods!" upon seeing their priests masked and disguised, and especially when they had donned the skins of the women offered up in sacrifice.[1]

The headdresses worn by the gods of the American Indians and the priests or medicine-men who served them were persistently called "miters" by the early Spanish writers. Thus Quetzalcoatl wore "en la cabeça una Mitra de papel puntiaguda."[2] When Father Felician Lopez went to preach to the Indians of Florida, in 1697, among other matters of record is one to the effect that "the chief medicine man called himself bishop."[3] Possibly this title was assumed because the medicine-men wore "miters."

Duran goes further than his fellows. In the headdress used at the spirit dances he recognizes the tiara. He says that the Mexican priests at the feast of Tezcatlipoca wore "en las cabezas tiaras hechas de barillas."[4] The ghost dance headdress illustrated in this paper (Fig. 13) is known to the Chiricahua Apache as the "ich-te," a contraction from "chas-a-i-wit-te," according to Ramon, the old medicine-man from whom

Fig. 13.—Ghost-dance headdress.

I obtained it. He explained all the symbolism connected with it. The round piece of tin in the center is the sun; the irregular arch underneath it is the rainbow. Stars and lightning are depicted on the side slats and under them; the parallelograms with serrated edges are clouds; the pendant green sticks are rain drops; there are snakes and snake heads on both horizontal and vertical slats, the heads in the former case being representative of hail.

There are feathers of the eagle to conciliate that powerful bird, turkey feathers to appeal to the mountain spirits, and white gull feathers for the spirits of the water. There are also small pieces of nacreous shells and one or two fragments of the "duklij," or chalchihuitl, without which no medicine-man would feel competent to discharge his functions.

The spirit dance itself is called "cha-ja-la." I have seen this dance a number of times, but will confine my description to one seen at Fort

---

[1] This fact is stated by Torquemada, Monarchia Indiana, lib. 10, cap. 33, and by Gomara, Hist. of the Conq. of Mexico, p. 446; see also Diego Duran, lib. 1, cap. 20, p. 226.

[2] Herrera, dec. 3, lib. 2, p. 67.

[3] John Gilmary Shea, The Catholic Church in Colonial Days, p. 472.

[4] Diego Duran, vol. 3, cap. 4, p. 217.

Marion (St. Augustine, Fla.), in 1887, when the Chiricahua Apache were confined there as prisoners; although the accompanying figure represents a ghost dance headdress seen among the Apache in the winter of 1885. A great many of the band had been suffering from sickness of one kind or another and twenty-three of the children had died; as a consequence, the medicine-men were having the Cha-ja-la, which is entered into only upon the most solemn occasions, such as the setting out of a war party, the appearance of an epidemic, or something else of like portent. On the terreplein of the northwest bastion, Ramon, the old medicine-man, was violently beating upon a drum, which, as usual, had been improvised of a soaped rag drawn tightly over the mouth of an iron kettle holding a little water.

Although acting as master of ceremonies, Ramon was not painted or decorated in any way. Three other medicine-men were having the finishing touches put to their bodily decoration. They had an under-coating of greenish brown, and on each arm a yellow snake, the head toward the shoulder blade. The snake on the arm of one of the party was double-headed, or rather had a head at each extremity.

Each had insignia in yellow on back and breast, but no two were exactly alike. One had on his breast a yellow bear, 4 inches long by 3 inches high, and on his back a kan of the same color and dimensions. A second had the same pattern of bear on his breast, but a zigzag for lightning on his back. The third had the zigzag on both back and breast. All wore kilts and moccasins.

While the painting was going on Ramon thumped and sang with vigor to insure the medicinal potency of the pigments and the designs to which they were applied. Each held, one in each hand, two wands or swords of lathlike proportions, ornamented with snake-lightning in blue.

The medicine-men emitted a peculiar whistling noise and bent slowly to the right, then to the left, then frontward, then backward, until the head in each case was level with the waist. Quickly they spun round in full circle on the left foot; back again in a reverse circle to the right; then they charged around the little group of tents in that bastion, making cuts and thrusts with their wands to drive the maleficent spirits away.

It recalled to my mind the old myths of the angel with the flaming sword guarding the entrance to Eden, or of St. Michael chasing the discomfited Lucifer down into the depths of Hell.

These preliminaries occupied a few moments only; at the end of that time the medicine-men advanced to where a squaw was holding up to them a little baby sick in its cradle. The mother remained kneeling while the medicine-men frantically struck at, upon, around, and over the cradle with their wooden weapons.

The baby was held so as successively to occupy each of the cardinal points and face each point directly opposite; first on the east side, facing the west; then the north side, facing the south; then the west side, facing the east; then the south side, facing the north, and back to the original position. While at each position, each of the medicine-men in succession, after making all the passes and gestures described, seized the cradle in his hands, pressed it to his breast, and afterwards lifted it up to the sky, next to the earth, and lastly to the four cardinal points, all the time prancing, whistling, and snorting, the mother and her squaw friends adding to the dismal din by piercing shrieks and ululations.

That ended the ceremonies for that night so far as the baby personally was concerned, but the medicine-men retired down to the parade and resumed their saltation, swinging, bending, and spinning with such violence that they resembled, in a faint way perhaps, the Dervishes of the East. The understanding was that the dance had to be kept up as long as there was any fuel unconsumed of the large pile provided; any other course would entail bad luck. It was continued for four nights, the colors and the symbols upon the bodies varying from night to night. Among the modes of exorcism enumerated by Burton, we find "cutting the air with swords."[1] Picart speaks of the "flèches ou les baguettes dont les Arabes Idolâtres se servoient pour deviner par le sort." He says that the diviner "tenoit à la main" these arrows, which certainly suggest the swords or wands of the Apache medicine-men in the spirit dance.[2]

There were four medicine-men, three of whom were dancing and in conference with the spirits, and the fourth of whom was general superintendent of the whole dance, and the authority to whom the first three reported the result of their interviews with the ghostly powers.

The mask and headdress of the first of the dancers, who seemed to be the leading one, was so elaborate that in the hurry and meager light supplied by the flickering fires it could not be portrayed. It was very much like that of number three, but so fully covered with the plumage of the eagle, hawk, and, apparently, the owl, that it was difficult to assert this positively. Each of these medicine-men had pieces of red flannel tied to his elbows and a stick about four feet long in each hand. Number one's mask was spotted black and white and shaped in front like the snout of a mountain lion. His back was painted with large arrowheads in brown and white, which recalled the protecting arrows tightly bound to the backs of Zuñi fetiches. Number two had on his back a figure in white ending between the shoulders in a cross. Number three's back was simply whitened with clay.

All these headdresses were made of slats of the Spanish bayonet, unpainted, excepting that on number two was a figure in black, which could not be made out, and that the horizontal crosspieces on number three were painted blue.

The dominos or masks were of blackened buckskin, for the two fastened around the neck by garters or sashes; the neckpiece of number three was painted red; the eyes seemed to be glass knobs or brass

[1] Anatomy of Melancholy, London, 1827, vol. 1, p. 337.
[2] Picart, Cérémonies et Coûtumes, etc., Amsterdam, 1729, vol. 5, p. 50.

buttons. These three dancers were naked to the waist, and wore beautiful kilts of fringed buckskin bound on with sashes, and moccasins reaching to the knees. In this guise they jumped into the center of the great circle of spectators and singers and began running about the fire shrieking and muttering, encouraged by the shouts and the singing, and by the drumming and incantation of the chorus which now swelled forth at full lung power.

THE SPIRIT OR GHOST DANCE HEADDRESS.

As the volume of music swelled and the cries of the on-lookers became fiercer, the dancers were encouraged to the enthusiasm of frenzy. They darted about the circle, going through the motions of looking for an enemy, all the while muttering, mumbling, and singing, jumping, swaying, and whirling like the dancing Dervishes of Arabia.

Their actions, at times, bore a very considerable resemblance to the movements of the Zuñi Shálako at the Feast of Fire. Klashidn told me that the orchestra was singing to the four willow branches planted near them. This would indicate a vestige of tree worship, such as is to be noticed also at the sun dance of the Sioux.

At intervals, the three dancers would dart out of the ring and disappear in the darkness, to consult with the spirits or with other medicine-men seated a considerable distance from the throng. Three several times they appeared and disappeared, always dancing, running, and whirling about with increased energy. Having attained the degree of mental or spiritual exaltation necessary for communion with the spirits, they took their departure and kept away for at least half an hour, the orchestra during their absence rendering a mournful refrain, monotonous as a funeral dirge. My patience became exhausted and I turned to go to my quarters. A thrill of excited expectancy ran through the throng of Indians, and I saw that they were looking anxiously at the returning medicine-men. All the orchestra now stood up, their leader (the principal medicine-man) slightly in advance, holding a branch of cedar in his left hand. The first advanced and bending low his head murmured some words of unknown import with which the chief seemed to be greatly pleased. Then the chief, taking his stand in front of the orchestra on the east side of the grove or cluster of trees, awaited the final ceremony, which was as follows: The three dancers in file and in proper order advanced and receded three times; then they embraced the chief in such a manner that the sticks or wands held in their hands came behind his neck, after which they mumbled and muttered a jumble of sounds which I can not reproduce, but which sounded for all the world like the chant of the "hooter" at the Zuñi Feast of Fire. They then pranced or danced through the grove three times. This was repeated for each point of the compass, the chief medicine-man, with the orchestra, taking a position successively on the east, south, west, and north and the three dancers advancing, receding, and embracing as at first.

This terminated the "medicine" ceremonies of the evening, the glad shouts of the Apache testifying that the incantations of their spiritual leaders or their necromancy, whichever it was, promised a successful

Fig. 14.—Apache kan or gods.　(Drawn by Apache.)

campaign. These dancers were, I believe, dressed up to represent their gods or kan, but not content with representing them aspired to be mistaken for them.

Plate III

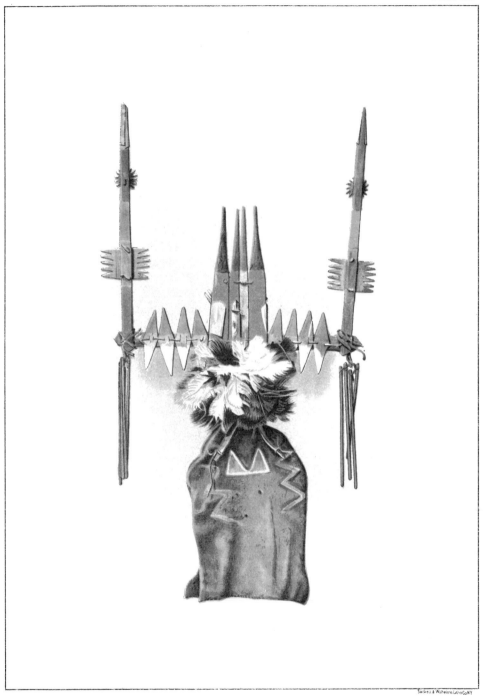

APACHE MEDICINE HAT USED IN GHOST DANCE.

AMULETS AND TALISMANS.

THE "TZI-DALTAI."

The Apache, both men and women, wear amulets, called tzi-daltai, made of lightning-riven wood, generally pine or cedar or fir from the mountain tops, which are highly valued and are not to be sold. These are shaved very thin and rudely cut in the semblance of the human form. They are in fact the duplicates, on a small scale, of the rhombus, already described. Like the rhombus, they are decorated with incised lines representing the lightning. Very often these are to be found attached to the necks of children or to their cradles. Gen-

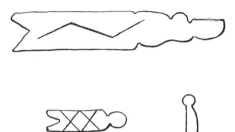

Fig. 15.—Tzi-daltai amulet (Apache).

erally these amulets are of small size. Below will be found figures of those which I was permitted to examine and depict in their actual size. They are all unpainted. The amulet represented was obtained from a Chiricahua Apache captive. Deguele, an Apache of the Klukaydakaydn clan, consented to exhibit a kan, or god, which he carried about his person. He said I could have it for three ponies. It was made of a flat piece of lath, unpainted, of the size here given, having drawn upon it this figure in yellow, with a narrow black band, excepting the three snake heads, a, b, and c, which were black with white eyes; a was a yellow line and c a black line; flat pearl buttons were fastened at m and k respectively and small eagle-down feathers at k on each side of the idol. The rear of the tablet, amulet, or idol, as one may be pleased to call it, was almost an exact reproduction of the front.

The owner of this inestimable treasure assured me that he prayed to it at all times when in trouble, that he could learn from it where his ponies were when stolen and which was the right direction to travel when lost, and that when drought had parched his crops this would never fail to bring rain in abundance to revive and strengthen them. The symbolism is the rain cloud and the serpent lightning, the rainbow, rain drops, and the cross of the four winds.

These small amulets are also to be found inclosed in the phylacteries (Fig. 19) which the medicine-men wear suspended from their necks or waists.

Sir Walter Scott, who was a very good witness in all that related to prehistoric customs and "survivals" among the Celtic Scots, may be introduced at this point:

> A heap of wither'd boughs was piled
> Of juniper and rowan wild,
> Mingled with shivers from the oak,
> Rent by the lightning's recent stroke.[1]

---

[1] Lady of the Lake, canto 3, stanza 4, Sir Rhoderick Dhu, summoning Clan Alpine against the king.

CHALCHIHUITL.

The articles of dress depicted in this paper are believed to represent all those which exclusively belong to the office of the Apache "diyi" or "izze-nantan." Of late years it can not be said that every medicine-man has all these articles, but most of them will be found in the possession of the man in full practice.

No matter what the medicine-man may lack, he will, if it be possible, provide himself with some of the impure malachite known to the whites of the Southwest as turquoise. In the malachite veins the latter stone

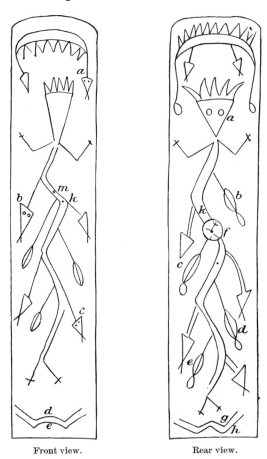

Front view.   Rear view.

Fig. 16.—Tzi-daltai amulet (Apache).

is sometimes found and is often of good quality, but the difference between the two is apparent upon the slightest examination. The color of the malachite is a pea green, that of the turquoise a pale sky blue. The chemical composition of the former is a carbonate of copper, mixed with earthy impurities; that of the latter, a phosphate of alumina, colored with the oxide of copper. The use of this malachite was widespread. Under the name of chalchihuitl or chalchihuite, it appears with fre-

Plate IV

APACHE MEDICINE SHIRT.

Plate V

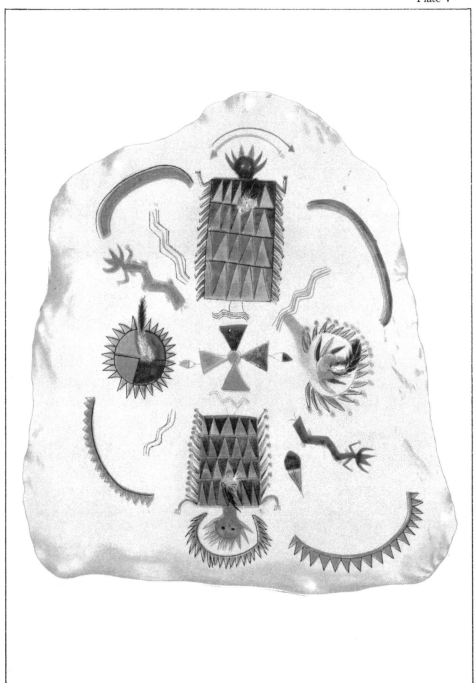

APACHE MEDICINE SHIRT.

quency in the old Spanish writings, as we shall presently see, and was in all places and by all tribes possessing it revered in much the same manner as by the Apache. The Apache call it duklij, "blue (or green) stone," these two colors not being differentiated in their language. A small bead of this mineral affixed to a gun or bow made the weapon shoot accurately. It had also some relation to the bringing of rain, and could be found by the man who would go to the end of a rainbow, after a storm, and hunt diligently in the damp earth. It was the Apache medicine-man's badge of office, his medical diploma, so to speak, and without it he could not in olden times exercise his medical functions.

Front view.   Rear view.

FIG. 17.—Tzi-daltai amulet (Apache).

In the curious commerce of the Indian tribes, some possessed articles of greater worth than those belonging to their neighbors. In the southwest the red paint sold by the tribes living in the Grand Canyon of the Colorado was held in higher repute than any other, and the green stone to be purchased from the Rio Grande Pueblos always was in great demand, as it is to this day. Vetancurt[1] speaks of the Apache, between the years 1630 and 1680, coming to the pueblo of Pecos to trade for "chalchihuites." John de Laet speaks of "petites pierres verdes" worn in the lower lip by the Brazilians.[2]

Among the Mexicans the chalchihuitl seems to have been the distinguishing mark or badge of the priesthood. Duran, in speaking of the consecration of a sacrificial stone in Mexico by Montezuma the elder, and his assistant or coadjutor, Tlacaclel, says: "Echáronse á las espaldas unas olletas [I do not know what this word means] hechas de piedras verdes

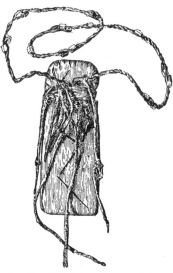

FIG. 18.—Tzi-daltai amulet (Apache).

muy ricas, donde significaban que no solamente eran Reyes, pero juntamente Sacerdotes."[3]

Among the tribes in Central America, a chalchihuitl was placed in

---

[1] Teatro Mexicano, vol. 3, p. 323.   [2] Lib. 14, cap. 4, and lib. 16, cap. 16.   [3] Lib. 1, cap. 23, pp. 251–252.

the mouths of the dying to receive their souls: "que era para que recibiese su ánima."[1]

One of the Mexican myths of the birth of Quetzalcoatl narrates that his mother, Chimalma, while sweeping, found a chalchihuitl, swallowed it, and became pregnant: "Andando barriendo la dicha Chimalma halló un chalchihuitl, (que es una pedrezuela verde) y que la tragó y de esto se empreñó, y que así parió al dicho Quetzalcoatl."[2] The same author tells us that the chalchihuitl (which he calls "pedrezuela verde") are mentioned in the earliest myths of the Mexicans.[3]

In South America the emerald seems to have taken the place of the chalchihuitl. Bollaert[4] makes frequent mention of the use of the emerald by the natives of Ecuador and Peru, "a drilled emerald, such as the Incas wore;" "large emeralds, emblematic of their [the Incas'] sovereignty."

From Torquemada we learn that the Mexicans adorned their idols with the chalchihuitl, and also that they buried a chalchihuitl with their dead, saying that it was the dead man's heart.[5]

"Whenever rain comes the Indians [Pima and Maricopa] resort to these old houses [ruins] to look for trinkets of shells, and a peculiar green stone."[6] The idols which the people of Yucatan gave to Juan de Grijalva in 1518 were covered with these stones, "cubierta de pedrecicas."[7] Among the first presents made to Cortes in Tabasco were "unas turquesas de poco valor."[8] The fact that the Mexicans buried a "gem" with the bodies of their dead is mentioned by Squier, but he says it was when the body was cremated.[9]

The people of Cibola are said to have offered in sacrifice to their fountains "algunas turquesas que las tienen, aunque ruines."[10]

"Turquesas" were given to the Spaniards under Coronado by the people of the pueblo of Acoma.[11]

"The Mexicans were accustomed to say that at one time all men have been stones, and that at last they would all return to stones; and, acting literally on this conviction, they interred with the bones of the dead a small green stone, which was called the principle of life."[12]

The great value set upon the chalchihuitl by the Aztecs is alluded to by Bernal Diaz, who was with the expedition of Grijalva to Yucatan

---

[1] Ximenez, Hist. Orig. Indios, p. 211.
[2] Mendieta, p. 83.
[3] Ibid., p. 78.
[4] Researches in South America, p. 83.
[5] Monarchia Indiana, vol. 2, lib. 13, cap. 45, and elsewhere.
[6] Emory, Reconnoissance, p. 88.
[7] Gomara, Historia de la Conquista de Méjico, Veytia's edition, p. 299.
[8] Ibid., p. 310.
[9] Smithsonian Contributions, "Ancient monuments of New York," vol. 2.
[10] Buckingham Smith, Relacion de la Jornada de Coronado á Cibola, Coleccion de Documentos para la Historia de Florida, London, 1857, vol. 1, p. 148.
[11] Ibid., vol. 1, p. 150.
[12] Brinton, Myths of the New World, p. 253.

before he joined that of Cortes to Mexico.[1] Diaz says that Montezuma sent to Charles V, as a present "a few chalchihuis of such enormous value that I would not consent to give them to any one save to such a powerful emperor as yours."[2] These stones were put "in the mouth of the distinguished chiefs who died."[3]

Torquemada[4] repeats the Aztec myth already given from Mendieta. He says that in 1537 Fray Antonio de Ciudad-Rodrigo, provincial of the Franciscans, sent friars of his order to various parts of the Indian country; in 1538 he sent them to the north, to a country where they heard of a tribe of people wearing clothes and having many turquoises.[5] The Aztec priesthood adopted green as the sacred color. The ceremony of their consecration ended thus: "puis on l'habillait tout en vert."[6]

Maximilian, Prince of Wied, saw some of the Piegans of northwestern Montana "hang round their necks a green stone, often of various shapes." He describes it as "a compact talc or steatite which is found in the Rocky Mountains."[7]

PHYLACTERIES.

The term phylactery, as herein employed, means any piece of buckskin or other material upon which are inscribed certain characters or symbols of a religious or "medicine" nature, which slip or phylactery is to be worn attached to the person seeking to be benefited by it, and this phylactery differs from the amulet or talisman in being concealed from the scrutiny of the profane and kept as secret as possible. This phylactery, itself "medicine," may be employed to enwrap other "medicine" and thus augment its own potentiality. Indians in general object to having their "medicine" scrutinized and touched; in this there is a wide margin of individual opinion; but in regard to phylacteries there is none that I have been able to discover, and the rule may be given as antagonistic to the display of these sacred "relics," as my Mexican captive interpreter persisted in calling them.

The first phylactery which it was my good fortune to be allowed to examine was one worn by Ta-ul-tzu-je, of the Kaytzentin gens. It was tightly rolled in at least half a mile of orange-colored saddlers' silk, obtained from some of the cavalry posts. After being duly uncovered, it was found to be a small piece of buckskin two inches square, upon which were drawn red and yellow crooked lines which the Apache said represented the red and yellow snake. Inside were a piece of green chalchihuitl and a small cross of lightning-riven twig (pine) and two very small perforated shells. The cross was called "intchi-dijin," the black wind.

A second phylactery which I was also allowed to untie and examine

[1] London, 1844, vol. 1, pp. 26, 29, 36, 93.
[2] Ibid., p. 278.
[3] Ibid., vol. 2, p. 389.
[4] Monarchia Indiana, lib. 6, cap. 45, p. 80.
[5] Ibid., lib. 19, cap. 22. pp. 357–358.
[6] Ternaux-Compans, vol. 10, p. 240.
[7] London, 1843, p. 248.

belonged to Na-a-cha and consisted of a piece of buckskin of the same size as the other, but either on account of age or for some other reason no characters could be discerned upon it. It, however, enwrapped a tiny bag of hoddentin, which, in its turn, held a small but very clear crystal of quartz and four feathers of eagle down. Na-a-cha took care to explain very earnestly that this phylactery contained not merely the "medicine" or power of the crystal, the hoddentin, and the itza-chu, or eagle, but also of the shoz-dijiji, or black bear, the shoz-lekay, or

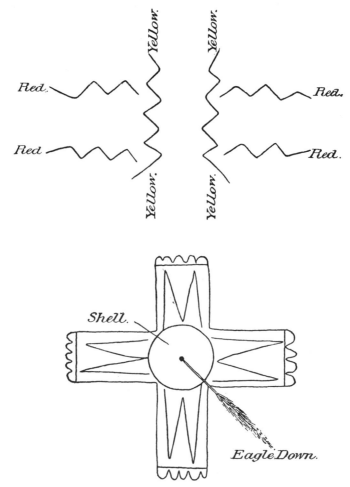

Fig. 19.—Phylacteries.

white bear, the shoz-litzogue, or yellow bear, and the ʞlij-litzogue or yellow snake, though just in what manner he could not explain.

It would take up too much time and space to describe the manner in which it was necessary for me to proceed in order to obtain merely a glimpse of these and other phylacteries, all of the same general type; how I had to make it evident that I was myself possessed of great "medicine" power and able to give presents of great "medicine" value,

Plate VI

APACHE MEDICINE SHIRT.

as was the case. I had obtained from cliff dwellings, sacred caves, and other places beads of talc, of chalchihuitl, and of shell, pieces of crystal and other things, sacred in the eyes of the Apache, and these I was compelled to barter for the information here given.

The medicine shirts of the Apaches, several of which are here represented, do not require an extended description. The symbolism is different for each one, but may be generalized as typical of the sun, moon, stars, rainbow, lightning, snake, clouds, rain, hail, tarantula, centipede, snake, and some one or more of the " kan " or gods.

The medicine sashes follow closely in pattern the medicine shirts, being smaller in size only, but with the same symbolic decoration. Similar ornamentation will be found upon the amulets (ditzi), made of lightning-struck pine or other wood. All of these are warranted, among other virtues, to screen the wearer from the arrows, lances, or bullets of the enemy. In this they strongly resemble the salves and other means by which people in Europe sought to obtain " magical impenetrability." The last writer to give receipts for making such salves, etc., that I can recall, was Etmüller, who wrote in the early years of the seventeenth century.

FIG. 20.—Apache medicine sash.

Such as the reader can imagine the medicine-man to be from this description of his paraphernalia, such he has been since the white man first landed in America. Never desirous of winning proselytes to his own ideas, he has held on to those ideas with a tenacity never suspected until purposely investigated. The first of the Spanish writers seem to have employed the native terms for the medicine-men, and we come across them as cemis or zemis, bohiti, pachuaci, and others; but soon they were recognized as the emissaries of Satan and the preachers of witchcraft, and henceforth they appear in the documents as " hechicheros" and " brujos" almost exclusively. " Tienan los Apaches profetas ó adivinos que gozan de la mas alta estimacion. Esos adivinos pratican la medicina la mas rudimental, la aplicacion de algunas yerbas y esto acompañado de ceremonias y cantos supersticiosos."[1] Pimentel seems to have derived his information from Cordero, a Spanish officer who had served against the Apache at various times between 1770 and 1795, and seemed to understand them well.

"There was no class of persons who so widely and deeply influenced the culture and shaped the destiny of the Indian tribes as their priests. In attempting to gain a true conception of the race's capacities and

---

[1] Pimentel, Lenguas Indígenas de México, vol. 3, pp. 498, 499.

history there is no one element of their social life which demands closer attention than the power of these teachers. . . . However much we may deplore the use they made of their skill, we must estimate it fairly and grant it its due weight in measuring the influence of the religious sentiment on the history of man."[1]

"Like Old Men of the Sea, they have clung to the neck of their nations, throttling all attempts at progress, binding them to the thraldom of superstition and profligacy, dragging them down to wretchedness and death. Christianity and civilization meet in them their most determined, most implacable foes."[2]

In spite of all the zeal and vigilance of the Spanish friars, supported by military power, the Indians of Bogotá clung to their idolatry. Padre Simon cites several instances and says tersely: "De manera que no lo hay del Indio que parece mas Cristiano y ladino, de que no tenga ídolos á quien adore, como nos lo dice cada dia la experiencia." (So that there is no Indian, no matter how well educated he may appear in our language and the Christian doctrine, who has not idols which he adores, as experience teaches us every day.)[3]

"The Indian doctor relied far more on magic than on natural remedies. Dreams, beating of the drum, songs, magic feasts and dances, and howling to frighten the female demon from the patient, were his ordinary methods of cure."[4]

In a very rare work by Padre José de Arriaga, published in Lima, 1621, it is shown that the Indians among whom this priest was sent on a special tour of investigation were still practicing their old idolatrous rites in secret. This work may be found quoted in Montesinos, Mémoires sur l'Ancien Pérou, in Ternaux-Compans, Voyages, vol. 17; the title of Arriaga's work is Extirpacion de la Idolatría de los Indios del Peru. Arriaga also states that the functions of the priesthood were exercised by both sexes.

It will only be after we have thoroughly routed the medicine-men from their intrenchments and made them an object of ridicule that we can hope to bend and train the mind of our Indian wards in the direction of civilization. In my own opinion, the reduction of the medicine-men will effect more for the savages than the giving of land in severalty or instruction in the schools at Carlisle and Hampton; rather, the latter should be conducted with this great object mainly in view: to let pupils insensibly absorb such knowledge as may soonest and most completely convince them of the impotency of the charlatans who hold the tribes in bondage.

Teach the scholars at Carlisle and Hampton some of the wonders of electricity, magnetism, chemistry, the spectroscope, magic lantern,

---

[1] Brinton, Myths of the New World, pp. 285, 286.
[2] Ibid., p. 264.
[3] Kingsborough, vol. 8, sup., p. 249.
[4] Parkman, Jesuits, introduction, p. lxxxiv.

ventriloquism, music, and then, when they return to their own people, each will despise the fraud of the medicine-men and be a focus of growing antagonism to their pretensions. Teach them to love their own people and not to despise them; but impress upon each one that he is to return as a missionary of civilization. Let them see that the world is free to the civilized, that law is liberty.

BIBLIOGRAPHY.

Acosta, José.
Histoire naturelle et moralle des Indes, tant Orientalles qu'Occidentalles. . . Composée en Castillian par Ioseph Acosta, & traduit en François par Robert Regnault Cauxois. Paris: 1600.

Adair, James.
History of the American Indians. London: 1775.

Adventure and Beagle.
Narrative of the surveying voyages of his majesty's ships *Adventure* and *Beagle*. Vols. I–III. London: 1839.

Alegre, Francisco Javier.
Historia de la compañia de Jesus en Nueva-España. Vols. I–III. Mexico: 1841–'42.

Arriaga, José de.
Extirpacion de la idolatría de los Indios del Peru. Lima: 1621.

Asiatick Researches or transactions of the society instituted in Bengal, etc. Vols. VII and VIII. Calcutta: 1801–'05.

Backus, E.
An account of the Navajo of New Mexico. (In Schoolcraft, Indian Tribes, IV, pp. 209–215, Philadelphia: 1854.)

Baegert, Jacob.
An account of the aboriginal inhabitants of the Californian peninsula. (In Smithsonian Reports for 1863 and 1864, Washington: 1864–'65.)

Baker, Frank.
Anthropological notes on the human hand. (In American Anthropologist, I, pp. 51–75, Washington: January, 1888.)

Baker, Samuel W.
The Albert N'yanza, great basin of the Nile, and explorations of the Nile sources. Vols. I–II. London: 1866. Ibid., Philadelphia: 1869.

Balboa, Miguel C.
Histoire du Pérou. (Forms Vol. XV of Ternaux-Compans, Voyages, Paris: 1840.)

Bancroft, Hubert H.
Native Races. Vols. I–V. San Francisco: 1882.

Barcia, Gabriel de Cardenas de.
Ensayo cronologico, para la historia general de la Florida. (Forms part II of Garcilaso de la Vega's La Florida del Inca.) Madrid: 1723.

Beckherius, Daniel.
Medicus microcosmus. London: 1660.

Benjamin, G. W.
Persia. London: 1877.

Benzoni, Girolamo.
History of the New World. Now first translated and edited by Rear-Admiral W. H. Smyth. (Forms Hakluyt Society's Works, vol. 21, London: 1857.)

Black, William G.
Folk-medicine; a chapter in the history of culture. London: 1883.

Blount, Thomas.
Tenures of land and customs of manors. London: 1874.

Bock, Carl.
The head-hunters of Borneo. London: 1881.

Bogle, George.
See Markham, Clements R.

Bollaert, William.
Antiquarian, ethnological and other researches in New Granada, Ecuador, Peru and Chile. London: 1860.

Boscana, Geronimo.
Chinigchinich. (In Robinson, Life in California, New York: 1846.)

Bourke, John G.
Snake dance of the Moquis of Arizona. New York: 1884.

Bourke, John G.
Scatalogic rites of all nations. Washington: 1891.

Brand, John.
Observations on the popular antiquities of Great Britain. Vols. I–III. London: 1882–'83.

Brasseur de Bourbourg.
Histoire des nations civilisées du Mexique et de l'Amérique Centrale. Vols. I–IV. Paris: 1857–'59.

Brasseur de Bourbourg.
See Popol Vuh.

Brinton, Daniel G.
Myths of the New World. New York: 1868.

Browne, Thomas.
Religio medici. (In Vol. II of his works.) London: 1835.

Bruce, James.
Travels to discover the source of the Nile, in the years 1768–1773. Vol. III. Dublin: 1791.

Buckle, Henry Thomas.
Wise and posthumous works of. Vol. II. Common place books. London: 1872.

Burton, Richard F.
A mission to Gelele, king of Dahome. Vols.
I–II. London: 1864.

Burton, Richard F.
A plain and literal translation of the Arabian
nights' entertainments, now entitled the
book of the thousand nights and a night.
Vol. VIII. London: [1886.]

Burton, Robert.
The anatomy of melancholy, what it is, with
all the kinds, causes, symptoms, prog-
nostics, and several cures of it. By De-
mocritus Junior. Vols. I–II. London:
1827.

Cabeza de Vaca, Alvar Nuñez.
Relation et naufrages; Valladolid, 1555. (In
Vol. VII of Ternaux-Compans, Voyages.
Paris: 1837.)

Cabeza de Vaca, Alvar Nuñez.
See Smith, Buckingham.

Cameron, Verney L.
Across Africa. Vols. I–II. London: 1877.

Campbell, Archibald.
A voyage round the world, from 1806 to 1812.
Second American edition. New York:
1819.

Catlin, George.
Illustrations of the manners, customs, and
condition of the North American Indians.
Vols. I–II. London: 1845.

Catlin, George.
O-kee-pa: A religious ceremony, and other
customs of the Mandans. Philadelphia:
1867.

Charlevoix, Pierre F. X. de.
History and general description of New
France. Translated, with notes, by John
Gilmary Shea. Vol. IV. New York: 1870.

Clavigero, Francisco Saverio.
History of Mexico. Translated by Charles
Cullen. Vols. I–III. Philadelphia: 1817.

Cockayne, Oswald.
Leechdoms, wortcunning, and starcraft of
early England. Vol. I. London: 1864.

Coleccion de documentos inéditos, relativos al
descubrimiento, conquista y organizacion
de las antiguas posesiones Españolas de
América y Oceanía. Vol. XIV. Madrid:
1870.

Coleman, Charles.
Mythology of the Hindus. London: 1832.

Columbus, Christopher.
Select letters of. Translated and edited by R.
H. Major. (Forms Vol. II of Hakluyt
Society's Works, London: 1847.)

Corbusier, William F.
The Apache-Yumas and Apache-Mohaves.
(In American Antiquarian, Chicago:
September and November, 1886.)

Coxe, William.
Account of Russian discoveries between Asia
and America. London: 1803.

Crantz, David.
The history of Greenland: containing a
description of the country, and its inhabitants. Vols. I–II. London: 1767.

Crónica seráfica y apostólica. Espinosa (Mexico):
1746.

Cushing, Frank H.
A study of Pueblo pottery as illustrative of
Zuñi culture growth. (In Ann. Rep. Bu.
Ethnology, 1882–'83, pp. 467–521, Washing-
ton: 1886.)

Dall, William H.
Masks, labrets, and certain aboriginal customs. (In Ann. Rep. Bu. of Ethnology,
1881–'82, Washington: 1884.)

Davis, T. W. Rhys.
See Hibbert Lectures, 1881.

Davis, W. W. H.
Spanish conquest of New Mexico. Doyles-
town (Pa.): 1869.

Deane, J. B.
Serpent worship. London: 1833.

Delano, Amasa.
Voyage. Boston: 1847.

Dennys, N. B.
The folk-lore of China, and its affinities with
that of the Aryan and Semitic races. London and Hongkong: 1876.

Diaz del Castillo, Bernal.
The memoirs of. Written by himself, con-
taining a true and full account of the dis-
covery and conquest of Mexico and New
Spain. Translated by John I. Lockhart.
Vols. I–II. London: 1844.

Dillon, P.
Narrative and successful result of a voyage in
the south seas to ascertain the actual fate
of La Perouse's expedition. Vols. I–II.
London: 1829.

Dobrizhoffer, Martin.
An account of the Abipones, an equestrian
people of Paraguay. Vol. I–III. London:
1822.

Dodge, Richard I.
Our wild Indians: thirty-three years' personal
experience among the red men of the great
West. Hartford (Conn.): 1882.

Domenech, Em.
Seven years' residence in the great deserts of
North America. Vols. I–II. London: 1860.

Dorman, Rushton M.
Origin of primitive superstitions. Philadelphia: 1881.

Dubois, J. A.
Description of the character, manners, and
customs of the people of India. London:
1817.

Du Cange, Charles du F.
Glossarium ad scriptores mediæ et infimæ
Latinitatis. Vols. I–VI. Paris: 1733.

Du Halde, P.
The general history of China. Containing a
geographical, historical, chronological,
political, and physical description of the
empire of China, Chinese-Tartary, Corea,
and Thibet. Vols. I, II, IV. London: 1836.

Dulaure, J. A.
Histoire abrégée de différens cultes. Vols. I–
II. Paris: 1825.

Dupuis.
Origine de tous le cultes, ou religion universelle. Vols. I–II. Paris: [N. D.].

Duran, Diego.
Historia antigua de la Nueva España con noticias de los ritos y costumbres de los Yndios y esplicacion del calendario Mexicano. Escrita en el año de 1585. Vols. I–III. Manuscript in the Library of Congress at Washington.

Eastman, Mary H.
Dacotah; or, life and legends of the Sioux around Fort Snelling. New York: 1849.

Emerson, Ellen R.
Indian myths or legends, traditions, and symbols of the aborigines of America. Boston: 1884.

Emory, William H.
Notes of a military reconnoissance from Fort Leavenworth, in Missouri, to San Diego, in California. (Senate ex. doc. 7; 30th cong., 1st sess.) Washington: 1848.

Etmuller, Michael.
Opera omnia. Lyons: 1690.

Eye, J. L. August von.
See Iconographic Encyclopædia.

Fernandez, Alonso.
Historia eclesiastica de nuestros tiempos. Toledo: 1611.

Flemming, Samuel Augustus.
De remediis ex corpore humano desumtis. Erfurt: 1738.

Fletcher, Robert.
On prehistoric trephining and cranial amulets. (In Contributions to North American Ethnology. Vol. V, Washington: 1882.)

Forlong, J. G. R.
Rivers of life, or the sources and streams of the faiths of man in all lands. Vols. I–II and chart. London: 1883.

Forster, George.
A voyage round the world, in his Britannic majesty's sloop *Resolution*. Vols. I–II. London: 1777.

Fosbrooke, Thomas Dudley.
British monachism; or, manners and customs of the monks and nuns of England. London: 1817.

Franklin, John.
Narrative of a second expedition to the shores of the Polar sea, in the years 1825, 1826, and 1827. London: 1828.

Fraser, John.
The aborigines of Australia: their ethnic position and relations. (In Jour. of Trans. of Victoria Institute, vol. XXII, pp. 154–186, London: 1889.)

Frazer, J. G.
Totemism. Edinburg: 1887.

French, B. F.
Historical collections of Louisiana. Compiled with historical and biographical notes by B. F. French, part 1—Historical documents from 1678 to 1691. New York: 1846.

Freycinet, Louis C. D. de.
Voyage round the world. London: 1823.

Frommann, Johannes Christianus.
Tractatus de fascinatione. Nuremberg: 1675.

Gabb, William M.
On the Indian tribes and languages of Costa Rica. (In Proc. Am. Philos. Soc., vol. XIV, pp. 483–602, Philadelphia: 1876.)

Gage, Thomas.
The English-American, his travail by sea and land: or, a new survey of the West-Indies. London: 1648.

Gallatin, Albert.
Notes on the semicivilized nations of Mexico, Yucatan, and Central America. (In Trans. Am. Ethnological Soc., vol. I, New York: 1845.)

Gatschet, Albert S.
Migration legend of the Creek Indians. Vol. I, Philadelphia: 1884. Vol. II, St. Louis: 1888.

Gayarre, Charles.
Louisiana: its colonial history and romance. New York: 1851.

Gilmour, James.
Among the Mongols. London: 1883.

Gomara, Francisco L. de.
Historia general de las Indias. (In Vedia, Historiadores primitivos de Indias, vol. I, pp. 157–294, Madrid: 1852.)

Gomara, Francisco L. de.
Conquista de Méjico. Segunda parte de la crónica general de las Indias. (In ibid., pp. 295–455.)

Gore, J. Howard.
Tuckahoe, or Indian bread. (In Smithsonian Institution Ann. Rep. for 1881, Washington: 1883.)

Gregg, Josiah.
Commerce of the prairies. Vols. I–II. New York and London: 1844.

Grimm, Jacob.
Teutonic mythology. Translated from the fourth edition, with notes and appendix by James Steven Sallybrass. Vols. I–IV. London: 1880–'88.

Grinnell, Fordyce.
The healing art as practiced by the Indians of the plains.

Grossman, F. E.
The Pima Indians of Arizona. (In Smithsonian Institution Ann. Rep. for 1871, pp. 407–419, Washington: 1873.)

Gubernatis, Angelo de.
Zoological mythology or the legends of animals. Vols. I–II. London: 1872.

Gumilla, Joseph.
El Orinoco ilustrado, historia natural, civil, y geographica, de este gran rio. Madrid: 1741.

Hakluyt, Richard.
Collection of the early voyages, travels, and discoveries of the English nation. Vols. III and V. London: 1810–'12.

Hakluyt Society.
Works. London: Vol. II, 1847; vol. XVI, 1854; vol. XXI, 1857; vol. XLI, 1869; vol. XLVIII, 1873.

Harmon, Daniel W.
Journal of voyages and travels in the interiour of North America. Andover: 1820.

Harris, W. Cornwallis.
The highlands of Æthiopia. Vols. I–III. London: 1844.

Hatch, Edwin.
See Hibbert Lectures, 1888.

Hawkesworth, John.
An account of the voyages undertaken by the order of his present majesty for making discoveries in the southern hemisphere. Vols. I–III. London: 1773.

Heath, Perry S.
A Hoosier in Russia. New York: 1888.

Henderson, John G.
Aboriginal remains near Naples, Illinois. (In Smithsonian Institution Ann. Rep. for 1882, Washington: 1884.)

Hennepin, Louis.
See French, B. F.

Herrera, Antonio de.
Historia general de los hechos de los Castellanos en las islas i tierra firme del mar Oceano. Vols. I–V. Madrid: 1726–'30.

Hibbert Lectures, 1879.
On the origin and growth of religion as illustrated by the religion of ancient Egypt, by P. Le Page Renouf. London: 1880.

Hibbert Lectures, 1881.
On the origin and growth of religion as illustrated by some points in the history of Indian Buddhism, by T. W. Rhys Davis. New York: 1882.

Hibbert Lectures, 1888.
The influence of Greek ideas and usages upon the Christian church, by Edwin Hatch. London: 1890.

Higgins, Godfrey.
Anacalypsis, an attempt to draw aside the veil of the Saitic Isis. Vol. I–II. London: 1836.

Hind, Henry Youle.
Narrative of the Canadian Red River exploring expedition of 1857 and of the Assiniboine and Saskatchewan exploring expedition of 1858. Vols. I–II. London: 1860.

Hoffman, Walter J.
Folk-lore of the Pennsylvania Germans. (In Jour. of Am. Folk-Lore, .vol. I, No. 2, Boston: 1888.)

Hone, William.
Every-day book and table book. Vol. II. London: 1838.

Humboldt, Alexander de.
Researches concerning the institutions and monuments of the ancient inhabitants of America. Translated by Helen Maria Williams. Vol. I. London: 1814.

Icazbalceta, Joaquin G.
See Mendieta, Gerónimo de.

Iconographic Encyclopædia.
Prehistoric archæology by Daniel G. Brinton. History of culture translated from the German of Dr. J. L. August von Eye. Vol. II. Philadelphia: 1886.

Inman, Thomas.
Ancient faiths embodied in ancient names: or an attempt to trace the religious belief, sacred rites, and holy emblems of certain nations. Vols. I–II. London and Liverpool: 1868–'69.

James, Edwin.
See Tanner, John.

Jarvis, Samuel F.
Discourse on the religion of the Indian tribes of North America. (In Collections of N. Y. Hist. Soc. for 1821, vol. III, New York: 1821.)

Joutel.
See French, B. F.

Kane, Paul.
Wanderings of an artist among the Indians of North America. London: 1859.

Kelly, Fanny.
Narrative of my captivity among the Sioux Indians. Cincinnati: 1871.

Kennon, George.
Tent life in Siberia. New York and London: 1888.

King, Edward (Lord Kingsborough).
Antiquities of Mexico: comprising facsimiles of ancient Mexican paintings and hieroglyphics. Vols. I–IX. London: 1831–'48.

King, P. P. (and others).
Narrative of the surveying voyages of the Adventure and Beagle, between the years 1826 and 1836. Vols. I–III, London: 1839.

Kingsborough.
See King, Edward.

Knox, J.
A new collection of voyages, discoveries, and travels. Printed for J. Knox. Vol. II. London: 1767.

Kohl, J. G.
Kitchi-gami. Wanderings around Lake Superior. London: 1860.

Kotzebue, Otto von.
A voyage of discovery into the South Sea and Beering's Straits. Vols. I–III. London: 1821.

Kraskenninikoff, S.
History of Kamtschatka, and the Kurilski islands, with the countries adjacent. Translated by James Grieve. Glocester: 1764.

Laet, Joannes de.
L'histoire du nouveau monde ou description des Indes Occidentales. Leyde: 1640.

Lafitau, Joseph François.
Mœurs des sauvages Ameriquains, comparées aux mœurs des premiers temps. Vols. I–II. Paris: 1724.

Landa, Diego de.
Relation des choses de Yucatan. (Translated and edited by Brasseur de Bourbourg.) Forms vol. III of Collection de documents dans les langues indigènes, pour servir à l'étude de l'histoire et de la philologie de l'Amérique ancienne. Paris: 1864.

Lang, Andrew.
Custom and myth. New York: 1885.

Langsdorff, G. H. von.
Voyages and travels in various parts of the world during the years 1803–'07. Parts I–II. London: 1813–'14.

Lanzoni, Joseph.
Ephemeridum physico-medicarum. Vols. I–II. Leipsig: 1694.

Lea, Henry Charles.
History of the inquisition of the middle ages. Vols. I–III. New York: 1888.

Le Clercq, Chrestien.
Nouvelle relation de la Gaspesie. Paris: 1691.

Le Jeune, Paul.
See Relations des Jésuites.

Lenormant, François.
Chaldean magic: its origin and development. London: 1877.

Lisiansky, Urey.
Voyage round the world, in the years 1803–1806. London: 1814.

Long, Stephen H.
Account of an expedition from Pittsburgh to the Rocky mountains, performed in the years 1819–'20. Compiled by Edwin James. Vol. I. Philadelphia: 1823.

Mackenzie, Alexander.
Voyages from Montreal, on the river St. Laurence, through the continent of North America, to the Frozen and Pacific oceans, in the years 1789 and 1793. London: 1801.

Madden, R. R.
The shrines and sepulchres of the old and new world. Vols. I–II. London: 1851.

Malte-Brun.
Universal geography, or a description of all the parts of the world, on a new plan. Vols. I, II, and III. Philadelphia, 1817; Ibid., 1827; Ibid., 1832.

Malte-Brun.
Universal geography. Vols. I–V. Boston: 1825–'26.

Manning, Thomas.
See Markham, Clements R.

Markham, Clements R.
First part of the royal commentaries of the Yncas by the Ynca Garcilasso de la Vega. (Forms Vol. 41 of "Works issued by the Hakluyt Society," London: 1869.)

Markham, Clements R.
Narratives of the rites and laws of the Yncas. Translated from the original Spanish manuscripts, and edited by Clements R. Markham. (Forms Vol. 48 of Hakluyt's Society's Works, London: 1873.)

Markham, Clements R.
Narratives of the mission of George Bogle to Tibet, and of the journey of Thomas Manning to Lhasa. London: 1876.

Massingberd, Francis C.
The English reformation. London: 1842; Ibid., 1857.

Matthews, Washington.
The mountain chant: a Navajo ceremony. (In Ann. Rep. Bu. Eth., 1883–'84, pp. 379–467, Washington: 1887.)

Matthews, Washington.
The prayer of a Navajo shaman. (In the American Anthropologist, Washington, D. C., vol. I, No. 2, April, 1888.)

Maurice, Thomas.
Indian antiquities: or, dissertations relative to . . . Hindostan. Vols. I–V. London: 1800–'01.

Maximilian Prince of Wied.
Travels in the interior of North America. London: 1843.

Meignan, Victor.
From Paris to Pekin. London: 1885.

Mendieta, Gerónimo de.
Historia eclesiástica Indiana; obra escrita á fines del siglo XVI. La publica por primera vez Joaquin Garcia Icazbalceta. Mexico: 1870.

Miles, W. Augustus.
How did the natives of Australia become acquainted with the demigods and dæmonia and with the superstitions of the ancient races? (In Jour. Ethnological Soc. of London, vol. III, London: 1854.)

Molina, Christoval de.
An account of the fables and rites of the Yncas. Translated by C. R. Markham. (In Hakluyt Society's Works, vol. 48, London: 1873.)

Molina, Ignacio.
Compendio de la historia geográfica, natural y civil del reyno de Chile. (Translation of Mendoza and Cruz y Bahamonde.) Vols. I–II. Madrid: 1788–'95.

Montesinos, Fernando.
Mémoires historiques sur l'ancien Pérou. (Forms Vol. XVII of Ternaux-Compans, Voyages, Paris: 1840.)

Montfaucon, Bernard de.
L'antiquité expliquée et representée en figures. Tom. II, pts. 1 and 2. Paris: 1722.

Mooney, James.
Holiday customs of Ireland. Reprinted from the Proceedings of the American Philosophical Society (May 3, 1889; pp. 377–427). Philadelphia: 1889.

Müller, Max.
Lectures on the science of religion. New York: 1872.

Müller, Max.
The sacred books of the East, translated by various oriental scholars and edited by Max Müller. Vol. V (the Bundahis, Bahman Yast, and Shâyast lâ-Shâyast), Oxford: 1880. Vol. XIV (the sacred laws of the Âryas—Vasishtha and Baudhâyana), Oxford: 1882.

New York Historical Society.
Collections . . . for the year 1821. Vol. III. New York: 1821.

Nightingale, J.
The religions and religious ceremonies of all nations. London: 1821.

North Carolina.
Colonial records. Vol. I—1662–1712. Raleigh: 1886.

Notes and Queries.
First series, London: Vol. IV, July–December, 1851. Fourth series, vol. V, January–June, 1870; Ibid., Vol. VIII, July–December, 1871.

Pane, Roman.
Des antiquités des Indiens. Translation of Brasseur de Bourbourg. Paris: 1864.

Parkman, Francis.
The Jesuits in North America in the seventeenth century. Boston: 1867.

Parr, Bartholomew.
London medical dictionary. Vol. I. Philadelphia: 1820.

Pennant, Thomas.
A tour in Scotland, 1769. (In Pinkerton, Collection of voyages and travels, vol. III, pp. 1–569, London: 1809.)

Perrot, Nicholas.
Memoire sur les mœurs, coustumes et relligion des sauvages de l'Amerique septentrionale. Leipzig and Paris: 1864.

Pettigrew, Thomas J.
On superstitions connected with the history and practice of medicine and surgery. Philadelphia: 1844.

Pettit, James S.
Apache campaign notes—'86. (In Jour. Military Service Institution, vol. VII, pp. 331–338, New York: 1886.)

Peyronie, Gauthier de la.
Voyages de M. P. S. Pallas. Tome 4, Paris: 1793.

Picart, Bernard.
Ceremonies et coutumes religieuses de tous les peuples du monde. Vols. I–IX. Amsterdam: 1733–'39.

Pimentel, Francisco.
Cuadro descriptivo y comparativo de las lenguas indígenas de México. Vol. III. México: 1875.

Pinkerton, John.
A general collection of the best and most interesting voyages and travels in all parts of the world. London: Vol. I, 1808; vol. III, 1809; vol. VII, 1811; vol. X, 1811; vol. XI, 1812; vol. XVI, 1814.

Pliny.
Natural history. Translation of Bostock and Riley. Vols. I–VI. London: 1855–'57,1887.

Popol Vuh.
Popol Vuh. Le livre sacré et les mythes de l'antiquité américaine. (Translation of Brasseur de Bourbourg.) Paris: 1861.

Powers, Stephen.
Tribes of California. (Contributions to North American Ethnology, vol. III, Washington: 1877.)

Purchas, Samuel.
Haklvytvs posthumus or Purchas his pilgrimage. Vols. I–V. London: 1625–'26.

Rau, Charles.
Ancient aboriginal trade in North America. (In Smithsonian Institution Ann. Rep. for 1872, pp. 348–394, Washington: 1873.)

Relations des Jésuites.
Relations des Jésuites contenant ce qui s'est passé de plus remarquable dans les missions des pères de la compagnie de Jésus dans la Nouvelle-France. Vol. I. Québec: 1858.

Renouf, P. Le Page.
See Hibbert Lectures, 1879.

Richardson, John.
Arctic searching expedition. Vols. I–II. London: 1851.

Robinson, A.
Life in California. New York: 1846.

Ross, Alexander.
The fur hunters of the far West. Vols. I–II. London: 1855.

Salverte, Eusebe.
Philosophy of magic, prodigies, and apparent miracles. With notes, etc., by Anthony Todd Thomson. Vols. I–II. London: 1846.

Saxon Leechdoms.
See Cockayne, Oswald.

Scheffer, John.
The history of Lapland wherein are shewed the original manners, habits, marriages, conjurations, etc., of that people. Oxford: 1674.

Schoolcraft, Henry R.
Information respecting the history, condition and prospects of the Indian tribes of the United States. Part IV. Philadelphia: 1854.

Schultze, Fritz.
Fetichism: a contribution to anthropology and the history of religion. Translated by J. Fitzgerald. (Forms No. 69 of Humboldt library of popular science literature.) New York: 1885.

Schweinfurth, Georg.
The heart of Africa. Translated by Ellen E. Frewer. Vols. I–II. London: 1873.

Scott, Walter.
Letters on demonology and witchcraft. Addressed to J. G. Lockhart, esq. New York: 1842.

Scott, Walter.
Lady of the lake.

Sextus Placitus.
De medicamentis ex animalibus. Lyons: 1537.

Shakespeare, William.
Macbeth. Collated with the old and modern editions [by Charles Jennens]. London: 1773.

Shâyast lâ-Shâyast.
See Müller, Max.

Shea, John G.
The Catholic church in colonial days. New York: 1886.

Simpson, J. H.
Report of an expedition into the Navajo country in 1849. (Forms part of senate ex. doc. 64, 31st cong.. 1st sess.). Washington: 1850.

Smart, Charles.
Notes on the "Tonto" Apaches. (In Smithsonian Institution Ann. Rep. for 1867, Washington: 1868).

Smet, P. J. de.
Oregon missions and travels over the Rocky mountains in 1845–'46. New York: 1847.

Smith, Buckingham.
Coleccion de varios documentos para la historia de la Florida y tierras adyacentes. Tom. I. London: 1857.

Smith, Buckingham.
Relation of Alvar Nuñez Cabeça de Vaca translated from the Spanish. New York: 1871.

Smith, Edmund R.
The Araucanians; or, notes of a tour among the Indian tribes of southern Chili. New York: 1855.

Smith, John.
True travels, adventures and observations. Vol. I. The generall historie of Virginia, New-England, and the Summer Iles, vol. II. Richmond: 1819.

Smyth, R. Brough.
Aborigines of Victoria: with notes relating to the habits of the natives of other parts of Australia and Tasmania. Vols. I–II. London: 1878.

Snyder, J. F.
Indian remains in Cass County, Illinois. (In Smithsonian Institution Ann. Rep. for 1881, pp. 568–579, Washington: 1883.)

Speke, John Hanning.
Journal of the discovery of the source of the Nile. Edinburgh and London: 1863.

Spencer, Herbert.
Descriptive sociology; or, groups of sociological facts, classified and arranged. Nos. I–V. New York: 1873–'76.

Spencer, Herbert.
Ecclesiastical institutions: being part VI of the principles of sociology. New York: 1886.

Squier, E. G.
The serpent symbol, and the worship of the reciprocal principles of nature in America. New York: 1851.

Squier, E. G.
Aboriginal monuments of the state of New York. (In Smithsonian Contributions to Knowledge, vol. II, Washington: 1851.)

Squier, E. G., and Davis, E. H.
Ancient monuments of the Mississippi valley. (Forms Smithsonian Contributions to Knowledge, vol. I, Washington: 1848.)

Staden de Homberg, Hans.
Histoire d'un pays dans le Nouveau Monde, nommé Amérique. Marbourg, 1557. (Forms Vol. III of Ternaux-Compans, Voyages, Paris: 1837.)

Stanley, H. M.
Through the dark continent. Vols. I–II. New York: 1878.

Strabo.
The geography of Strabo. Literally translated by H. C. Hamilton and W. Falconer. Vol. I. London: 1854.

Strutt, Joseph.
Sports and pastimes of the people of England. London: 1855.

Tanner, John.
Narrative of the captivity and adventures of John Tanner . . . during three years' residence among the Indians. Prepared for the press by Edwin James. New York: 1830.

Ternaux-Compans.
Voyages, relations et mémoires originaux pour servir à l'histoire de la découverte de l'Amérique. Paris: Vols. III, VII, 1837; vols. IX, X, 1838; vols. XV, XVII, 1840.

Theal, George McC.
Kaffir folk-lore. London: 1882.

Thiers, Jean-Baptiste.
Traité des superstitions que regardent les sacremens. Vols. I–IV. Paris: 1741.

Thomas, Cyrus.
Notes on certain Maya and Mexican manuscripts. (In Ann. Rep. Bu. Ethnology for 1881–'82, pp. 1–65, Washington: 1884.)

Thurn, Everard F. im.
Among the Indians of Guiana. London: 1883.

Torquemada, Juan de.
Primera [-tercera] parte de los veinte i un libros rituales i monarchia Indiana. Vols. I–III. Madrid: 1723.

Tylor, Edward B.
Researches into the early history of mankind and the development of civilization. London: 1870.

Tylor, Edward B.
Primitive culture. Vols. I–II. London: 1871.

Vaca.
See Cabeça de Vaca; Smith, Buckingham.

Vasishtha and Baudhâyana.
See Müller, Max.

Vedia, Enrique de.
Historiadores primitivos de Indias. Vols. I–II. Madrid: 1852–'53.

Vega, Garcilasso de la.
First part of the royal commentaries of the Yncas by the Ynca Garcilasso de la Vega. Translated and edited by Clements R. Markham. (Forms vol. XLI of Hakluyt Society's Works, London: 1869.)

Venegas, Miguel.
A natural and civil history of California. Vols. I–II. London: 1759.

Vetancurt, Agustin de.
Teatro Mexicano. Descripcion breve de los sucesos ejemplares, historicos, politicos. militares y religiosos del nuevo mundo occidental de las Indias. Vols. I–III. Mexico: 1870–'71.

Villagra, Gaspar de.
Historia de la Nveva Mexico. Alcala: 1610.

Villagutierre, Juan de.
Historia de la conquista de la provincia de el Itza. [Madrid: 1701.]

Vining, Edward P.
An inglorious Columbus. New York: 1885.

Waitz, Theodor.
Introduction to anthropology. Edited by J. Frederick Collingwood. London: 1863.

Wallace, Alfred R.

A narrative of travels on the Amazon and Rio Negro, with an account of the native tribes. London: 1853.

Whipple, A. W.

Reports of explorations and surveys to ascertain the most practicable and economical route for a railroad from the Mississippi river to the Pacific ocean. Vol. III. Washington: 1856.

Whitney, W. Norton.

Notes from the history of medical progress in Japan. Yokohama: 1885.

Williams, Monier.

Modern India and the Indians. London: 1878.

Winstanley, W.

A visit to Abyssinia: an account of travel in modern Ethiopia. Vols. I–II. London: 1881.

Wrangell, Ferdinand P. von.

Narrative of an expedition to the Polar Sea. New York: 1841.

Wright, Thomas.

Narratives of sorcery and magic, from the most authentic sources. Vols. I–II. London: 1851.

Ximenez, Francisco.

Las historias del origen de los Indios de esta provincia de Guatemala. Translated by C. Scherzer. Vienna: 1857.

INDEX

A.

Acosta, José, cited on sacrifices of Indian corn, 75

Alarcon, quoted on Indian customs, 41, 44, 61

    quoted on Indian sacred cords, 105

Albinos, not medicine-men among the Apaches, 10

Alegre, Francisco J., cited on Indian remedies, 22

    cited on ceremonial scratching among Indians, 42

Amulets of the Apache, 137–139

Arriaga, José de, cited on Indian medicine men, 144

Ashes, use of, in religious formalities, 86

Asylum, right of, among Apache and other Indians, 3–4

B.

Backus, E., quoted on magic powder of Indians, 62–63

Baker, Frank, cited on "hand of glory," 36

Baker, Samuel, cited on African customs, 39

Baking, origin of, 92

Balboa, Vasco Nuñez, cited on Indian medicine-men, 17

    cited on Peruvian festival, 77

Bancroft, H. H., cited on Indian medicine men, 7, 61

    cited on multilation by Indians, 33

    cited on scratching, by Indians, 41

    cited on Indian cakes, 74

    cited on Indian use of feathers, 84, 85

Barcia, Gabriel de Cardenas, cited on sacred meal of Indians, 62

    quoted on magic powder of Indians, 99

Bean, aversion to, by Egyptians and Abyssinians, 67

Beans, string of, used as signal by Tecumseh, 105

Benzoni, Girolami, cited on Indian medicine-men, 11

Black, William G., cited on magic knots and cords, 120, 122, 123, 125, 126, 127, 128, 129, 130

Blankets, blessed, used at Zuñi feasts, 76

Bledos, meaning of the term, 72

Blindness among Indian medicine-men, 20

Blount, Thomas, cited on symbolic use of meal, 63, 64

Bock, Carl, cited on Borneo water vessels, 44

Bollaert, William, cited on emeralds of Peruvians, 140

Brand, John, cited on bell-ringing, 15

    "hand of glory," 36

    cited on powders, 64, 82, 86

    cited on sacred cakes, 91, 94, 95, 96, 97

    cited on cords and girdles, 120, 121, 123, 125, 126, 128, 129, 130

Brasseur de Bourbourg, cited on Indian medicine-men, 16

    cited on origin of labrets, 48

    cited on tzoalli, 73

Bread, sacred, 91–97

    unleavened, 93, 94

Brinton, Daniel G., cited on Indian medicine-men, 7, 30, 82

    cited on Peruvian quipu, 112

    cited on chalchihuitl among Mexicans, 140

    quoted on influence of Indian medicine-men, 143, 144

Bruce, James, quoted on Abyssinian hair dressing, 42

Bull-roarer, use of among Indians, 26–29

Buns, hot cross, of Good Friday, 94–95

Burton, Robert, cited on magic cords and girdles, 118, 119, 125

    cited on exorcism, 134

C.

Cakes, sacred, 68, 91–97

Cameron, V. Lovett, cited on African customs, 44, 64, 65

Castañeda, cited on Indian bread, 72

Castration of Indian priests and medicine-men, 4

Catlin, George, cited on Indian medicine-men, 13

    cited on Indian wigs, 25

Chalchihuitl, an Indian amulet, 138–141

Christmas foods, 97

Clavigero, Francisco S., cited on Indian labret, 47

    cited on Indian mats of reeds, 77–78

    cited on Indian food, 73

Clay-eating, 87–90

Coleman, Charles, cited on Hindu powders, 65

    cited on sacred cords, 115

Columbus, Christopher, quoted on magic powder of Indians, 63

Commerce between "Buffalo" Indians and Pueblos, 79, 80

Confessions of patient to Indian medicine-men, 15, 16

Corbusier, Wm. F., quoted on galena among the Indians, 99

    cited on use of pollen by Indians, 55

    cited on Indian medicine-men, 10

    cited on Indian wigs, 24

Cord of St. Francis, the, 106–107

Cords, used in casting lots, 108–109

    magic wind, of the Lapps, 110–111

    mnemonic, 111–113

    sacred, of the Parsis and Brahmins, 113–117

    Mahometan belief concerning, 116

    measuring, 122–123

    sacred, ophic origin of, 124

    formerly used in binding prisoners, 124–125

    unclassified superstitions concerning, 126–130

    superstitions concerning, 103–130

Countercharms to Indian "medicine," 9–10

Coxe, William, quoted on Indian magic powder, 98

Crantz, David, cited on scratching among Eskimo, 41

Crispellæ, 91

Cross, place of the, in Indian symbolism, 29–30

Cushing, F. H., cited on Zuñi watervessels, 44

    cited on Zuñi Indians, 2

    cited on Zuñi drinking tubes, 44

D.

Dall, William H., cited on Eskimo labrets, 46

Davis, John, cited on Pueblo rebellion, 105

Diaz, Bernal, cited on Indian medicine-women, 19

cited on chalchihuitl among the Mexicans, 141

Diaz, Melchior, cited on Indian wig-making, 25

Disease, method of treating by Indian medicine-men, 12–18

Divination with grains and seeds, 4, 82, 83

Dobrizhoffer, Father, quoted on Abipones medicine-men, 9, 13

Dorman, Rushton M., cited on Peruvian priests, 6

Dorsey, J. Owen, cited on Siouan medicine, 2

Down of birds in ceremonial observances, 83–85

Drinking reed and tubes, use of among Indians, 43–48

Drinks and drugs used by Indian medicine-men, 4, 5–6

Du Halde, P., cited on cords worn by Lamas, 111

Dupuis, cited on castration of priests of Cybele, 4

Duran, Diego, cited on Mexican priests, 4, 6, 14

cited on Indian drinking tubes, 45, 46

cited on sacred meal of Indians, 60

cited on Indian idol of dough, 74, 75, 79

quoted on clay eating by Mexicans, 88

cited on cords among Mexicans, 108

cited on Mexican headdress, 132

Dust from churches, superstitions concerning, 87

E.

Earth eating, 87–90

Emerson, Mrs. Ellen Russell, cited on Indian customs, 40, 45

Epileptic and insane, how regarded by Apache, 10–11

Etmüller, Michael, quoted on girdles and cords, 121, 122

F.

"Far," radical of "farina," etc., 95–96

Feathers, use of, in ceremonial observances, 83–85

use of, in medicine hat, 132

Fernandez, Alonso, quoted on sacrificial bread of Pueblos, 95

Forlong, J. G. R., quoted on manna, 67

quoted on sacred cakes, 68, 94

cited on sacred cords, 114, 115, 128

Fosbrooke, Thomas D., quoted on use of rushes at Easter, 78

cited on symbolic use of ashes, 86

Franklin, Sir John, cited on earth-eating by Eskimo, 89

Frazer, J. G., cited on Indian customs, 35

Frommann, J. C., on magic knots, 119

G.

Galena, powdered, ceremonial use of, by Indians, 98–99

pieces of, used in sacrifices, 99

Gibberish always used by Indian medicine-men, 14

Girdles, superstitions concerning, 107–108, 120–122, 127

use of, in parturition, 120–121

of human skin, 121

Gomara cited on Indian medicine-men, 9, 13, 14, 20, 22, 62

cited on Indian medicine-women, 19

cited on Indian necklaces, 38

cited on Indian cakes, 76

cited on Indian mats, 77

cited on clay-eating by Indians, 88, 89

cited on chalchihuitl among Mexicans, 140

Gonzales de Mendoza quoted on Indians throwing meal, 59–60

Graffenreid, Baron de, cited on magic powder of Indians, 62

Grimm, Jacob, cited on ancient German superstitions, 37, 41, 91, 111, 118, 120, 123

Grossman, Capt., cited on Apache purification, 25

H.

Harris, W. Cornwallis, quoted on magic cords, 124, 125

Hawkins,—, cited on scratching among Indians, 41

Hair and wigs, use of, by Indian medicine-men, 24, 25

"Hand of glory," superstitions concerning, 36

Hangman's rope, superstitions concerning, 124, 125

Headdresses of Indian gods, 132

of Apache medicine-men, 134

Heath, Perry S., cited on use of down at Russian weddings, 85

cited on Russian cakes, 92

cited on Russian kostia, 97

Hereditary priesthood among Indians, 5–6

Herodotus cited on Egyptian priests, 4

Herrera, Antonio, quoted on Indian medicine-men, 9, 11, 13, 22

quoted on Indian medicine-women, 19

quoted on cross among Indians, 30

quoted on Indian labrets, 47

quoted on sacred meal of Indians, 60

quoted on "powder of grass," 69

cited on Indian cakes, 77

Herrera, Antonio, quoted on cords among Indians, 108, 109, 124

cited on Indian headdress, 132

Higgins, Godfrey, cited on hierophants of Athens, 4

cited on Hindu powders, 66

cited on use of flour in sacrifice, 67

cited on use of pollen by the ancients, 82

cited on girdles, 107

Hind, Henry Youle, cited on Indian medicine-men, 14, 63

cited on finger necklace, 33

cited on Indian powder, 63

Hoddentin, employment of, by the Apache, 49–57

bags for carrying, 50

offered to sun, moon, etc., 51–52

employment in cornculture, 52

employment in sickness, 52–55

employment as an amulet, 53–56

a prehistoric food, 68–71

the yiauhtli of the Aztecs, 71–72

analogues of, 80–82

Hoffman, W. J., cited on Ojibwa medicine, 61

Hutchinson, consul, cited on African magic powders, 65

I.

Impotence, self-induced in Indian medicine-men, 4

Indian corn, sacrifice of, 75

Insanity, how regarded in Apache "medicine," 10

Izze-kloth of the Apache, 100–108

Izze-kloth, analogues of other people, 108

J.

James, Edwin, cited on Indian sacrifices, 76
Jus primæ noctis claimed by Indian medicine-men, 11

K.

Kalm, quoted on use of roots of rushes by Indians, 70, 71
Kan or Apache gods, 131–132
Kane, Paul, cited on scratching by Indians, 41
Kelly, Fanny, cited on Sioux medicine-men, 3
quoted on Sioux games with bones, 36
Kennan, Geo., quoted on use of roots by Siberians, 71
Kingsborough, Edward, quoted on Indian medical practice, 144
Knots, magic wind, of the Lapps, 110–111
mnemonic use of, 112–113
magic, preventive of sexual intercourse, 117, 119, 120
true lovers, 117, 118, 126
magic, various powers of, 118–120
nuptial, 118–120
use of in parturition, 120–121
used in capturing hyena, 124
used in finding lost animal, 124
in garments, 126
cure for warts, scrofula, epilepsy, etc., 128–129
Kohl, J. G., cited on mutilation by Indians, 33, 34
cited on Ojibwa customs, 40, 61, 81
Kolben, Peter, cited on Hottentot customs, 35, 86
Kraskenninikoff, cited on Eskimo remedies, 22, 23
Kunque, use of by the Apache and Pueblo, 58–61
analogy of to flour in Spanish carnival, 59–60

L.

Lafitau, Joseph François, cited on sacred powder of Indians, 62
La Flèche, Francis, cited on Indian ghost food, 77
La Salle, Robert C., quoted on use of corn by Indians in burials, 63
Lea, Henry Charles, cited on sacred cords, 117
Le Clercq, Chrestien, quoted on cross as an Indian symbol, 30
Lucky days and seasons, 11
Lycanthropy, power of, claimed by Indian medicine-men, 8–9

M.

Malte-Brun, cited on earth-eating by Siberians, 89
cited on cords and girdles, 111, 112, 114
Mason, Otis T., cited on superstition connected with scratching, 43
Maurice, Thomas, cited on sacred cords, 116
Meal, sacred, use of, by Apache and Pueblo, 58–61
use of, by other people, 60–65
Measuring cords, 122–123
Meat, sacred, of the Zuñis, 95
Medicine cord of the Apache, 100–108
Medicine hat of the Apache, 102–103, 130–131
symbolism of, 132
Medicine-men of the Apache, paper on, by John G. Bourke, 1–158
Medicine-men of the Indians, who may be, 1–7
no organization of, 2
manner of becoming one, 3–4

powers claimed by, 4–9, 12, 20–21
penalty for failure of, to cure disease, 16–17
food of, 20
disposal of, when dead, 20
Medicine-women of the Indians, 18–19
Medidas, 122
Mendieta, Geronimo, cited on Indian medicine-women, 19
quoted on Indian idols of flour or seeds, 76
quoted on Indian divination with corn, 83
Metamorphosis, power of, claimed by Indian medicine-men, 8–9
Montesinos, Fernando, cited on Peruvian sacred flour, 61
Montfaucon, Bernard de, cited on girdles of Saliens, 109
Mud, plastering the head with, by Indians, 25–26
Müller, Max, cited on scratching among the Parsi, 43
cited on parched grain among the Hindus, 96
cited on Hindu drinking custom, 46
cited on sacred cords of Hindus, 113, 117
Music, use of, by Indian medicine-men, 15

N.

Name of an American Indian not to be divulged by himself, 11
when given, 11–12
battle or agnomen, 12
Necklaces, of human fingers, 30–37
of various parts of the human body, 33–39
of human teeth, 37–39

P.

Painting in Apache ceremonies, 133
Pancakes, superstitions concerning, 91, 92, 93
Parkman, Francis, cited on Indian medicine-men, 5, 9, 25
Parturition, use of cords and knots in, 20–22
Payment of Indian medicine-men, 17–18
Pennant, Thomas, quoted on magic-knots, 119, 128
Perrot, Nicolas, quoted on magic powder of Indians, 64
Pettit, Lieut., cited on Indian medicine-men, 23
Phylacteries of the Apache, 141–142
Picart, Bernard, cited on Indian medicine-men, 7, 62
cited on Indian necklaces, 38
cited on Indian drinking tubes, 45
cited on Indian labrets, 48
cited on sacred powders of Hindus, 66
cited on reeds among the Romans, 78
quoted on hair powder, 85
quoted on cords, 106–107, 108, 109, 111, 113, 114, 126
cited on Arab divination, 134
Pimentel, Francisco, quoted on Indian medicine-men, 143
Pliny, Caius, cited on Roman superstitions, 36, 37, 118, 120, 122, 124, 125, 128, 129
Pollen, use of by Israelites and Egyptians, 67–68
use of among Hindus and Romans, 82
Polo, Marco, cited on cords worn by Brahmans, 113
Porter, J. Hampden, cited on ceremonial scratching among Indians, 42
Powder, sacred, use of, by various peoples, 63–67
Powder of grass and straw used as food, 69–70
sacred, general use of, among Indians, 78–79
hair, use by Indians, 85–86
Prehistoric foods used in convenant, 90–91
sacrificed by Romans, 95

Purchas, Samuel, quoted on Indian "mud-heads," 26

Q.

Quipu of the Peruvians, 103

R.

Rain-making one of the powers ascribed to Indian medicine-men, 5–6
Rebellion of the Pueblos, 105
Reeds or rushes, superstitious uses of, 77–78
Remedies of the Indian medicine-men, 21–24
Rhombus, or bull-roarer, use of, among Indians, 26–29
Richardson, Sir John, cited on Indian medicine-women, 19
Rockhill, W. W., cited on flour-throwing by Tibetans, 66
Rosary, origin of, 104
    used as a mnemonic cord, 111

S.

Sage, seeds and roots of, used in tzoalli, 76–77
Sahagun cited on Aztec customs, 14, 36, 45, 68, 73, 78, 88, 109, 171
Salverte, Eusebe, cited on Indian medicine-men, 8, 14
    cited on Roman covenant bread, 90
    cited on amulets, 128
Sashes, medicine, of the Apache, 143
Scalp shirts in Indian "medicine," 26
Schultze, Fritz, cited on Indian medicine-men and women, 20
Schweinfurth, Georg A., cited on African customs, 38, 110
Scott, Walter, cited on lycanthrophy, 9
    quoted on lightning-riven wood, 37
Scratch stick, employment of, among uncivilized peoples, 40–43
    not used for combs, 41
    origin of, 42
Shirts of scalps in Indian "medicine," 26
Shirts, medicine, of the Apache, 143
Simon, Padre, quoted on Indian idolatry, 144
Simpson, John, cited on use of magic powder by Indians, 59
Smith, John, cited on sacred meal of Indians, 61, 62
Smyth, Brough, cited on Australian aboriginal customs, 35, 85, 87, 90, 124
Snake-killing, prohibition of, by Indian medicine-men, 20
Soul cakes, 96
Speke, John H., cited on African customs, 38, 44, 64, 65, 110
Spencer, Charles, cited on Indian medicine-men, 8
Spencer, Herbert, cited on Indian medicine-men, 7, 8, 11, 17, 18, 22
    cited on ancient German priests, 13
    cited on Indian customs, 42
Spirit dance of the Apache, 132–134, 135–136

Stanley, Henry M., quoted on African amulets, 35, 110
    cited on African customs, 65, 125
Stolen property, power to recover claimed by Indian medicine-men, 11
Strutt, Joseph, quoted on magic cakes, 97
Stuart, King James, quoted on magic knots, 119
Sweat bath, a necessary part of Indian medicine, 5

T.

Talismans of the Apache, 137–140
Tanner, John, cited on Indian sacks of human skin, 34
    cited on scratching by Indians, 40
    cited on Indian powders, 63
    cited on Indian headdress, 105–106
Theal, Geo. M., quoted on rhombus among Kaffirs, 29
Torquemada, Juan de, quoted on Aztec customs, 72, 73, 74, 75
    cited on Indian headdresses, 132
Tule or flag, roots used as food, 70, 71
Tylor, E. B., cited on Indian medicine-men, 8
    cited on bull-roarer, 28
Tzi-daltai of the Apaches, 137
Tzoalli, cakes of, used in Indian sacrifices, 73–78
    idols formed of, 75–76

U.

Unleavened bread, 93–94

V.

Vaca, Cabeza de, cited on Mexican customs, 5
    cited on Floridian medicine-men, 20, 22
    cited on clay-eating by Indians, 88
    quoted on galena among the Indians, 98
Vetancurt, Augustin de, quoted on Aztec customs, 72
    cited on Apache commerce, 80
Villagrá, quoted on throwing meal by Indians, 60
Vining, Edward P., cited on mnemonic knots of Japanese, 112

W.

Wheat, origin of, 92
Whipple, A. W., cited on Indian commerce, 80
Whitney, W. Norton, cited on Japanese "medicine," 81
Wigs, use of by Indian medicine-men, 24–25
Winstanley, W., cited on cords worn by Abyssinians, 110
Wounds by wild beasts a qualification for Indian priest-hood, 7–8

X.

Ximenez, Francisco, cited on myths of Guatemala, 78
    quoted on divination by Guatemalan Indians, 83
    quoted on chalchihuitl among the Mexicans, 140

A CATALOG OF SELECTED
DOVER BOOKS
IN ALL FIELDS OF INTEREST

A CATALOG OF SELECTED

DOVER BOOKS

IN ALL FIELDS OF INTEREST

DRAWINGS OF REMBRANDT, edited by Seymour Slive. Updated Lippmann, Hofstede de Groot edition, with definitive scholarly apparatus. All portraits, biblical sketches, landscapes, nudes. Oriental figures, classical studies, together with selection of work by followers. 550 illustrations. Total of 630pp. 9⅛ × 12¼.
21485-0, 21486-9 Pa., Two-vol. set $29.90

GHOST AND HORROR STORIES OF AMBROSE BIERCE, Ambrose Bierce. 24 tales vividly imagined, strangely prophetic, and decades ahead of their time in technical skill: "The Damned Thing," "An Inhabitant of Carcosa," "The Eyes of the Panther," "Moxon's Master," and 20 more. 199pp. 5⅜ × 8½.   20767-6 Pa. $4.95

ETHICAL WRITINGS OF MAIMONIDES, Maimonides. Most significant ethical works of great medieval sage, newly translated for utmost precision, readability. Laws Concerning Character Traits, Eight Chapters, more. 192pp. 5⅜ × 8½.
24522-5 Pa. $5.95

THE EXPLORATION OF THE COLORADO RIVER AND ITS CANYONS, J. W. Powell. Full text of Powell's 1,000-mile expedition down the fabled Colorado in 1869. Superb account of terrain, geology, vegetation, Indians, famine, mutiny, treacherous rapids, mighty canyons, during exploration of last unknown part of continental U.S. 400pp. 5⅜ × 8½.   20094-9 Pa. $8.95

HISTORY OF PHILOSOPHY, Julián Marías. Clearest one-volume history on the market. Every major philosopher and dozens of others, to Existentialism and later. 505pp. 5⅜ × 8½.   21739-6 Pa. $9.95

ALL ABOUT LIGHTNING, Martin A. Uman. Highly readable nontechnical survey of nature and causes of lightning, thunderstorms, ball lightning, St. Elmo's Fire, much more. Illustrated. 192pp. 5⅜ × 8½.   25237-X Pa. $5.95

SAILING ALONE AROUND THE WORLD, Captain Joshua Slocum. First man to sail around the world, alone, in small boat. One of great feats of seamanship told in delightful manner. 67 illustrations. 294pp. 5⅜ × 8½.   20326-3 Pa. $4.95

LETTERS AND NOTES ON THE MANNERS, CUSTOMS AND CONDI-TIONS OF THE NORTH AMERICAN INDIANS, George Catlin. Classic account of life among Plains Indians: ceremonies, hunt, warfare, etc. 312 plates. 572pp. of text. 6⅛ × 9¼.   22118-0, 22119-9, Pa., Two-vol. set $17.90

THE SECRET LIFE OF SALVADOR DALÍ, Salvador Dalí. Outrageous but fascinating autobiography through Dalí's thirties with scores of drawings and sketches and 80 photographs. A must for lovers of 20th-century art. 432pp. 6½ × 9¼. (Available in U.S. only)   27454-3 Pa. $9.95

THE BOOK OF BEASTS: Being a Translation from a Latin Bestiary of the Twelfth Century, T. H. White. Wonderful catalog of real and fanciful beasts: manticore, griffin, phoenix, amphivius, jaculus, many more. White's witty erudite commentary on scientific, historical aspects enhances fascinating glimpse of medieval mind. Illustrated. 296pp. 5⅜ × 8¼. (Available in U.S. only) 24609-4 Pa. $7.95

FRANK LLOYD WRIGHT: Architecture and Nature with 160 Illustrations, Donald Hoffmann. Profusely illustrated study of influence of nature—especially prairie—on Wright's designs for Fallingwater, Robie House, Guggenheim Museum, other masterpieces. 96pp. 9¼ × 10¾. 25098-9 Pa. $8.95

LIMBERT ARTS AND CRAFTS FURNITURE: The Complete 1903 Catalog, Charles P. Limbert and Company. Rare catalog depicting 188 pieces of Mission-style furniture: fold-down tables and desks, bookcases, library and octagonal tables, chairs, more. Descriptive captions. 80pp. 9⅜ × 12¼. 27120-X Pa. $6.95

YEARS WITH FRANK LLOYD WRIGHT: Apprentice to Genius, Edgar Tafel. Insightful memoir by a former apprentice presents a revealing portrait of Wright the man, the inspired teacher, the greatest American architect. 372 black-and-white illustrations. Preface. Index. vi + 228pp. 8¼ × 11. 24801-1 Pa. $10.95

THE STORY OF KING ARTHUR AND HIS KNIGHTS, Howard Pyle. Enchanting version of King Arthur fable has delighted generations with imaginative narratives of exciting adventures and unforgettable illustrations by the author. 41 illustrations. xviii + 313pp. 6⅛ × 9¼. 21445-1 Pa. $6.95

THE GODS OF THE EGYPTIANS, E. A. Wallis Budge. Thorough coverage of numerous gods of ancient Egypt by foremost Egyptologist. Information on evolution of cults, rites and gods; the cult of Osiris; the Book of the Dead and its rites; the sacred animals and birds; Heaven and Hell; and more. 956pp. 6⅛ × 9¼. 22055-9, 22056-7 Pa., Two-vol. set $22.90

A THEOLOGICO-POLITICAL TREATISE, Benedict Spinoza. Also contains unfinished *Political Treatise*. Great classic on religious liberty, theory of government on common consent. R. Elwes translation. Total of 421pp. 5⅜ × 8½. 20249-6 Pa. $7.95

INCIDENTS OF TRAVEL IN CENTRAL AMERICA, CHIAPAS, AND YUCATAN, John L. Stephens. Almost single-handed discovery of Maya culture; exploration of ruined cities, monuments, temples; customs of Indians. 115 drawings. 892pp. 5⅜ × 8½. 22404-X, 22405-8 Pa., Two-vol. set $17.90

LOS CAPRICHOS, Francisco Goya. 80 plates of wild, grotesque monsters and caricatures. Prado manuscript included. 183pp. 6⅝ × 9⅜. 22384-1 Pa. $6.95

AUTOBIOGRAPHY: The Story of My Experiments with Truth, Mohandas K. Gandhi. Not hagiography, but Gandhi in his own words. Boyhood, legal studies, purification, the growth of the Satyagraha (nonviolent protest) movement. Critical, inspiring work of the man who freed India. 480pp. 5⅜ × 8½. (Available in U.S. only) 24593-4 Pa. $6.95

HOW TO WRITE, Gertrude Stein. Gertrude Stein claimed anyone could understand her unconventional writing—here are clues to help. Fascinating improvisations, language experiments, explanations illuminate Stein's craft and the art of writing. Total of 414pp. 4⅝ × 6⅜. 23144-5 Pa. $6.95

ADVENTURES AT SEA IN THE GREAT AGE OF SAIL: Five Firsthand Narratives, edited by Elliot Snow. Rare true accounts of exploration, whaling, shipwreck, fierce natives, trade, shipboard life, more. 33 illustrations. Introduction. 353pp. 5⅜ × 8½. 25177-2 Pa. $9.95

THE HERBAL OR GENERAL HISTORY OF PLANTS, John Gerard. Classic descriptions of about 2,850 plants—with over 2,700 illustrations—includes Latin and English names, physical descriptions, varieties, time and place of growth, more. 2,706 illustrations. xlv + 1,678pp. 8½ × 12¼. 23147-X Cloth. $89.95

DOROTHY AND THE WIZARD IN OZ, L. Frank Baum. Dorothy and the Wizard visit the center of the Earth, where people are vegetables, glass houses grow and Oz characters reappear. Classic sequel to *Wizard of Oz*. 256pp. 5⅜ × 8. 24714-7 Pa. $5.95

SONGS OF EXPERIENCE: Facsimile Reproduction with 26 Plates in Full Color, William Blake. This facsimile of Blake's original "Illuminated Book" reproduces 26 full-color plates from a rare 1826 edition. Includes "The Tyger," "London," "Holy Thursday," and other immortal poems. 26 color plates. Printed text of poems. 48pp. 5¼ × 7. 24636-1 Pa. $3.95

SONGS OF INNOCENCE, William Blake. The first and most popular of Blake's famous "Illuminated Books," in a facsimile edition reproducing all 31 brightly colored plates. Additional printed text of each poem. 64pp. 5¼ × 7. 22764-2 Pa. $3.95

PRECIOUS STONES, Max Bauer. Classic, thorough study of diamonds, rubies, emeralds, garnets, etc.: physical character, occurrence, properties, use, similar topics. 20 plates, 8 in color. 94 figures. 659pp. 6⅛ × 9¼. 21910-0, 21911-9 Pa., Two-vol. set $21.90

ENCYCLOPEDIA OF VICTORIAN NEEDLEWORK, S. F. A. Caulfeild and Blanche Saward. Full, precise descriptions of stitches, techniques for dozens of needlecrafts—most exhaustive reference of its kind. Over 800 figures. Total of 679pp. 8⅛ × 11. 22800-2, 22801-0 Pa., Two-vol. set $26.90

THE MARVELOUS LAND OF OZ, L. Frank Baum. Second Oz book, the Scarecrow and Tin Woodman are back with hero named Tip, Oz magic. 136 illustrations. 287pp. 5⅜ × 8½. 20692-0 Pa. $5.95

WILD FOWL DECOYS, Joel Barber. Basic book on the subject, by foremost authority and collector. Reveals history of decoy making and rigging, place in American culture, different kinds of decoys, how to make them, and how to use them. 140 plates. 156pp. 7⅞ × 10¾. 20011-6 Pa. $14.95

HISTORY OF LACE, Mrs. Bury Palliser. Definitive, profusely illustrated chronicle of lace from earliest times to late 19th century. Laces of Italy, Greece, England, France, Belgium, etc. Landmark of needlework scholarship. 266 illustrations. 672pp. 6⅛ × 9¼. 24742-2 Pa. $16.95

SUNDIALS, Albert Waugh. Far and away the best, most thorough coverage of ideas, mathematics concerned, types, construction, adjusting anywhere. Over 100 illustrations. 230pp. 5⅜ × 8½. 22947-5 Pa. $5.95

PICTURE HISTORY OF THE NORMANDIE: With 190 Illustrations, Frank O. Braynard. Full story of legendary French ocean liner: Art Deco interiors, design innovations, furnishings, celebrities, maiden voyage, tragic fire, much more. Extensive text. 144pp. 8⅜ × 11¾. 25257-4 Pa. $11.95

THE FIRST AMERICAN COOKBOOK: A Facsimile of "American Cookery," 1796, Amelia Simmons. Facsimile of the first American-written cookbook published in the United States contains authentic recipes for colonial favorites—pumpkin pudding, winter squash pudding, spruce beer, Indian slapjacks, and more. Introductory Essay and Glossary of colonial cooking terms. 80pp. 5⅜ × 8½. 24710-4 Pa. $3.50

101 PUZZLES IN THOUGHT AND LOGIC, C. R. Wylie, Jr. Solve murders and robberies, find out which fishermen are liars, how a blind man could possibly identify a color—purely by your own reasoning! 107pp. 5⅜ × 8½. 20367-0 Pa. $2.95

ANCIENT EGYPTIAN MYTHS AND LEGENDS, Lewis Spence. Examines animism, totemism, fetishism, creation myths, deities, alchemy, art and magic, other topics. Over 50 illustrations. 432pp. 5⅜ × 8½. 26525-0 Pa. $8.95

ANTHROPOLOGY AND MODERN LIFE, Franz Boas. Great anthropologist's classic treatise on race and culture. Introduction by Ruth Bunzel. Only inexpensive paperback edition. 255pp. 5⅜ × 8½. 25245-0 Pa. $7.95

THE TALE OF PETER RABBIT, Beatrix Potter. The inimitable Peter's terrifying adventure in Mr. McGregor's garden, with all 27 wonderful, full-color Potter illustrations. 55pp. 4¼ × 5½. 22827-4 Pa. $1.75

THREE PROPHETIC SCIENCE FICTION NOVELS, H. G. Wells. *When the Sleeper Wakes, A Story of the Days to Come* and *The Time Machine* (full version). 335pp. 5⅜ × 8½. (Available in U.S. only) 20605-X Pa. $8.95

APICIUS COOKERY AND DINING IN IMPERIAL ROME, edited and translated by Joseph Dommers Vehling. Oldest known cookbook in existence offers readers a clear picture of what foods Romans ate, how they prepared them, etc. 49 illustrations. 301pp. 6⅛ × 9¼. 23563-7 Pa. $8.95

SHAKESPEARE LEXICON AND QUOTATION DICTIONARY, Alexander Schmidt. Full definitions, locations, shades of meaning of every word in plays and poems. More than 50,000 exact quotations. 1,485pp. 6½ × 9¼. 22726-X, 22727-8 Pa., Two-vol. set $31.90

THE WORLD'S GREAT SPEECHES, edited by Lewis Copeland and Lawrence W. Lamm. Vast collection of 278 speeches from Greeks to 1970. Powerful and effective models; unique look at history. 842pp. 5⅜ × 8½. 20468-5 Pa. $12.95

THE BLUE FAIRY BOOK, Andrew Lang. The first, most famous collection, with many familiar tales: Little Red Riding Hood, Aladdin and the Wonderful Lamp, Puss in Boots, Sleeping Beauty, Hansel and Gretel, Rumpelstiltskin; 37 in all. 138 illustrations. 390pp. 5⅜ × 8½. 21437-0 Pa. $6.95

THE STORY OF THE CHAMPIONS OF THE ROUND TABLE, Howard Pyle. Sir Launcelot, Sir Tristram and Sir Percival in spirited adventures of love and triumph retold in Pyle's inimitable style. 50 drawings, 31 full-page. xviii + 329pp. 6½ × 9¼. 21883-X Pa. $7.95

THE MYTHS OF THE NORTH AMERICAN INDIANS, Lewis Spence. Myths and legends of the Algonquins, Iroquois, Pawnees and Sioux with comprehensive historical and ethnological commentary. 36 illustrations. 5⅜ × 8½.
25967-6 Pa. $8.95

GREAT DINOSAUR HUNTERS AND THEIR DISCOVERIES, Edwin H. Colbert. Fascinating, lavishly illustrated chronicle of dinosaur research, 1820s to 1960. Achievements of Cope, Marsh, Brown, Buckland, Mantell, Huxley, many others. 384pp. 5¼ × 8¼. 24701-5 Pa. $8.95

THE TASTEMAKERS, Russell Lynes. Informal, illustrated social history of American taste 1850s–1950s. First popularized categories Highbrow, Lowbrow, Middlebrow. 129 illustrations. New (1979) afterword. 384pp. 6 × 9.
23993-4 Pa. $8.95

NORTH AMERICAN INDIAN LIFE: Customs and Traditions of 23 Tribes, Elsie Clews Parsons (ed.). 27 fictionalized essays by noted anthropologists examine religion, customs, government, additional facets of life among the Winnebago, Crow, Zuni, Eskimo, other tribes. 480pp. 6⅛ × 9¼. 27377-6 Pa. $10.95

AUTHENTIC VICTORIAN DECORATION AND ORNAMENTATION IN FULL COLOR: 46 Plates from "Studies in Design," Christopher Dresser. Superb full-color lithographs reproduced from rare original portfolio of a major Victorian designer. 48pp. 9¼ × 12¼. 25083-0 Pa. $7.95

PRIMITIVE ART, Franz Boas. Remains the best text ever prepared on subject, thoroughly discussing Indian, African, Asian, Australian, and, especially, Northern American primitive art. Over 950 illustrations show ceramics, masks, totem poles, weapons, textiles, paintings, much more. 376pp. 5⅜ × 8. 20025-6 Pa. $8.95

SIDELIGHTS ON RELATIVITY, Albert Einstein. Unabridged republication of two lectures delivered by the great physicist in 1920–21. *Ether and Relativity* and *Geometry and Experience.* Elegant ideas in nonmathematical form, accessible to intelligent layman. vi + 56pp. 5⅜ × 8½. 24511-X Pa. $3.95

THE WIT AND HUMOR OF OSCAR WILDE, edited by Alvin Redman. More than 1,000 ripostes, paradoxes, wisecracks: Work is the curse of the drinking classes, I can resist everything except temptation, etc. 258pp. 5⅜ × 8½. 20602-5 Pa. $4.95

ADVENTURES WITH A MICROSCOPE, Richard Headstrom. 59 adventures with clothing fibers, protozoa, ferns and lichens, roots and leaves, much more. 142 illustrations. 232pp. 5⅜ × 8½. 23471-1 Pa. $4.95

PLANTS OF THE BIBLE, Harold N. Moldenke and Alma L. Moldenke. Standard reference to all 230 plants mentioned in Scriptures. Latin name, biblical reference, uses, modern identity, much more. Unsurpassed encyclopedic resource for scholars, botanists, nature lovers, students of Bible. Bibliography. Indexes. 123 black-and-white illustrations. 384pp. 6 × 9. 25069-5 Pa. $9.95

FAMOUS AMERICAN WOMEN: A Biographical Dictionary from Colonial Times to the Present, Robert McHenry, ed. From Pocahontas to Rosa Parks, 1,035 distinguished American women documented in separate biographical entries. Accurate, up-to-date data, numerous categories, spans 400 years. Indices. 493pp. 6½ × 9¼. 24523-3 Pa. $11.95

THE FABULOUS INTERIORS OF THE GREAT OCEAN LINERS IN HISTORIC PHOTOGRAPHS, William H. Miller, Jr. Some 200 superb photographs capture exquisite interiors of world's great "floating palaces"—1890s to 1980s: *Titanic, Ile de France, Queen Elizabeth, United States, Europa,* more. Approx. 200 black-and-white photographs. Captions. Text. Introduction. 160pp. 8⅞ × 11¾. 24756-2 Pa. $10.95

THE GREAT LUXURY LINERS, 1927-1954: A Photographic Record, William H. Miller, Jr. Nostalgic tribute to heyday of ocean liners. 186 photos of *Ile de France, Normandie, Leviathan, Queen Elizabeth, United States,* many others. Interior and exterior views. Introduction. Captions. 160pp. 9 × 12. 24056-8 Pa. $12.95

A NATURAL HISTORY OF THE DUCKS, John Charles Phillips. Great landmark of ornithology offers complete detailed coverage of nearly 200 species and subspecies of ducks: gadwall, sheldrake, merganser, pintail, many more. 74 full-color plates, 102 black-and-white. Bibliography. Total of 1,920pp. 8⅝ × 11¼. 25141-1, 25142-X Cloth., Two-vol. set $100.00

THE COMPLETE "MASTERS OF THE POSTER": All 256 Color Plates from "Les Maîtres de l'Affiche", Stanley Appelbaum (ed.). The most famous compilation ever made of the art of the great age of the poster, featuring works by Chéret, Steinlen, Toulouse-Lautrec, nearly 100 other artists. One poster per page. 272pp. 9¼ × 12¼. 26309-6 Pa. $29.95

THE TEN BOOKS OF ARCHITECTURE: The 1755 Leoni Edition, Leon Battista Alberti. Rare classic helped introduce the glories of ancient architecture to the Renaissance. 68 black-and-white plates. 336pp. 8⅜ × 11¼. 25239-6 Pa. $14.95

MISS MACKENZIE, Anthony Trollope. Minor masterpieces by Victorian master unmasks many truths about life in 19th-century England. First inexpensive edition in years. 392pp. 5⅜ × 8½. 25201-9 Pa. $8.95

THE RIME OF THE ANCIENT MARINER, Gustave Doré, Samuel Taylor Coleridge. Dramatic engravings considered by many to be his greatest work. The terrifying space of the open sea, the storms and whirlpools of an unknown ocean, the ice of Antarctica, more—all rendered in a powerful, chilling manner. Full text. 38 plates. 77pp. 9¼ × 12. 22305-1 Pa. $4.95

THE EXPEDITIONS OF ZEBULON MONTGOMERY PIKE, Zebulon Montgomery Pike. Fascinating firsthand accounts (1805-6) of exploration of Mississippi River, Indian wars, capture by Spanish dragoons, much more. 1,088pp. 5⅜ × 8½. 25254-X, 25255-8 Pa., Two-vol. set $25.90

A CONCISE HISTORY OF PHOTOGRAPHY: Third Revised Edition, Helmut Gernsheim. Best one-volume history—camera obscura, photochemistry, daguerreotypes, evolution of cameras, film, more. Also artistic aspects—landscape, portraits, fine art, etc. 281 black-and-white photographs. 26 in color. 176pp. 8⅜ × 11¼.
25128-4 Pa. $14.95

THE DORÉ BIBLE ILLUSTRATIONS, Gustave Doré. 241 detailed plates from the Bible: the Creation scenes, Adam and Eve, Flood, Babylon, battle sequences, life of Jesus, etc. Each plate is accompanied by the verses from the King James version of the Bible. 241pp. 9 × 12.
23004-X Pa. $9.95

WANDERINGS IN WEST AFRICA, Richard F. Burton. Great Victorian scholar/adventurer's invaluable descriptions of African tribal rituals, fetishism, culture, art, much more. Fascinating 19th-century account. 624pp. 5⅜ × 8½. 26890-X Pa. $12.95

HISTORIC HOMES OF THE AMERICAN PRESIDENTS, Second Revised Edition, Irvin Haas. Guide to homes occupied by every president from Washington to Bush. Visiting hours, travel routes, more. 175 photos. 160pp. 8¼ × 11.
26751-2 Pa. $9.95

THE HISTORY OF THE LEWIS AND CLARK EXPEDITION, Meriwether Lewis and William Clark, edited by Elliott Coues. Classic edition of Lewis and Clark's day-by-day journals that later became the basis for U.S. claims to Oregon and the West. Accurate and invaluable geographical, botanical, biological, meteorological and anthropological material. Total of 1,508pp. 5⅜ × 8½.
21268-8, 21269-6, 21270-X Pa., Three-vol. set $29.85

LANGUAGE, TRUTH AND LOGIC, Alfred J. Ayer. Famous, clear introduction to Vienna, Cambridge schools of Logical Positivism. Role of philosophy, elimination of metaphysics, nature of analysis, etc. 160pp. 5⅜ × 8½. (Available in U.S. and Canada only)
20010-8 Pa. $3.95

MATHEMATICS FOR THE NONMATHEMATICIAN, Morris Kline. Detailed, college-level treatment of mathematics in cultural and historical context, with numerous exercises. For liberal arts students. Preface. Recommended Reading Lists. Tables. Index. Numerous black-and-white figures. xvi + 641pp. 5⅜ × 8½.
24823-2 Pa. $11.95

HANDBOOK OF PICTORIAL SYMBOLS, Rudolph Modley. 3,250 signs and symbols, many systems in full; official or heavy commercial use. Arranged by subject. Most in Pictorial Archive series. 143pp. 8¼ × 11. 23357-X Pa. $8.95

INCIDENTS OF TRAVEL IN YUCATAN, John L. Stephens. Classic (1843) exploration of jungles of Yucatan, looking for evidences of Maya civilization. Travel adventures, Mexican and Indian culture, etc. Total of 669pp. 5⅜ × 8½.
20926-1, 20927-X Pa., Two-vol. set $13.90

DEGAS: An Intimate Portrait, Ambroise Vollard. Charming, anecdotal memoir by famous art dealer of one of the greatest 19th-century French painters. 14 black-and-white illustrations. Introduction by Harold L. Van Doren. 96pp. 5⅜ × 8½.
25131-4 Pa. $4.95

PERSONAL NARRATIVE OF A PILGRIMAGE TO AL-MADINAH AND MECCAH, Richard F. Burton. Great travel classic by remarkably colorful personality. Burton, disguised as a Moroccan, visited sacred shrines of Islam, narrowly escaping death. 47 illustrations. 959pp. 5⅜ × 8½.
21217-3, 21218-1 Pa., Two-vol. set $19.90

PHRASE AND WORD ORIGINS, A. H. Holt. Entertaining, reliable, modern study of more than 1,200 colorful words, phrases, origins and histories. Much unexpected information. 254pp. 5⅜ × 8½.
20758-7 Pa. $5.95

THE RED THUMB MARK, R. Austin Freeman. In this first Dr. Thorndyke case, the great scientific detective draws fascinating conclusions from the nature of a single fingerprint. Exciting story, authentic science. 320pp. 5⅜ × 8½. (Available in U.S. only)
25210-8 Pa. $6.95

AN EGYPTIAN HIEROGLYPHIC DICTIONARY, E. A. Wallis Budge. Monumental work containing about 25,000 words or terms that occur in texts ranging from 3000 B.C. to 600 A.D. Each entry consists of a transliteration of the word, the word in hieroglyphs, and the meaning in English. 1,314pp. 6⅝ × 10.
23615-3, 23616-1 Pa., Two-vol. set $35.90

THE COMPLEAT STRATEGYST: Being a Primer on the Theory of Games of Strategy, J. D. Williams. Highly entertaining classic describes, with many illustrated examples, how to select best strategies in conflict situations. Prefaces. Appendices. xvi + 268pp. 5⅜ × 8½.
25101-2 Pa. $7.95

THE ROAD TO OZ, L. Frank Baum. Dorothy meets the Shaggy Man, little Button-Bright and the Rainbow's beautiful daughter in this delightful trip to the magical Land of Oz. 272pp. 5⅜ × 8.
25208-6 Pa. $5.95

POINT AND LINE TO PLANE, Wassily Kandinsky. Seminal exposition of role of point, line, other elements in nonobjective painting. Essential to understanding 20th-century art. 127 illustrations. 192pp. 6½ × 9¼.
23808-3 Pa. $5.95

LADY ANNA, Anthony Trollope. Moving chronicle of Countess Lovel's bitter struggle to win for herself and daughter Anna their rightful rank and fortune—perhaps at cost of sanity itself. 384pp. 5⅜ × 8½.
24669-8 Pa. $8.95

EGYPTIAN MAGIC, E. A. Wallis Budge. Sums up all that is known about magic in Ancient Egypt: the role of magic in controlling the gods, powerful amulets that warded off evil spirits, scarabs of immortality, use of wax images, formulas and spells, the secret name, much more. 253pp. 5⅜ × 8½.
22681-6 Pa. $4.95

THE DANCE OF SIVA, Ananda Coomaraswamy. Preeminent authority unfolds the vast metaphysic of India: the revelation of her art, conception of the universe, social organization, etc. 27 reproductions of art masterpieces. 192pp. 5⅜ × 8½.
24817-8 Pa. $6.95

CHRISTMAS CUSTOMS AND TRADITIONS, Clement A. Miles. Origin, evolution, significance of religious, secular practices. Caroling, gifts, yule logs, much more. Full, scholarly yet fascinating; non-sectarian. 400pp. 5⅜ × 8½.
23354-5 Pa. $7.95

THE HUMAN FIGURE IN MOTION, Eadweard Muybridge. More than 4,500 stopped-action photos, in action series, showing undraped men, women, children jumping, lying down, throwing, sitting, wrestling, carrying, etc. 390pp. 7⅞ × 10⅝.
20204-6 Cloth. $24.95

THE MAN WHO WAS THURSDAY, Gilbert Keith Chesterton. Witty, fast-paced novel about a club of anarchists in turn-of-the-century London. Brilliant social, religious, philosophical speculations. 128pp. 5⅜ × 8½.
25121-7 Pa. $3.95

A CÉZANNE SKETCHBOOK: Figures, Portraits, Landscapes and Still Lifes, Paul Cézanne. Great artist experiments with tonal effects, light, mass, other qualities in over 100 drawings. A revealing view of developing master painter, precursor of Cubism. 102 black-and-white illustrations. 144pp. 8¾ × 6⅜.
24790-2 Pa. $6.95

AN ENCYCLOPEDIA OF BATTLES: Accounts of Over 1,560 Battles from 1479 B.C. to the Present, David Eggenberger. Presents essential details of every major battle in recorded history, from the first battle of Megiddo in 1479 B.C. to Grenada in 1984. List of Battle Maps. New Appendix covering the years 1967–1984. Index. 99 illustrations. 544pp. 6½ × 9¼.
24913-1 Pa. $14.95

AN ETYMOLOGICAL DICTIONARY OF MODERN ENGLISH, Ernest Weekley. Richest, fullest work, by foremost British lexicographer. Detailed word histories. Inexhaustible. Total of 856pp. 6½ × 9¼.
21873-2, 21874-0 Pa., Two-vol. set $19.90

WEBSTER'S AMERICAN MILITARY BIOGRAPHIES, edited by Robert McHenry. Over 1,000 figures who shaped 3 centuries of American military history. Detailed biographies of Nathan Hale, Douglas MacArthur, Mary Hallaren, others. Chronologies of engagements, more. Introduction. Addenda. 1,033 entries in alphabetical order. xi + 548pp. 6½ × 9¼. (Available in U.S. only)
24758-9 Pa. $13.95

LIFE IN ANCIENT EGYPT, Adolf Erman. Detailed older account, with much not in more recent books: domestic life, religion, magic, medicine, commerce, and whatever else needed for complete picture. Many illustrations. 597pp. 5⅜ × 8½.
22632-8 Pa. $9.95

HISTORIC COSTUME IN PICTURES, Braun & Schneider. Over 1,450 costumed figures shown, covering a wide variety of peoples: kings, emperors, nobles, priests, servants, soldiers, scholars, townsfolk, peasants, merchants, courtiers, cavaliers, and more. 256pp. 8⅜ × 11¼.
23150-X Pa. $9.95

THE NOTEBOOKS OF LEONARDO DA VINCI, edited by J. P. Richter. Extracts from manuscripts reveal great genius; on painting, sculpture, anatomy, sciences, geography, etc. Both Italian and English. 186 ms. pages reproduced, plus 500 additional drawings, including studies for *Last Supper*, *Sforza* monument, etc. 860pp. 7⅞ × 10¾.
22572-0, 22573-9 Pa., Two-vol. set $35.90

THE ART NOUVEAU STYLE BOOK OF ALPHONSE MUCHA: All 72 Plates from "Documents Decoratifs" in Original Color, Alphonse Mucha. Rare copyright-free design portfolio by high priest of Art Nouveau. Jewelry, wallpaper, stained glass, furniture, figure studies, plant and animal motifs, etc. Only complete one-volume edition. 80pp. 9⅜ × 12¼. 24044-4 Pa. $10.95

ANIMALS: 1,419 Copyright-Free Illustrations of Mammals, Birds, Fish, Insects, Etc., edited by Jim Harter. Clear wood engravings present, in extremely lifelike poses, over 1,000 species of animals. One of the most extensive pictorial sourcebooks of its kind. Captions. Index. 284pp. 9 × 12. 23766-4 Pa. $10.95

OBELISTS FLY HIGH, C. Daly King. Masterpiece of American detective fiction, long out of print, involves murder on a 1935 transcontinental flight—"a very thrilling story"—*NY Times.* Unabridged and unaltered republication of the edition published by William Collins Sons & Co. Ltd., London, 1935. 288pp. 5⅜ × 8½. (Available in U.S. only) 25036-9 Pa. $5.95

VICTORIAN AND EDWARDIAN FASHION: A Photographic Survey, Alison Gernsheim. First fashion history completely illustrated by contemporary photographs. Full text plus 235 photos, 1840–1914, in which many celebrities appear. 240pp. 6½ × 9¼. 24205-6 Pa. $8.95

THE ART OF THE FRENCH ILLUSTRATED BOOK, 1700–1914, Gordon N. Ray. Over 630 superb book illustrations by Fragonard, Delacroix, Daumier, Doré, Grandville, Manet, Mucha, Steinlen, Toulouse-Lautrec and many others. Preface. Introduction. 633 halftones. Indices of artists, authors & titles, binders and provenances. Appendices. Bibliography. 608pp. 8⅜ × 11¼. 25086-5 Pa. $24.95

THE WONDERFUL WIZARD OF OZ, L. Frank Baum. Facsimile in full color of America's finest children's classic. 143 illustrations by W. W. Denslow. 267pp. 5⅜ × 8½. 20691-2 Pa. $7.95

FOLLOWING THE EQUATOR: A Journey Around the World, Mark Twain. Great writer's 1897 account of circumnavigating the globe by steamship. Ironic humor, keen observations, vivid and fascinating descriptions of exotic places. 197 illustrations. 720pp. 5⅜ × 8½. 26113-1 Pa. $15.95

THE FRIENDLY STARS, Martha Evans Martin & Donald Howard Menzel. Classic text marshalls the stars together in an engaging, nontechnical survey, presenting them as sources of beauty in night sky. 23 illustrations. Foreword. 2 star charts. Index. 147pp. 5⅜ × 8½. 21099-5 Pa. $3.95

FADS AND FALLACIES IN THE NAME OF SCIENCE, Martin Gardner. Fair, witty appraisal of cranks, quacks, and quackeries of science and pseudoscience: hollow earth, Velikovsky, orgone energy, Dianetics, flying saucers, Bridey Murphy, food and medical fads, etc. Revised, expanded In the Name of Science. "A very able and even-tempered presentation."—*The New Yorker.* 363pp. 5⅜ × 8. 20394-8 Pa. $6.95

ANCIENT EGYPT: Its Culture and History, J. E. Manchip White. From predynastics through Ptolemies: society, history, political structure, religion, daily life, literature, cultural heritage. 48 plates. 217pp. 5⅜ × 8½. 22548-8 Pa. $5.95

CATALOG OF DOVER BOOKS

SIR HARRY HOTSPUR OF HUMBLETHWAITE, Anthony Trollope. Incisive, unconventional psychological study of a conflict between a wealthy baronet, his idealistic daughter, and their scapegrace cousin. The 1870 novel in its first inexpensive edition in years. 250pp. 5⅜ × 8½.   24953-0 Pa. $6.95

LASERS AND HOLOGRAPHY, Winston E. Kock. Sound introduction to burgeoning field, expanded (1981) for second edition. Wave patterns, coherence, lasers, diffraction, zone plates, properties of holograms, recent advances. 84 illustrations. 160pp. 5⅜ × 8¼. (Except in United Kingdom)   24041-X Pa. $4.95

INTRODUCTION TO ARTIFICIAL INTELLIGENCE: Second, Enlarged Edition, Philip C. Jackson, Jr. Comprehensive survey of artificial intelligence—the study of how machines (computers) can be made to act intelligently. Includes introductory and advanced material. Extensive notes updating the main text. 132 black-and-white illustrations. 512pp. 5⅜ × 8½.   24864-X Pa. $10.95

HISTORY OF INDIAN AND INDONESIAN ART, Ananda K. Coomaraswamy. Over 400 illustrations illuminate classic study of Indian art from earliest Harappa finds to early 20th century. Provides philosophical, religious and social insights. 304pp. 6⅜ × 9⅜.   25005-9 Pa. $11.95

THE GOLEM, Gustav Meyrink. Most famous supernatural novel in modern European literature, set in Ghetto of Old Prague around 1890. Compelling story of mystical experiences, strange transformations, profound terror. 13 black-and-white illustrations. 224pp. 5⅜ × 8½.   25025-3 Pa. $7.95

PICTORIAL ENCYCLOPEDIA OF HISTORIC ARCHITECTURAL PLANS, DETAILS AND ELEMENTS: With 1,880 Line Drawings of Arches, Domes, Doorways, Facades, Gables, Windows, etc., John Theodore Haneman. Sourcebook of inspiration for architects, designers, others. Bibliography. Captions. 141pp. 9 × 12.
24605-1 Pa. $8.95

BENCHLEY LOST AND FOUND, Robert Benchley. Finest humor from early 30s, about pet peeves, child psychologists, post office and others. Mostly unavailable elsewhere. 73 illustrations by Peter Arno and others. 183pp. 5⅜ × 8½.
22410-4 Pa. $4.95

ERTÉ GRAPHICS, Erté. Collection of striking color graphics: *Seasons, Alphabet, Numerals, Aces* and *Precious Stones.* 50 plates, including 4 on covers. 48pp. 9⅜ × 12¼.
23580-7 Pa. $7.95

THE JOURNAL OF HENRY D. THOREAU, edited by Bradford Torrey, F. H. Allen. Complete reprinting of 14 volumes, 1837–61, over two million words; the sourcebooks for *Walden*, etc. Definitive. All original sketches, plus 75 photographs. 1,804pp. 8½ × 12¼.   20312-3, 20313-1 Cloth., Two-vol. set $130.00

CASTLES: Their Construction and History, Sidney Toy. Traces castle development from ancient roots. Nearly 200 photographs and drawings illustrate moats, keeps, baileys, many other features. Caernarvon, Dover Castles, Hadrian's Wall, Tower of London, dozens more. 256pp. 5⅜ × 8¼.   24898-4 Pa. $7.95

AMERICAN CLIPPER SHIPS: 1833–1858, Octavius T. Howe & Frederick C. Matthews. Fully-illustrated, encyclopedic review of 352 clipper ships from the period of America's greatest maritime supremacy. Introduction. 109 halftones. 5 black-and-white line illustrations. Index. Total of 928pp. 5⅜ × 8½.
25115-2, 25116-0 Pa., Two-vol. set $21.90

TOWARDS A NEW ARCHITECTURE, Le Corbusier. Pioneering manifesto by great architect, near legendary founder of "International School." Technical and aesthetic theories, views on industry, economics, relation of form to function, "mass-production spirit," much more. Profusely illustrated. Unabridged translation of 13th French edition. Introduction by Frederick Etchells. 320pp. 6⅛ × 9¼. (Available in U.S. only)
25023-7 Pa. $8.95

THE BOOK OF KELLS, edited by Blanche Cirker. Inexpensive collection of 32 full-color, full-page plates from the greatest illuminated manuscript of the Middle Ages, painstakingly reproduced from rare facsimile edition. Publisher's Note. Captions. 32pp. 9⅜ × 12¼. (Available in U.S. only)
24345-1 Pa. $5.95

BEST SCIENCE FICTION STORIES OF H. G. WELLS, H. G. Wells. Full novel *The Invisible Man*, plus 17 short stories: "The Crystal Egg," "Aepyornis Island," "The Strange Orchid," etc. 303pp. 5⅜ × 8½. (Available in U.S. only)
21531-8 Pa. $6.95

AMERICAN SAILING SHIPS: Their Plans and History, Charles G. Davis. Photos, construction details of schooners, frigates, clippers, other sailcraft of 18th to early 20th centuries—plus entertaining discourse on design, rigging, nautical lore, much more. 137 black-and-white illustrations. 240pp. 6⅛ × 9¼.
24658-2 Pa. $6.95

ENTERTAINING MATHEMATICAL PUZZLES, Martin Gardner. Selection of author's favorite conundrums involving arithmetic, money, speed, etc., with lively commentary. Complete solutions. 112pp. 5⅜ × 8½.
25211-6 Pa. $3.95

THE WILL TO BELIEVE, HUMAN IMMORTALITY, William James. Two books bound together. Effect of irrational on logical, and arguments for human immortality. 402pp. 5⅜ × 8½.
20291-7 Pa. $8.95

THE HAUNTED MONASTERY and THE CHINESE MAZE MURDERS, Robert Van Gulik. 2 full novels by Van Gulik continue adventures of Judge Dee and his companions. An evil Taoist monastery, seemingly supernatural events; overgrown topiary maze that hides strange crimes. Set in 7th-century China. 27 illustrations. 328pp. 5⅜ × 8½.
23502-5 Pa. $6.95

CELEBRATED CASES OF JUDGE DEE (DEE GOONG AN), translated by Robert Van Gulik. Authentic 18th-century Chinese detective novel; Dee and associates solve three interlocked cases. Led to Van Gulik's own stories with same characters. Extensive introduction. 9 illustrations. 237pp. 5⅜ × 8½.
23337-5 Pa. $5.95

Prices subject to change without notice.

Available at your book dealer or write for free catalog to Dept. GI, Dover Publications, Inc., 31 East 2nd St., Mineola, N.Y. 11501. Dover publishes more than 400 books each year on science, elementary and advanced mathematics, biology, music, art, literary history, social sciences and other areas.